The Principal Reader

Narratives of Experience

Praise for The Principal Reader

These narratives from the "trenches" are a refreshing change from the empty prescriptions we get from politicians, edu-businesses, and those who have given up on public schooling. This book is testament to the fact that there are committed educators struggling one day at a time to transform public schools in spite of their armchair critics. — *Gary L. Anderson, Professor of Educational Leadership at NYU Steinhardt.*

In the 1970s, as an elementary school teacher in North York's Jane-Finch Corridor, I had the good fortune to be mentored by an outstanding and innovative principal, Jim Montgomerie. He transformed my understanding of educational leadership and what it means to become a teacher. While a young professor in the United States in the 1980s, I had the good fortune to meet and learn from Brazilian educator, Paulo Freire. Over the years, I have grown to appreciate more and more the role of educational leaders whose actions and reflections on those actions constitute a praxis of possibility and transformation. The Principal Reader is an outstanding collection of narratives that conveys the lived texture of learning and the deep ecology of leadership. This is a book that should be required for all educators, especially at a time when public education is becoming overrun by business models and commodified by corporate initiatives. — *Peter McLaren, Distinguished Professor in Critical Studies, Co-Director, the Paulo Freire Democratic Project, College of Educational Studies, Chapman University, and author of Life in Schools (Routledge) and Pedagogy of Insurrection (Peter Lang).*

Griffiths and Lowrey have gone to the very heart of what it means to be a principal in schools today, by bringing together a beautiful anthology of stories by educational leaders who daily contend with the challenges, mishaps, and joys of school leadership in the name of social justice. By so doing, this volume humanizes the labor of principals in ways that expand our understanding of the struggles they face, as well as the powerful impact they can have in the building of a more just world. — *Antonia Darder, Leavey Endowed Chair of Ethics & Moral Leadership, Loyola Marymount University.*

An impressive collection of genuine narratives that get into the heart, soul and mind of educational leadership exposing the real tensions and possibilities and offering insights. — *John P. Portelli, Professor, OISE, University of Toronto.*

"The Principal Reader" is truly a unique resource in educational leadership studies. The narratives in this volume provide insight into how educational leadership theory might be enacted and understood and how practical wisdom is exercised on a daily basis by highly skilled and thoughtful educational leaders. Editors Griffiths and Lowrey have bought together a collection of commentaries and narratives that will provoke productive conversations about the contemporary principalship. — *Paul Newton, Department Head, Department of Educational Administration, University of Saskatchewan, Canada.*

The Principal Reader is a banquet of reflective thinking. The insights provided will be illuminating for nearly anyone interested in schools. — *Douglas J. Simpson, Texas Christian University & Texas Tech University.*

Griffiths's and Lowrey's The Principal Reader is a compelling assemblage of voices from the ground that resists simplistic renderings of school leadership and dissolves artificial divides between leadership theory and practice. The vivid narratives told by experienced school leaders provide an insider's view of leadership as a complex, holistic craft of leading, teaching, learning and advocacy. The text is humanizing and hopeful, bringing school leaders to the foreground as active participants in the struggle for social justice within diverse societies. — *Tricia M. Kress, Associate Professor of Leadership in Education and Graduate Program Director of the Leadership in Urban Schools Ed.D./Ph.D. program at the University of Massachusetts Boston.*

This unique collection of voices from across North America brings theories, challenges and rewards of educational leadership to life. The diverse perspectives of its many authors are sure to provoke discussion and reflection amongst aspiring and practicing principals. The Principal Reader is an excellent resource for educational leadership students and professors. — *Sue Winton, Associate Dean of Research and Community, Faculty of Education, York University.*

The Principal Reader

Narratives of Experience

Darrin Griffiths and Scott Lowrey

Editors

Word & Deed Publishing Incorporated & Edphil Books
1860 Appleby Line, Suite #778
Burlington, Ontario, Canada, L7L 7H7
(Toll Free) 1-866-601-1213

Edited by Darrin Griffiths, Ed.D., & Scott Lowrey Ed.D.
Copy-Edited by Mark Cassar, M.Ed. and Steve Viau.
Book design by Jim Bisakowski – www.bookdesign.ca

ISBN 978-0-9918626-2-7

Word & Deed Publishing Incorporated
1860 Appleby Line, Suite #778
Burlington, Ontario, Canada, L7L 7H7
(Toll Free) 1-866-601-1213

Visit our website at
www.wordanddeedpublishing.com

Dedication

Darrin – *To Sheila Tait and Helen Evans, two superb educational leaders who have taught me so much about leadership and about making a difference in students' lives.*

Scott - *To the memories of Susan Mawson and Tess Lowrey who both exemplified unconditional fidelity, friendship, and patience.*

Acknowledgements

This collection has been in production for over a year and we thank our contributors for sharing their experiences, insights, and expertise. Their dedication to sharing their stories will certainly be a powerful contributor to leadership practice across the world. We also thank Mark Cassar and Steve Viau for their excellent copy-editing and Jim Bisakowski for his terrific interior design work.

Contents

PART I
Leadership Theories In Practice

PART II
Confronting The Status Quo

PART III
Leading The Instructional Practice

PART IV
Leadership And Adversity

PART V
It's All About The People

PART VI
The Challenge of Change

PART VII
Reflections On Educational Leadership

PART VIII
In the Principal's Office

Foreword

My students enjoy hearing stories, and I enjoy telling them. It seems as if there is always some lesson that can be learned through the telling of the story of a life experience – often my own – that has some implication for the lesson at hand.

The personal narrative, or story, can be a powerful learning experience for the student. For some students, it's comfortable to hear a story they can relate to, and possibly to remind them of an experience from their own lives. For others, the story could provide an interesting lead-in to a lesson that might otherwise have no obvious relevance.

However, this is not a new approach to learning. As I pointed out in my book *The Canadian Writer's Workplace*, narration is the oldest and best-known form of communication. It is, quite simply, the telling of a story.

Every culture in the world, past and present, has used narration to provide entertainment as well as information for the people of that culture. Since everyone likes a good story, the many forms of narration, such as novels, short stories, lectures and narration in teaching, are always popular.

Aboriginal people have used the narrative as a teaching tool for centuries. Since nothing in Aboriginal culture was written down until recently, the narrative became the principle means of transmitting information from generation to generation, and that information transmittal often included life lessons and cultural teachings.

Throughout time, Aboriginal people have attempted to answer questions about the mystery of their existence and to answer things that are beyond our control. "Where did we as a people come from?" "Who am I?" "Where will I go when I die?" Each Aboriginal culture has responded with its own explanation – stories that are unique to that culture.

Storytelling, for example, is part of an oral tradition that is used by many cultures to pass down knowledge of themselves to future generations. "Oral tradition" can be defined as information that is passed from one person to another by word of mouth. Storytellers in each culture are considered unique in that they have the power to mesmerize their audiences with their eloquence and their ability to spark the imagination. To use the Aboriginal culture again as an example, because few Native tribes devised a written method of communication to keep records of their history, culture and traditions, and to instruct their youth; the oral tradition was vital, linking the past with the present and the future.

The Aboriginal tradition of passing information along to the next generation is seen in the following passage from Beck, Walters and Francisco (1992), *The Sacred: Ways of Knowledge, Sources of Life*, concerning the oral tradition in a Navaho community:

> When I was young, my grandfather and I, almost every evening we would sit on the west side of the summer house and watch the sun set or we would sit on the east side and watch the colours cover the mountains. My grandmother would join us. Then they would tell me about the mountain, about the evening sounds, my grandfather would sing a particular song and tell me "remember it." I would try. Sometimes I would ask my grandmother to help me remember. She would only tell me that was between my grandfather and me. She would not interfere and it was the same when my grandmother was teaching – my grandfather did not interfere. And these things they were advising me, their thoughts were the same.

This is an example of the power of story, of the use of the narrative in teaching and learning among people since before recorded time.

The essays in this book reflect the power of the oral tradition and show how we as humanity can connect with one another through the narrative story. We can, as the book points out, share one another's experiences and learn to see the world from a perspective different from our own. The narrative is seen as a valuable teaching tool.

Dr. John A. Roberts
Hamilton, Ontario
January, 2017

About the Author: *John Roberts is a Metis who has retired from Mohawk College in Hamilton, Ontario. He has served as President of the Canadian Metis Council for 11 years and has written 30 books, mainly textbooks in the areas of communications and Indigenous studies.*

Introduction

There is no doubt that neoliberalism has had an immense impact on the thinking and practices of educators in the western world. Neoliberalism, with its emphasis on excessive individualism, positivist notions of neutrality and evidence, and a restricted form of accountability that marginalizes moral responsibility, has hindered educators, including school principals, from properly considering and understanding that there is no genuine education for all without equity and meaningful inclusion. As much as the current dominant ideology might espouse that educational leadership can be commodified, and packaged in a group of practices or a set of recipes to blindly follow, educational leadership is much more complex. It cannot be reduced to prescribed actions that align or mirror practices that have been adopted in the business world. The neoliberal influence places extensive value on standardized testing, standardization and a one-size-fits-all mentality, and teaching without considering that schools work with students - not widgets or some other manufacturing product.

Educational leadership, at its core, is about supporting students reaching their full potential, in a holistic sense. Academic progress and learning are critically important; but students need to feel safe, included, and valued for the experiences, histories, and cultures they bring to school. Without a meaningful sense of belonging that builds on a variety of values and ways of being, exclusion and marginalization will occur. And to overcome such alienation from oneself, the school, and the community, the standards and criteria of what we deem education to be, and the practices that support that education, need revising. This must happen, even if such revisions create tensions for us if we feel that our traditional beliefs and practices need to be abandoned for more just ones. We cannot simply expose a diverse student body to practices that do not connect with their lives. To do so does not amount to meaningful inclusion.

Schools, unfortunately, are often places where socially constructed beliefs such as racism, sexism, homophobia, classism, etc., play out. Oppressive practices and ideologies that often pervade institutions are not always overt and explicit but they exist nonetheless.

How then can schools become places where all students are genuinely included and nurtured to become citizens in a democratic society? There is no simple or straight forward answer to this question, especially given the demands and pressures on school principals. A lack of resources, time, freedom to innovate, and strait-jacket approaches to school improvement create problems on a daily basis for an overwhelming majority of principals. While as a realist I do not envision such issues and problems will abate overnight, there is hope, much hope, that challenges and changes to the existing paradigm can take place at the local level. My reason for hope lies directly in the chapters and experiences shared by the contributors of this book. The contributors share maps and routes of their journey to improve students' lives; these maps and routes help them circumvent, challenge, out manoeuvre, and elude the tentacles of systems more concerned with quantitative data than with supporting students holistically.

The local level for me is the school where learning and teaching and leadership synergize on a daily basis. My hope is directly connected to what Roland Barth characterized as sharing of "craft knowledge." For principals, craft knowledge would be about learning about leadership, about infusing both rigorous academic and socially-just practices in the daily operation of a school, and developing a beginning understanding of how our current society operates to marginalize and oppress some while at the same time providing others with a "passport to success."

The principal is the key individual to any and all reforms to public education. While teachers are more important and more influential to students than is a principal, the value of the principal reaching students through supporting, protecting, and nurturing socially-just (which always includes a demanding academic program and learning) programs and practices with teachers can not be underestimated. Even with the challenges of time and an over-prescription of practices and bureaucratic requirements, principals can manoeuvre within their schools. Such manoeuvering requires principals to have opportunities to share their craft knowledge and to learn from others outside of their regular network of mentors and work colleagues. Manoeuvering is not associated or connected with the principal's charisma or lack thereof, but with understanding the different maps and routes to circumvent and/or overcome systemic barriers to supporting students holistically. Said otherwise, these authors, through their experiences and expertise, offer us all insight into how to work within the systemic confines and demands of the principal's role.

The expertise is available because there are thousands and thousands of principals who are effectively challenging these neoliberal-influenced practices and ideologies. Sadly, there are few opportunities for practicing principals to share their voices and their learning outside of their school district. It is vital that there are opportunities for learning that extends beyond, while still including, school level expertise.

The narratives have been organized into themes and are presented in recognition of the amazing work principals are doing. The themes provide guidance for us all in the various areas and demands of the role of principal. These chapters can be revisited multiple times, and over time, as the core components of educational leadership are evident throughout.

Theme I examines how leadership theories have been applied to the school contexts; in essence it examines the exact points where theory meets practice. The focus of Theme II is squarely on challenging the status quo, and shares contributors' insights of how they applied socially-just practices to challenge exclusionary and oppressive practice. Theme III showcases our authors' being able to facilitate improving the instructional program, while Theme IV outlines how contributors led during significant adversity in their schools. Theme V examines the importance of building and nurturing relationships within the school in order to support students. Theme VI examines the complexity of change, both as a process and as the moral imperative of principal leadership significantly nuanced by individual and collective reflective practice. Theme VII shares personal reflections on educational leadership from principals along various stages of their career trajectory. Theme VIII pulls back the curtain of one principal's office to reinforce the role of humor, joy, humility, and collegiality in maintaining a healthy work-life balance.

Nearly ten years ago when I was interviewing principals about inclusive leadership practices for my doctorate research, I realised something very important: these principals had incredible ideas, insights and expertise to share and likely had little opportunity to do so outside of their local district. Their narratives changed me; they challenged me to reflect on my own leadership practices, biases/prejudices, and privileges. I immediately became a better school leader after learning from their experiences and insights; their narratives remain with me and continue to shape me. The power of the narrative is undeniable if we are open to listening and learning and accepting some internal cognitive dissonance.

This is where the value and necessity of this book resides: there are fifty-six leadership narratives from practising educational leaders from the United States and Canada. The power of their stories lies in their lived realities and in the informal style of presentation; they are written as if you were meeting them for a coffee or sitting together at a conference. Let the stories sink in so that you can digest them, reflect on them, connect them with your unique context, and then take steps to make the learning real for yourself, the staff, and most importantly your students.

PART I
Leadership Theories In Practice

Foundational to the health of a democratic society is the leadership that influences public education. Every day, and in complex contexts, principals demonstrate leadership towards fostering more socially just, equitable, and inclusive learning environments. As middle managers, principals are uniquely situated to influence those both above and below them in an organizational hierarchy. Leveraging their leadership, principals demonstrate moral commitment to ethical leadership succession and sustainability. Research literature outlines numerous leadership models, with each model configured to honor the moral purpose of public education. Theory informs practice, and practice informs theory, in a highly iterative process. Behind every leadership practice, there is a theory influencing how principals approach complex situations. Over time, principals develop a complex repertoire of leadership practices, expertly nuanced by a deepening understanding of leadership theories.

Chapter 1

Transformational Leadership

Warman Hall, Ed.D.

Transformational leadership is such an attractive idea that it has become a catch phrase in modern leadership literature. The concept of leadership that transforms followers has certainly proven to be rich tilling ground for scores of theorists since James M. Burns first brought the idea to prominence in 1978. Following in Burns' footsteps, Joseph Rost argued for a central definition of leadership to guide scholarly inquiry into organizational leadership. Others, like Bernard Bass, have explored the sociological and psychological mechanisms that influence the transformational effect leaders have on their organizations. Nearly all this study has sought to focus on the measurable factors of influence between leaders and followers. In my own practice, I have most felt the pull between defining leadership and understanding its impact on my school when I have collaborated with other school leaders.

One does not need to practice school leadership very long before you come to the realization that becoming a better principal has a lot to do with being ready for unanticipated dilemmas. Much of the public perception of a school's quality is set by social or legislative influences that can feel too large for the school leader's scope of control. Additionally, local problems affecting enrollment, school climate or educational programming can arise that no one leader can hope to have the experience to deal with on his or her own. Theory can only go so far to help and there are no guidebooks for good principal leadership in a dynamic and ever-changing profession. By taking part in a local community of practice, I have found that like-minded school leaders can access one another's tacit knowledge to face a wider set of problems than one leader can hope to face alone.

I have been a consumer of leadership literature and research as a public school leader for 15 years now. In 2014 I finished my dissertation, having struggled through my studies on a 7-year program; I concurrently worked as a principal. This practical experience gave me many opportunities to reflect on leadership theory. My tacit experiences in school leadership have led me to think that Burns' transformational leadership cannot be understood, as he proposed it, if we divest that concept of the direct moral context that Burns (1978) placed it in. To be fair, neither Rost nor Bass intended to separate transformational leadership from the moral leadership that Burns places it in when writing his prologue to the book *Leadership*. However, a good deal of the more recent literature on leadership has eroded the original moral context of transformational leadership by focusing on how to do leadership rather than how to be the moral agent that transformational leadership needs.

From my perspective, the guiding moral imperative of public school leadership is to work with the parents and local community to give the best possible opportunity for a better life to everyone's children. Furthermore, my striving to create the best possible opportunity for my community's children should not come at the expense of children in other communities. If you lead long enough in a public school, you quickly find like-minded leaders around you. By nurturing open conversation within this community of practice we can all support one another's schools and gain valuable tacit knowledge to lead our own campuses.

In his chapter from the book *Leaders as Communicators and Diplomats*, Paul Houston (2009) made this moral leadership connection and touched a nerve with me by comparing the diplomatic authority of a superintendent with the moral authority of a minister. As a life-long church goer, I have listened to a lot of preachers. And it has always impressed me how a good preacher can bring the word of God to his congregation in a way that steps on everyone's toes on Sunday; then turn around and minister to those same pride-wounded believers when they need God's love while hurting in their daily lives. Clearly, this ministerial relationship is strong when it is based in trust, mutual respect and need. Equally clear to me is that the bonds of such a relationship are weak when trust is broken or mutual needs are neglected.

Just as healthy clerical leadership can move a church member to a more God-fearing life, moral leadership can be the catalyst in a secular moral context that turns transactional leadership into transforming leadership. Burns roughly defined moral leadership as leadership that meets the needs of followers to make more leaders; who might, in turn, evolve into moral agents of change themselves. To me, this moral leadership is a practice of ministering to followers in a way that reinforces the moral contract between leader and follower. Anything less in the practice of one's leadership is a transactional exercise that may be good and beneficial, but cannot transform the relationship because it does not mutually press for anything greater than what is needed in the here and now.

In New Mexico we have seen the last few years bring policy and evaluation changes that have demoralized teachers. To be sure, the teacher evaluation system needed attention in our State. However, by establishing rules that base 50% of a teacher's annual evaluation on their students' standardized test scores, the state has significantly sidelined the local administrator's ability to grow average new teachers into effective educators. Furthermore, like the rest of the nation, we are losing teachers and cannot fill vacancies as promising young educators leave the profession feeling a lack of hope. This scenario has galvanized local educational leadership to seek out others with a moral aim to help their community. In recent years the county I serve in has seen our superintendents and high school principals cross district lines to find ways to work together to share resources, stretch budget dollars, and find ways to improve the work in our schools. Among principals, one of the most personal of these collaborations has been an effort to meet regularly for coffee to discuss issues in our state that impact teaching and learning in high schools, as well as to share professional learning we might have picked up at conferences and workshops.

The support and encouragement I get from the local community of practice that I take part in helps me to be a better leader to my students, teachers, and families. Several pastors that I have spoken with have shared how isolating leadership can feel when the church community needs their leadership, but can be deaf to the pastors' needs to be inspired or counseled. It is the same for the public school leader. Superintendents and principals have layers of responsibility and the teachers we lead need our honest feedback, effective decision-making and informed organizational management. If we truly feel the moral impulse to help give opportunity to the children of our communities, we must seek out the professional wisdom and tacit knowledge around us.

Paraphrasing Paul Houston's language, I have come to see myself as a minister of democratic culture. I am entrusted with the education of my friends and neighbors' most precious treasure: their children. The school I build for those little treasures is going to mold the men and women they become. By holding fast to this moral contract with the families I serve, I will support students, teachers, and families; I will also encourage them and even challenge them in ways that move us collectively into the higher purpose of building a democratic society for our children. Hopefully, that society will be ready to meet the unknown challenges of the future.

At the time of this writing, my leadership career is hopefully far from over. The four districts in our corner of New Mexico are meeting the challenges we face. As a public servant I am continually amazed at the on-going nature of local educational ministry in our public schools. No one leader can claim singular success, and the need for schooling goes on well after any singular failure. Public school administration is the practice of managing programs to serve an on-going need for learning. Failure might be the outcome of any well-intended act of administrative moral leadership. However, when funding or policy challenges make transactional leadership in a static system no longer plausible for our schools and our children, a moral leader has no other choice than to act with moral integrity and play out his leadership with the same sense of mission that drives a pastor to continue in ministry.

About the Author: *Dr. Warman Hall has had leadership positions in schools in Albuquerque and Aztec, New Mexico since 2002. Currently, Warman serves as principal at Aztec High School. His research interests include tacit knowledge acquisition and servant leadership. He received both an Ed.D. in Leadership and a M.A.. in US History from the University of New Mexico. Warman is married to an elementary music teacher, Anjee, and they have two children, Serenity and Daniel, all of whom make coming home a joy every day.*

Chapter 2

Distributive Leadership: Real Leaders Lead and Follow

Donnell McLean

In today's typical school dynamic, leaders are not always the people presenting at the front of the room or even leading school-related projects. I argue that most leaders in today's schools come in many forms and positions other than that of the principal. As I begin my eighteenth year in education and sixth year in school administration, I continue to discover the importance and need for "Distributive Leadership". Distributive leadership is a leader's ability to properly distribute duties to other members of administration and/or staff.

This form of leadership definitely looks to augment many traditional administrative processes that were often undertaken by the head principal of schools. In fact, a principal's ability to properly delegate through distributive leadership is not only important to the equity and fidelity of school programming, but also to the longevity of school principals as a whole.

During the 2015– 2016 school year, my school virtually went through an entire administrative change. Only I remained as the school principal. It became very important that we minimized each other's areas of need and maximized our strengths. Our administrative team consisted of two other school administrators with various areas of experiences.

These experiences ranged from being a beginning administrator to an administrator with several years of expertise.

In order to achieve fidelity, equity of duties and delegated responsibilities, the three of us each took a character strengths survey. As an administrative team we began to converse about the importance of maximizing the strengths of each team member by empowering each other. Therefore, we all had to hone in on each other's strengths by continuing to build personal relationships with each other. Generally speaking, off-campus lunch meetings and other gatherings provided a much needed environment for fostering our personal relationships to the fullest extent.

The character survey was provided through our Intervention Services Department. The link for the character survey is as follows: http://www.viacharacter.org/www/Character-Strengths-Survey

But you may ask why a character survey was necessary. Well, in the identifying of a person's strengths, there is an immediate understanding of delegated strengths that is based solely on the human character. For example, one of our administrator's top character strengths was in the area of love and perseverance. This particular administrator has been identified to work in the area of student relations, student discipline, building staff relationships and heading up our Positive Behavior Intervention Support (PBIS) system (this aligned with the results from the survey).

In order to ensure the equity of the process, we constantly scheduled informal debriefing meetings. This entire process allowed every administrator to provide clarity and to ask clarifying questions to each other. We not only looked to address areas of strength, but we also examined our areas of need (weaknesses) by clearly identifying and conversing about them. Cultural biases were also addressed and eliminated by holding very candid, open conversations as well.

Unfortunately many school head principals continue to hold all the responsibilities and yet refuse any thoughts of distributive leadership. Some principals fear the loss of what they see as their monarchial control of their school and school programming. Simply put, this kind of leader refuses to become a follower to the leader of an assigned school delegation. This type of leader continues to adopt an old and archaic administrative stance. This type of leadership will also have negative consequences for all school participants.

As I aspire to my first head principal's appointment, I will not only implement the distributive leadership model amongst the administrative team, but teachers will have many opportunities to take the character survey in order to grasp their character strengths.

Many school administrators would wait for at least the first couple of years of taking over a particular school to develop trust. I totally disagree. With any staff, distributive leadership can be implemented by allowing every staff member to gain a piece of autonomy with the building of trust in mind. I believe that by working through the mistakes teachers and staff make, trust is built and fostered. Mistakes allow all stakeholders to have crucial conversations and compare very important thoughts, opinions and openness. As a result of these conversations my hope is that all hats are removed and trust is built with integrity, equity and fidelity.

Real leaders should not be afraid to become followers at times when distributive leadership is implemented. Fear of loss of control is a personal matter that should be eradicated internally, but definitely not at the detriment of one's school and/or school programming.

About the Author: *Donnell McLean is an eighteen-year educator – who has had assignments in several school districts. He began his career as a Special Educator and worked with special education students for thirteen years. In 2011, he began his school administrative career with Wake County Public Schools (Raleigh, NC). Donnell specializes in working with students, staff and parents from all walks of life. Plans for Donnell include starting school to finalize his Doctorate, and to earn his first appointment as head principal of a thriving school and school community.*

Chapter 3

A Few Thoughts on Mentoring-Coaching

Mary Nanavati

The longer I work as a school leader the more I realize that leadership is a team sport in education and all other organizations. Leaders must continuously develop the knowledge, skills and dispositions needed to work successfully with a myriad of individuals and groups in complex settings. Education is a people-intensive profession, and while it has so many joys and rewards, the challenges often involve working to bring out the best in those we interact with daily. Mentor-coaches are a key part of this team, supporting the growth and development as professionals and as leaders. After eight years and two schools later as a principal, I increasingly appreciate the importance of a leadership style that includes mentoring-coaching as its foundation, and I offer a few reflections on this incredible leadership learning journey.

I have had the good fortune to coordinate a Mentoring-Coaching pilot project for the Ontario Principals' Council (OPC)[1] in 2007-2008, working with six districts to set up mentoring-coaching supports for new school administrators. For the past two years, I have enjoyed teaching OPC's Mentoring Qualification Program, an Additional Qualification course that attracts school administrators and others in leadership positions who work daily with many students, staff, and parents. My lived experiences as a school leader align with those of the course participants who overwhelmingly believe that leaders working in complex school contexts need the kind of support that derives from the combination of both mentoring and coaching, and their positive impact on mentor-coaches, mentees, and organizations.

While mentoring and coaching are unique in many ways, the line between them is becoming increasingly blurred. Lois Zachary continues to be influential in my understanding of mentoring as being foremost a learning relationship focused on the mentee's goals. Mentoring is learning for both the mentor and the mentee. From Zachary (2012), I have learned that effective mentoring is no longer about the mentor imparting knowledge to the mentee. Mentoring has become a collaborative relationship "rooted in principles and practices of adult learning" (p. 3). In this important role, one develops a learning partnership focused on the mentee's learning goals.

Table 1: *Distinguishing Between Mentoring and Coaching*[2]

Mentoring	Coaching
A self-directed learning relationship driven by the learning needs of the mentee	A self-directed learning relationship driven by the learning needs of the client
More process-oriented than service-driven	More product-oriented, that is, the skills of the client
Focuses more on achievement of personal or professional development goals; may focus on broader, 'softer,' intangible issues as learning goals e.g., getting to know the corporate culture, as well as more tangible, specific goals	Focuses more on boosting performance and skill enhancement; usually focuses on the specific skills of the client as learning goals; goals of the client can be personal or professional
Mentoring relationships are voluntary	Coaching relationships are often contracted for pay
Mentoring lacks standardization and is not a professional field of practice; relationships evolve organically over time time	Coaching is a growing professional field with certification, established standards and practices
Mentors usually come from within the organization	Coaches can come from within the organization but are often hired outside an organization
Usually one-to-one relationship but can include peer and group mentoring	Usually one-to-one relationship but can include peer and group coaching

What do we gain when we combine mentoring and coaching? In examining the research literature on professional learning, one must conclude that both mentoring and coaching support those aspects of professional learning that we know to have a positive impact on participants. For example, mentoring and coaching support learning that is context-specific and has greater breadth and depth. An increase in self-knowledge through dialogue contributes to understanding and implementation as mentees develop clarity of thinking and decision-making, focusing on goals related to their personal and professional lives (Pask and Joy, 2007, p. 111). In pairing mentoring and coaching, the learning involves inquiry, reflection, and collaboration. The mentee benefits from not only the support that would be given by the mentor – but also the conversational, goal setting and accountability skills of the coach – all focused on the needs of the mentee. As a principal trained in both mentoring and coaching, I have realized that both learning experiences build positive, professional relationships and community which are essential to school improvement. I learned that combining mentoring and coaching provides benefits to mentees, mentor-coaches and organizations. Mentees develop a greater sense of efficacy which is key to personal and professional growth. Mentoring-coaching empowers mentees, enabling individuals to set goals and find their own solutions to problems in their personal and professional lives. Mentor-Coaches hold mentees accountable to reach their goals. Through mentoring-coaching, mentees can use their own personal strengths and emerge far more self-aware as they reflect on all facets of their lives. They develop their own critical thinking skills and become empowered to solve their own problems, becoming more reflective in the process. Learning for the mentee is the outcome of mentoring-coaching. Ultimately, I have learned that mentees experience a sense of renewal as many go on to become mentor-coaches themselves. I have seen many mentees giving back to others, their professions, and their organizations.

Mentor-coaches find that the learning is always reciprocal and through this supportive process, they are honing their own skills and experiences as leaders. Mentor-coaches are integral to building a culture of support within their organizations as they offer leadership in renewing their profession. Mentor-coaches often comment that the skills they develop in this process inevitably impact positively on their personal lives as they become more effective in such skills as listening deeply, coming to conversations from a point of curiosity, and asking impactful questions.

Mentoring-coaching also benefits organizations. In education, schools, districts, and systems become more focused on the art of powerful conversations, inquiry, reflection, collaboration, and community. As a powerful form of professional learning, mentoring-coaching can have a positive impact on the implementation of new practices and leadership skills. As reflected in the *Ontario Leadership Framework*, building relationships and developing people are foundational to school improvement.

Having supported this field for a considerable length of time now, there are key practices that make for success and sustainability:

- Convene a team to design, implement and renew your mentoring-coaching supports
- Secure training in both mentoring and coaching for your mentor-coaches
- Offer training for your mentees so that they become aware of the process
- Ensure that mentoring-coaching in your organization rests on trust and confidentiality as foundational supports
- Offer time for mentees and mentor-coaches to meet, ideally at times during the work day, while acknowledging that meetings will also happen outside the work day, at times mutually convenient for participants
- Include differentiation and flexibility to meet unique circumstances

While your committee might initially focus on one or two employee groups and individuals new to a role, ensure that mentoring-coaching eventually permeates the organization with fair access by all employee groups, creating a continuous culture of support.

Experience has taught me that there is a need for mentoring-coaching for all school leaders. School leadership is increasingly challenging and offering continuous support can make a positive difference for our front-line school leaders. Having the good fortune to network with many school leaders across several districts, many of these organizations are beginning to give these same supports to non-teaching staff, recognizing that mentoring-coaching is helpful to all employee groups. While those new to a role certainly need support, we must look beyond that and extend mentoring-coaching to anyone at any time in our school systems. As those new to a role or location gain experience, their goals inevitably change and a culture of mentoring-coaching can extend supports to these individuals whenever the need arises.

As an experienced principal, I have learned that education is one of the most rewarding, and at times, one of the most challenging professions that exist. Our students deserve the very best from those working in leadership positions, in the classroom and in support roles. Building a culture of Mentoring-Coaching for all can ensure that supports are available to all employees throughout their professional journey. Those working and leading in education deserve nothing less.

References

Kimsey-House, H., Kimsey-House, K., Sandahl, P. & Whitworth, L. (2011). *Co-active coaching: Changing business, transforming lives* (3rd ed.). Boston, MA: Nicholas Brealey Publishing.

Nanavati, M. S. B. (2011). *Knowledge and learning strategies in principal mentoringcoaching relationships.* (Unpublished master of education thesis). Ontario Institute for Studies in Education, University of Toronto.

Ontario Ministry of Education. (2016-17). *Mentoring for all.* Version 2. Available at https://www.teachontario.ca/community/explore/mentoring-for-all.

Pask, R. & Joy, B. (2007). *Mentoring-coaching: A guide for education professionals.* Berkshire, England: Open University Press.

Sharpe, K. & Nishimura, J. (2017). *When mentoring meets coaching: Shifting the stance in education.* Toronto, ON: Pearson Canada Inc.

Zachary, L. J. (2005). *Creating a mentoring culture: The organization's guide.* San Francisco, CA: Jossey-Bass.

Zachary, L. J. (2012). *The mentor's guide: Facilitating effective learning relationships.* San Francisco, CA: Jossey-Bass.

About the Author: *Mary Nanavati is a secondary school principal with the Peel District School Board in Ontario. She is also an instructor and program lead for the Ontario Principals' Council's Mentoring Qualification Program.*

Chapter 4

The Dynamics for Team Success

Vincent Potts

As I transitioned from a high school English teacher to an elementary school Assistant Principal, I felt some sadness because I enjoyed the camaraderie of working alongside my department's grade level team and the thrill of coaching my flag football teams. I would miss all that. Although I did not give it much thought at the time, I later came to the epiphany that these two cherished parts of my work had something in common: I gained extreme joy collaborating with a team of teachers who relentlessly worked alongside me to reach common goals. Moreover, through coaching I was able to help children develop into cohesive, effective teams and support them in their efforts to achieve the common goal of winning championships. For some time, I was curious about the successful development of teams. I often wondered, "How is it that some teams thrived despite obstacles, while other teams never seemed to reach their full potential?" It was during a "school turnaround" professional development session that my question seemed to be answered. Since then, I have attempted to apply the knowledge of team performance and the concept of "flow" to my role as a school leader.

Several years ago I settled down in a spacious lecture hall at the University of Virginia's Darden School of Business for leadership-based professional development. Instead, what I received was enlightened insight from a high performing team of teachers which has impacted my leadership practice ever since. I listened intently as this team of teachers from Ohio responded to questions about how they helped steer an underperforming school to high levels of academic achievement. It was especially poignant when they addressed the challenges faced when a new teacher joined their team who was not meeting their standard of performance. I sat in awe thinking to myself, "Oh no, she is sitting right next to them, this is not going to go well!" To the contrary, the teachers laughed as they explained how they brought the teacher along to meet their high expectations. The teacher gratefully spoke about how her teammates put in extra time to support her plan and execution to meet their common goals and support student achievement. During the session, I marveled at how happy these teachers seemed as they explained the obstacles they had to overcome to achieve success. I first thought, that they sure are giggling quite a bit, it must be nerve wracking to speak in front of this audience. However, as they continued I realized, that this was not nervous laughter, and these teachers are truly passionate and extremely overjoyed about their work. I continued to listen for the key components to turn around struggling schools, and it struck me that these teachers were engaged in making seemingly ordinary work, extraordinary—some might call it 'cutting edge'. Their special undertaking did not involve a new curriculum, extra resources, or additional money. What were they doing particularly well? These teachers were reflecting on and sharing how they worked cohesively as a team—one unit (even when those moving human parts were changed) with a laser-like focus on their goals and how they were going to achieve them.

I subsequently visited high performing urban public schools in Chicago, Houston, and Cincinnati. Through extensive classroom walk-throughs and discussions with key internal stakeholders, I concluded that the teacher teams in these buildings possessed common elements which led to increased student achievement. Teachers found great joy in the work they were performing within highly effective teams. As we continue to evolve further away from the notion of teachers working in isolation, the importance of team performance becomes more apparent. I believe that it is imperative for leaders to be in tune with meeting the needs of individuals within the context of a team framework to meet goals and obtain results.

A 'team' is generally defined as a group of people possessing complementary skills who are committed to working collaboratively toward achieving common purposes and goals to which they are mutually accountable. Psychologists Tuckman and Jensen (1977) outlined the phases (forming, storming, norming, performing, adjourning) teams encounter as they grow, encounter challenges, address issues, problem solve, plan, and take action on their journey to achieving. To optimize team performance, however, individual needs must be met. According to psychologist Mihalyi Csikszentmihalyi (1990), when people are engaged deeply in attempting to reach goals through challenging activities within the reach of their skill set, they experience a state of being termed "flow." Within this state, sometimes referred to as being "in the zone," people find happiness in working toward pursuing long term goals that are meaningful to them. Csikszentmihalyi (1990) identifies several components to the "flow" experience, including: 1) clear goals; 2) immediate feedback; and 3) a balance between challenges versus skill sets (so that success feels possible). His work asserts that a state of "flow" can be achieved once individuals face increasing challenges and their skill sets are developed to handle these obstacles. Additionally, due to various levels of experience present within teams, I find differentiated professional development for teachers to be helpful. Teachers may also take part in individualized coaching cycles so that skill deficits do not frustrate efforts to meet challenges.

As school leader, I find it important to identify individual teacher needs and simultaneously recognize what phase teaching teams are currently in to provide the best level of support. In the *forming* stage, teams need the school leader to help define roles and responsibilities, which may be unclear or undefined. During this phase, I establish clear communication regarding team and individual goals as they begin to engage in the work. I get to know individuals, determine if they have proper resources at their disposal, and work to establish common team goals and direction. Clear objectives make it easier to provide helpful feedback to teachers after classroom walk-throughs, observations, and assessment data reviews to ensure alignment between goals and practices. This clarity and resource support helps establish "flow" by allowing individuals to feel success is possible. School leaders need to develop strategies for coaching teams entering the *storming* stage to help manage the discomfort, frustration, and stress experienced by team members as differences arise over established roles and team goals. Here, individual "flow" may be jeopardized due to uncertainty or confusion present during the storming phase. The storming phase is the most precarious stage because initial enthusiasm will erode and variances in individual skill sets may require additional feedback and professional development. This support helps "flow" by allowing individuals to remain deeply engaged in the work while mitigating feelings of being overwhelmed. I make sure that issues are addressed head on before they become larger problems that erode team trust. I find that close guidance and follow up works best when working with teachers during this stage.

It is particularly important for me to identify and celebrate bright spots during this phase to continue building morale. Teams that are *norming* will experience a rise in enthusiasm as their skill sets increase and they begin to utilize one another's strengths to collaborate and make progress toward common goals. During this phase, I look to work in a facilitative capacity with the team to allow room for reciprocal feedback and search for opportunities that allow individuals the opportunity to deepen their leadership skills. This supports individual "flow" by increasing challenges as skill sets improve and confidence emerges. Teams begin *performing* as their enthusiasm increases along with their skill sets. Team members will hold themselves accountable and start to see the fruits of their labor in the form of results. As teams emerge in this phase individuals are "in the zone" and truly experiencing happiness in their work. Here, I make sure to publicly recognize individual and team accomplishments, evaluate achievements against the goals set, and seek continuous improvement. Although teams may fluctuate back and forth between phases, early recognition and proper intervention to support individual "flow" supports team development and helps keep focus on the goals at hand. During the *adjourning phase*, teachers may occupy new roles or loop to other grades. I work with teams to develop transition plans that will alleviate feelings of loss that may occur as a result of change and spark enthusiasm for new challenges ahead. Due to change, teachers may experience loss of enthusiasm during this phase which may impact individual "flow." These feelings could be offset by clarifying new goals and providing exciting challenges that align with increased skill sets.

Most people would agree that school decline takes place over time. Likewise, school growth occurs gradually. I believe school growth takes place within an environment that supports individual growth while cultivating collaborative learning and teamwork. School leaders can leverage the work of Tuckman and Csikszentmihalyi to harness the human power within their building. Teachers who are supported in their pursuit of individualized happiness through their work will help develop teams that achieve, sustain continuous improvement, and produce positive academic outcomes for students.

References

Csikszentmihalyi, M. (1990). *Flow: The psychology of optimal experience*. New York: Harper Perennial.

Tuckman, B.W. & Jensen, M.A.C. (1977). Stages of small-group development revisited. *Group & Organizational Studies, 2*(4), 419-427.

About the Author: *Vincent Potts holds degrees from Truman State University and the University of Missouri-Kansas City. Since 2011, he has held leadership positions and served students with diverse cultural and linguistic backgrounds as an Elementary School Administrator in both the charter school and large public school district settings in Kansas City, Missouri, U.S.A. He currently serves as Assistant Principal at Crestview Elementary in the North Kansas City School District.*

Chapter 5

Inclusive Leadership and Inclusive Education

Kimberly Lefevre-Walke

During my career as a teacher, vice-principal and principal, I have worked in thirteen elementary schools in three school districts over the course of thirty years. I have worked in schools of all sizes in a variety of school communities; I have experience in single-track English, double-track English, French Immersion, and single-track French Immersion settings. In the last sixteen years, I have been the principal of four elementary schools. Although all my experiences as a principal have been worthwhile, I think my most memorable and rewarding experience as an educator unfolded when I was the principal of a large, diverse, suburban dual-track English and French Immersion school (ABC school for our purposes) for a seven-year period. What I would like to share with you is the journey I was a part of in our work to make ABC school a "good" school, and how the concept that inclusive leadership and inclusive education became opposite sides of the same coin. You cannot have one without the other.

I will start from the beginning. I was appointed to ABC School at a time when the school was two years old and the principal who had opened the school had just gone on a leave of absence. The school had opened in a new developing suburban community, served a diverse community comprised of twenty-seven different cultural and linguistic backgrounds, and had grown in size at an accelerated rate. In this dual-track English/French immersion school, we had fifty-five staff working with approximately 750 K-8 students. We had 400 students in our K-8 program and 350 students in our Grade 1-8 French Immersion program. As part of my entry plan, I spoke with staff and with school council executive members. What I found at the outset was a divided staff and disgruntled school council along with no clear processes, structures or routines in place for communication or school operations.

In the first few months I met with each staff member and school council executive [an elected committee of parents and community members, students and staff] to find out how they viewed our school, and their ideas on how we could co-create a path forward to make the school the best it could be. I took that input and coalesced staff and our school council around a shared vision focused on quality educational programs, high expectations for all students, and the use of whole school leadership and collaboration to make that happen. We instituted processes, structures and routines for communication and school operations. Both the school staff and school council responded well to the changes we instituted and our new-found shared vision as these changes infused a sense of stability and direction in the school.

Once that was in place, we moved to the most important work of the principalship; building the culture and conditions to create the collaborative, professional learning community necessary to support student well-being and success. To that end, in my second month, we assembled a school leadership team comprised of divisional lead teachers, our teacher librarian, special education teachers, an English as a second language teacher, and a Reading Recovery teacher. At the outset, as a leadership team, we identified one critical thing about our school's ability to support the well-being and success of all students. We recognized that we had many special educational students and not enough staff to support their needs. We also identified that the structure of special education program delivery (withdrawal assistance and partial integration) was not meeting student needs.

Through our first year together as a leadership team, we discussed the need to transform the way we were delivering special education in our school. I positioned to the staff that we needed to dismantle our two special education student support center-rooms. Here, students received "withdrawal support" and/or modified language/math programs for a half-day. Students were then integrated into the regular classroom for the remaining half day. The team listened and agreed to co-implement this approach to serving students. Parallel to this, our staffing and time-table committees then subsequently worked each year to have teachers from both our English and French programs cross over and teach in the other program to further build a whole school team approach and school capacity, and tap into the skills and expertise of staff in both programs. Between our second to seventh year together, we had a fully integrated model of special education delivery from K-8, and served students with a gamut of exceptionalities in our English and French Immersion classrooms.

You might ask how we did that. We formulated a special education support team comprised of two special education resource teachers, two child and youth workers, four educational assistants, one vice-principal and one principal (me). We carried walkie-talkies and moved through classes based on a fluid schedule each day to support about 80 students across the school and their teachers. We were literally on roller skates most days! To support this fully inclusive model we had to have parents and guardians on board, and we did! Moreover, we began identifying the level of student support to be the "regular class with resource assistance" on the statement of decision at IPRCs (Identification, Placement, and Review Committee). Parents and guardians wholeheartedly agreed. To support our fully integrated model we also spent a great of time each year working together a whole staff to build our capacity in writing and implementing IEPs. This wasn't easy work by any stretch of the imagination, but it was meaningful and rewarding work.

We used this approach for delivering special education for six years. During that time we witnessed and documented great success based on both qualitative and quantitative data we collected. It would be worth mentioning that the most powerful effect of our approach to special education was a decrease in negative student behavior and increase in student engagement. We also saw an increase in student skills development as documented on school report cards and demonstrated on grade 3 and 6 provincial assessments (EQAO). We documented increased parent/guardian engagement in their child's learning and school life, and the development and sustainment of a collaborative, inclusive leadership approach to school governance.

In my seventh year a new superintendent came to our district and made a school visit. He asked us about our inclusive education model. This superintendent was the first in seven years to ask us how we were organizing our special education delivery; he recognized and praised our collective commitment and success in serving all our students, especially those with special educational needs. As a leadership team and school, we felt proud of our journey and success in creating a "good" school - a fully inclusive school.

At the end of our seventh year, our school became too large and as a result, the student population splintered to other schools in the area. Many of the staff moved on. I went on to be the principal of an English K-8 school where a number of special education programs existed. When I met my new superintendent, I enthusiastically shared the experience we had had at my previous school and explained how I would like to implement an inclusive leadership and inclusive education approach here at this school. My new superintendent said, "You are not supposed to do that. It is against board policy." That message resonated with me for a long time, but it has never changed my resolve to do what I believe is best for students. Soon after that, this new superintendent got a promotion and moved on. I went through my first year and worked to influence staff and parents, and infuse the groundwork for inclusive leadership and inclusive education. After that year, I went on to do the same at another school. My goal was simple: plant the seeds to promote the growth of educators and inclusive leadership and inclusive education.

Upon reflection on my journey as an educational leader, I have learned five overarching lessons. *First*, no matter how schools may differ in structure, setting or demographics, all schools share at least two common elements: i) they have teachers who want to make a difference and ii) they have students who look to belong and learn. *Second*, inclusive leadership and inclusive education are the keys to making the teacher-learning process blossom; and in fact, you cannot have one without the other. *Third*, next to teachers, the principal is the strongest influence on student learning and success. *Fourth*, principals can be in a position to influence the co-creation of professional learning communities. These learning communities can support the culture and conditions needed for student success, as well as the pursuit of equity and excellence for all. They can also promote teacher self-efficacy. *Fifth*, as educational leaders, principals must assume their role as "public intellectuals" and challenge current structures, policies and practices in public education that impede equity and excellence for all. Going forward, reform in the area of special education to promote full inclusion must be at the core of 21st century educational reform in teaching, learning and leading. Hear the call to action! If we do not advocate for our students, who will?

About the Author: *Kimberly Lefevre-Walke is currently a K-8 school principal. She is a firm believer in the power of teacher leadership, and the need for all educational leaders to challenge the status quo and create the organizational culture and conditions for student success in pursuit for equity and excellence for all. Over the last three years, she has spoken at various conferences to join the discourse on educational equity and excellence. As a doctoral student in the Department of Educational Leadership & Policy, at the Ontario Institute for the Study of Education, University of Toronto, Kimberly is currently working on her thesis proposal entitled "K-12 Superintendents Creating the Culture and Conditions for Student Success in Pursuit of Equity and Excellence for All."*

PART II

Confronting The Status Quo

P rincipals are deeply committed to leading in cultures of complex change. This work cannot be done in isolation. Confronting status quo situations of domination, marginalization and oppression, often deeply embedded in community and organizational culture, is the work of principals. Schools and school systems articulate the promise of equitable and inclusive environments, and yet some voices remain either unheard or silent. Moreover, the evidence of equity and inclusion provided can be superficial. Interestingly, and upon reflection, confronting the status quo has dimensions of both internal and external accountability. Confronting the status quo, principals learn much about themselves. Also, communities learn much about the moral imperative of such principals through observation and interaction. Collective community efficacy transpires.

Chapter 6

A Place at the Table

Tony Lamair Burks II, Ed.D.

I relocated to Greensboro, North Carolina in 2002 to establish one of the first early college high schools in the nation. Imagine arriving at a high school with no textbooks, no computers, nothing. No mission nor philosophy, no traditions nor heritage, nothing. Such was the case when we opened The Early College at Guilford that fall. Two teaching positions were vacant and many of our textbooks were trapped on a delivery truck a few weeks before students were to arrive. Computers were stolen from the school's main office just hours before the first day of school. And what's more, we didn't have a single student club, a school mascot, a school song, or school colors.

It has been well over a decade since we gave birth to a school that has been replicated across the continental United States and beyond. The school has been recognized many times as among the best in the country (e.g., Rank 5, America's Top High Schools 2016). We've grown a little older—and hopefully a little wiser—since we first huddled around a red-draped table at *Elizabeth's Pizza* in hopes of creating something transformative.

Whenever I am asked to speak about the early college experience, I think of my students and students like Trelliot*, who left an established high school that had more than a century of history as an academic and athletic powerhouse to enroll in a fledgling early college high school that did not have athletic teams or a proven record as a school. Trelliot was disadvantaged for admissions to The Early College at Guilford (ECG) by the intersectionality of race, gender, and socio-economics. The perceptions of the parents and guardians of identified gifted and talented students, the perceptions of my immediate supervisor, and perhaps the perceptions of some students at ECG, were that Trelliot—and students like him—had no place at a school established for high achieving gifted students. I wrestled with a decision to accept his application for admission. As one of the first early college high schools, we were "designing, building, and flying the plane" all at once and were developing protocols and procedures along the way. I embraced a moral commitment to educational access, equity, and excellence, and then I admitted Trelliot.

Through the decision to admit Trelliot, and other decisions like this, I embraced the notion of transformative leadership espoused by Astin and Astin (as cited in Shields, 2004, p. 113) and the hope they have for its widespread use:

> We believe that the value ends of leadership should be to enhance equity, social justice, and the quality of life; to expand access and opportunity; to encourage respect for difference and diversity; to strengthen democracy, civic life, and civic responsibility; and to promote cultural enrichment, creative expression, intellectual honesty, the advancement of knowledge, and personal freedom coupled with responsibility.

In retrospect, my decision to admit Trelliot was an effort on my part to "expand access and opportunity." The national, state, and local emphasis on rigor, relevance, relationships, and results is designed to advance the basic principle of equity which posits that the greatest inequity is to treat "unequals" equally. School reputations and demographics are wedded in today's age of accountability, and in this race to the top, some educators would rather protect schools from students whose test scores might lower a school's overall performance. The politics of equity suggest that when educators know a school's test score results, they can predict with great accuracy the demographics of the school. It this is plausible, then the reverse is equally feasible: tell a person the race and socio-economic status of students and that person can predict the students' achievement and performance on standardized tests. Schools populated by those on the "right side" of everything tend to have funding that equitably supports rigor. Those on the other side—often students of color—are more likely to attend schools that have lower per student funding which results in less support for teaching and learning.

The Early College at Guilford could have easily been exclusively populated by students who were white, wealthy, and advantaged. This necessitated that we as an admissions team maintain a moral commitment to equity. Our equity work did not stop at the end of the admissions process. I chose to be courageous and resist the ongoing question posed by naysayers along the way: Could Trelliot handle it? When rigor and equity are a part of a solid education all students are intellectually (and appropriately) stretched.

Trelliot was challenged beyond measure by interactions with high school peers, college classmates, and professors. I knew that whatever I designed for Trelliot would benefit all students. We met with each grade level each week to nurture and grow school culture and climate. Students led assemblies and taught fellow students during four- to six-week long mini-courses on everything from the use of scientific calculators and cooking with a microwave to public speaking and knitting (yes, knitting). We introduced students to the "office hours" concept and empowered them to meet with their teachers about coursework. Students took ownership of their learning and radically shifted the pendulum from "getting" grades to "earning grades". The goal was to achieve mastery of a subject all while exploring a diversity of opinions, ideas, and beliefs. For students who struggled to experience success, we reviewed their overall performance each quarter, and held Student-Centered Success Conferences with students and their families to generate process and protocols to ensure students were achieving academically and socially. Students established over 25 clubs and organizations—this a testament to the 150 students enrolled at the school at the time and their commitment to creating spaces to welcome all. Over time, even the notion of teaching and learning evolved to be student-centered and hands-on in support of all students.

Because of his experiences at our school, wherever he ventured, educators and peers alike recognized and respected his pioneering nature, convivial spirit, and dedication to academic and social excellence. And for these traits I am proud to call Trelliot one of my shining stars.

This story of Trelliot—a composite of two students of color who attended The Early College at Guilford—explores a series of culturally courageous decisions I made as a principal.

Reference

Shields, C. M. (2004, February). Dialogic leadership for social justice: Overcoming pathologies of silence. *Educational Administration Quarterly*, 40(1), 109-132.

About the Author: *Dr. Tony Lamair Burks II is an award-winning education expert who helps individuals and organizations as a thought partner and coach in his role as Chief Learning Officer of LEADright. He is the former Superintendent-in-Residence (2011-2015) with the National Center for Urban School Transformation (NCUST) and the author of three books: The Tale of Imani the Bunny, The Journey to Authenticity: 8 Secrets to Getting the Life You Desire (with Mitchell L. Jones), and Bought Wisdom: Tales of Living and Learning. A master whistler and story weaver, he is among five educators featured in Walking the Equity Talk: A Guide for Culturally Courageous Leadership in School Communities by John Robert Browne II.*

Chapter 7

A Beautiful Fall Day

Carole Dufort

I remember vividly a beautiful fall school day in October 2013. I arrived at our community center early and I waited anxiously for the 300 students, teachers and system leaders to come to our first Board Forum supporting LGBTQ+ students and their allies. It was unknown territory for our small and rural schools, and although everything had been carefully planned, there was a sense of responsibility, trepidation and high expectations associated with this Board Forum.

When the students arrived at the Forum, one could immediately feel an air of enthusiasm and excitement. It was not about getting the materials, the agenda, or signing up for the workshops. What was taking place that day was so much bigger than anything I could have ever imagined. I watched in awe as the kids skipped and hugged. I heard comments such as, "I never believed that this day would come" and "I wish school could be like this all the time". One could feel the energy and electricity grow throughout the day as students and staff came together, completely engaged with the presenters, and excited about the possibilities for the future. Kids felt that they belonged. Students who came in with their heads down could not stop talking, smiling, and participating. I observed with a sense of astonishment all that was taking place around me. I was at a loss for words. I went home that night and sobbed. My tears were tears of joy for a process where people finally came together and put aside their own beliefs to do what was right for the kids. I also shed tears for the staff, parents, and students who suffered in silence hoping that one day, together, we would start having open and honest dialogue so that every student has the opportunity to succeed. This happened on the beautiful day in the fall.

Equity work is hard. It takes commitment, dedication, and the ability to rebound after setbacks. It takes patience and dedicated leadership. It is imperative that students feel supported equitably through the identification and removal of discriminatory barriers. In order to achieve this goal, I believe that one of the key qualities of a leader is the commitment to reflection, analysis, and to the questioning of how and why we do what we do. I listened to the students' voices and the songs that they created that fall day. I felt the emotion in the students' poems, and clearly understood their commitment to making a difference in their schools. I also wondered what took us so long to get to this place and I asked myself, what I could have done differently. I know, without a doubt, that there still is much learning to do. As administrators, we must have a steadfast commitment to all of our students. If we want all our learners to feel safe, successful and healthy, we must take further action.

For years school-based equity teams have planted the seeds of change. Now, more than ever, schools and communities need to work together. We need to develop respectful and relational partnerships so we can share resources, knowledge, and skills. This in turn will assist us in developing a better understanding of community-based assets and challenges and how they influence our students, families and schools.

Life in small and rural communities is extremely different than in big cities. Small and rural communities often have a deep-rooted heritage and cultural identity. Each community is unique, exquisite, and has strengths and challenges. Small and rural communities, however, often lack the community agencies and supports found in larger urban centres, and are separated from each other by large geographic territory, and with limited access to transportation. As a school principal in a rural community, I must be resourceful, seek to break down geographic isolation, and build a network of supports to better address the issues of student belonging and achievement. I have always thought that my role was to serve in my school community and to cultivate a sense of well-being so that my students could flourish in all areas of life.

Being a principal is a complex, challenging and rewarding job, and so are the problems that we face every day. It is a unique position of responsibility and privilege; one in which we get to make a difference, educate, encourage, inspire, support, champion, spark and mentor. We give hope and are "merchants of hope" to many students. My commitment to an inclusive, respectful, and equitable school culture is unwavering. It goes beyond the legislative and political will; it is my moral imperative and my passion.

I believe that in order to succeed and to be meaningfully engaged, students need to feel that they belong, they have a voice, and they see themselves valued by the curriculum. We need to renew our commitment to moving beyond our differences and provide equitable opportunities for all children. This starts with us - the leaders. We set the tone in our buildings through leading by example and 'walking the talk'. We must lead in such a manner that anyone who walks through our doors knows that our commitment to equity and inclusion is non-negotiable.

We also need to build our own leadership practice, seek to understand, be a learner first, and ask ourselves some hard questions. Looking inward at our own biases, prejudices, power and privileges is key for leaders who want to engage in equitable and inclusive best practices. To do this, we must ask what do we know about our lesbian, gay, bisexual, transgender and two-spirit students. What do we know about race, culture, class, ableism, and identity? What can we do to get the information? Who can help us? Whose voices can we seek out to help guide us in this journey? The onus is on us as school administrators to take the lead as co-learners with our community in search of the answers.

When administrators confront issues such as racism, homophobia, sexism or ableism, complex cases involving conflicting rights, beliefs and practices may arise. We must have a good working knowledge of the Education Act, the Human Rights Code and other pertinent laws, legislation, policies and procedures that are relevant in Ontario's education system today. Our job, however, is much more than that; it is also about leading from the heart. If we truly believe that all students can learn, progress and achieve, we must refuse to accept the status quo, understand that diversity is an asset, challenge assumptions and preconceptions, and begin to understand the ways our own practices, schools, and systems impede or foster student success.

In order to achieve an inclusive environment each stakeholder must understand that they have a role to play. There needs to be a place for openness, learning, curiosity, and respect for differences. We must have honest and open discussions and crucial conversations at all levels of education. We must be prepared to be uncomfortable.

One of the most beautiful assets in Ontario is our diversity. How do we move beyond tolerance to acceptance, inclusivity and respect? It is imperative that we increase awareness and understanding in our schools, boards, and communities. We must foster safe, inclusive, and accepting environments for all students and staff. We must fully support the whole child and the well-being of all children. We must understand the legislative part of our roles, and use an equity lens as a way to inform our decisions and actions. We are the role models, and everything from our words to our actions is under scrutiny. This generation is like no other; they have access to information at the tip of their fingers. They will not accept the status quo and they want to have a voice. They want to play an important role for positive change on issues that affect their schools, and when you give them that opportunity, they shine.

I applaud leaders who recognize that we need to be learners first, we need to reach out and seek support, and we need to show an openness and vulnerability. This is a powerful example of leadership in action. At the Fall Forum, there were educators and administrators who felt that they belonged for the first time in their career. Think about this: many LGTBQ+ adults and colleagues in our system do not feel safe in their schools. In light of this, how can a child blossom, have dreams and build self-confidence when adults themselves do not feel accepted and safe?

It is our obligation to support all of our students. As leaders, we must explicitly embed equity in our daily work, pay attention to who is not at the decision-making table, listen to all stories, and give voice to all students whether in urban or rural Ontario. By addressing inequities and systemic barriers, leaders give a clear message to the students that they matter. Providing opportunities for kids to dream, belong, and hope, can only help us move beyond tolerance and guide us in the direction of a truly equitable and inclusive education where all students not only succeed, but thrive. Our students deserve nothing less.

About the Author: *Carole Dufort is a twenty-nine year veteran in education who currently works for the Ontario Ministry of Education in Ottawa. She has been an administrator since 2002; serving the entirety of her career in small and rural communities. She has taught the Principal's Qualification Program for York University and in 2013 she won the Canada's Outstanding Principals Award from The Learning Partnership. She is passionate about equity and inclusive education and ensuring the well-being and success of all students.*

Chapter 8

Students as Teacher Educators

Florita Cotto

I am very interested in the practice of teachers who effectively teach students who are economically poor and of color, particularly Latino students. I am also interested in the lived academic experience of those students. My interest in this topic not only stems from my experiences as an inner-city student, but from my current position as a school principal.

Careful reflection and my own course studies have led me to take an interest in Culturally Relevant Pedagogy. Often teachers in urban districts are not prepared adequately to teach diverse learners or a diverse population of students. The exploration of this topic helped me realize that a student led PD [professional development] is a profound way to discuss some of these issues with the teachers. It is student driven and led because with some support, students would plan and facilitate the PD session. It was my hope that the students would help pre-service teachers develop an awareness of the need to better support Latino students. My other goal was to help pre-service teachers understand the teaching practice and dispositions that have been successful with students from diverse cultural backgrounds.

It all began with a conversation I was having with some students regarding their learning experiences in the school. Our conversation eventually shifted to their perception of quality instruction, and I grew increasingly intrigued at the students' ability to identify aspects of teacher personality or practice that they deemed most important to their academic success.

This conversation became one of several which took place during part of their lunch periods (approximately five to six times over the course of the year). The students were asked about circumstances and experiences taking place when they were academically successful, as well as teacher qualities and other aspects that they deemed important to their learning. I developed questions and talking points that pertained to teacher practice, interpersonal relationships as related to their growth, and teacher disposition.

To obtain a range of perspectives to my questions, I met with three seventh grade Latino students. The group consisted of two boys and one girl. They were represented as being academically high, average, and a struggling student. I asked questions to name teaching and learning experiences when they felt successful and unsuccessful.

Student Interviews

Overall the students had clear opinions about each teacher. They were able to describe positive educational experiences as well as negative ones. They also understood the role that the teachers played in these experiences. For example, when asked what teacher qualities made them successful, S#1 responded that the teacher showed him tricks to memorize concepts, and S#2 said there was a teacher she got to know well, and that if she did not understand something the teacher would explain it simply. They all agreed these teachers inspired them to do better. I arranged to meet with teachers who were deemed as "strong teachers" so I could learn about their teaching practice and disposition. I wanted to understand the practices that made them successful at supporting Latino students.

Teacher Interviews

The most important implications of the interview were that all three teachers were committed to the students' success. They discussed their philosophies, and what they deemed as critical attributes when educating

Latino students. Two of the teachers interviewed determined that establishing trust was most important; the other teacher noted that preparation for high school was most important. One important aspect that came across during the interview was that the teachers all employed some form of Culturally Relevant Teaching (CRT). They used the students' culture as a point of reference so that the students could understand the content being presented. At first I only shared my student discussions with the middle school focus group of teachers who would later go on to help students prepare and facilitate the PD. Later, I shared the discussion with the staff at a faculty meeting.

Action Plan

The following year I wanted to continue to explore how to prepare teachers to teach Latino students. I elicited the cooperation of my teacher focus group to help me prepare a PD session. In addition to the original teacher focus group, I included a first year teacher who graduated from MSU. These teachers were like-minded and showed a commitment to Culturally Responsive Teaching in their classroom.

Initially, I wanted the PD for our practicing teachers, but I quickly realized that it would not be as effective, since many had or were now teaching the students who were presenting. I contacted a professor from a nearby university and arranged for the PD to take place with her pre-service/student-teachers. After some brainstorming with the teacher focus group, the following survey questions were developed, and the survey was given to the entire eighth grade class:

1. Describe the teaching of your favorite teacher.
2. Describe your academic performance (grade) in that class compared to what you usually earn in similar classes.
3. How do you define academic success?
4. What year did you experience the most (academic) success?
5. Describe your relationship with that teacher.
6. Describe your worst class.
7. Based on your responses, what teaching strategies help you succeed?
8. Based on your responses, what teacher qualities help you to succeed?

9. Is it important for teachers to have a relationship with your parents?
10. Describe your biggest learning obstacle.

In addition to the survey, I met with my newly expanded student focus group several times to speak about their experiences. By the time we conducted our PD the following year, my group of students expanded to include additional seventh grade students: one high achieving, one struggling academically, and one with multiple disciplinary infractions. In all, my group consisted of seventh and eighth graders.

Once the survey was completed, the teachers and I looked at the notes and drafted the Powerpoint for the students based on our discussions and surveys. We then met as a group and the students rearranged some slides and decided who would speak on each slide. They made these decisions based on their conversations with me; the student who made the points on a topic was selected to lead the discussion on the slide. They reminded each other of what they had shared that would be interesting to share in the PD. This made me realize that they do pay close attention to each other and are attuned to each other's thoughts, feelings and experiences.

Professional Development (PD)

I found the entire process to be an amazing experience. The structure worked well and the PD was powerful for all. The PD was approximately 2.5-3 hours long and took place in one of the bigger classrooms. Approximately 13 pre-service teachers attended and participated in the PD. The students each opened with an introduction of themselves and a very short bio. Next, they presented the demographic of the city and later the school. The students proceeded to conduct an icebreaker activity where everyone stands at the same point and proceeds or takes steps backwards depending on their responses to the questions being read. This activity helped the pre-service teachers understand a lot about our students.

Our next activity involved a fishbowl activity where students responded to misconceptions about the city's Latino students and their families such as: they do not value education nor have a support system/

parental involvement. The students led small group breakout sessions where they engaged in a discussion about the fishbowl activity with the pre-service teachers. Through these shared experiences, the student teachers were able to help us see the importance of CRT.

The next activity involved the students sharing their greatest learning challenges. According to the survey and our data, language is a huge challenge. The students discussed what it is like to struggle with the language and how they help English learners in the classroom. They also shared how they are academically impacted by not having English speaking parents at home to help them. The students conveyed the measures they take to complete homework assignments and how the families identify relatives and neighbors to assist them when needed. In relating this, it was important to them that they convey that their parents still cared but could not help them. The students also discussed the challenges of learning academic language, since they learn Spanish first, then everyday English.

The students continued to discuss what practices make them successful and shared a Successful Teacher Cheat Sheet from the eyes of a student. Finally, they conducted a reflection activity "Walk a Day in My Shoes." Pre-service teachers were asked to think of 5-10 important points from the day that have helped them to better understand urban youth, and prepare them as a future educator. The university professor said that this was a powerful PD. Some of the reflections left behind from the pre-service teachers were:

"Get to know your students first. They are aware of the biases placed on them."

"Teachers can learn from students."

"I am becoming a teacher but today you all have taught me a great unforgettable lesson." "What I had learned about urban districts has been completely changed."

The students wrote:

"I really enjoyed talking to the pre-service teacher about the type of teacher they want to be."

"I learned that teachers are not as scary as I thought they would be. I had a great time expressing myself as a student."

The middle school students presented the information. I found the age of the students perfect since they were able to accurately convey how socio-economic factors play a role in their learning by speaking about how they navigate the lack of access and resources. The students also explained which teaching practices they have found to be successful and explained the academic areas where they have the biggest struggle (for these students the biggest struggle was language). I was particularly pleased that the information came across in a natural way that did not demean or degrade the students. The answers were in the context of their lived experiences. The teachers appreciated the reality of their everyday life, the day-to-day obstacles the students face in their academic life.

In these professional development sessions, teachers must employ higher-order thinking as they listen. They were asked to critically analyze and evaluate what they are hearing, apply the knowledge to their teaching and reflect on their practice. The students shared advice with the pre-service teachers that they thought would assist them to teach Latino students in the future.

Many may not see the value of CRT, but the topic is relevant because teachers that are equipped with a sense of social consciousness tend to be fair and equitable. They set high expectations for all students and they hold them accountable. With school populations increasing in student diversity, teachers are expected to create an inclusive classroom for all students.

About the Author: *Florita Cotto has been in school administration since 2008 and works in Paterson, NJ. She has administration experience at the high school and elementary school levels. She has an interest in urban education and student voice in professional development. Florita recently presented at the 2016 37th Annual Ethnography in Education Research Forum at U Penn. Also, she is a doctoral student at Montclair State University.*

Chapter 9

Protecting the Educational Environment or Pandering?

Matthew Boucher

Racial injustice is a volatile subject today, and schools are not insulated from this societal debate. Productive discourse on this issue is in short supply. As a white male, I do not presume to understand the lived experiences of citizens of color. Moreover, I am aware that as a beneficiary of white privilege, I may not be able to fully understand the pervasiveness of racism in our society today. I have observed how white denial of the existence of a "problem" only seems to exacerbate the issue. Last year I also observed that if there is no agreement on the existence of a societal problem, then there is a tendency to blame and fear those that want to confront the uncomfortable issue. Then I learned I played a role in this.

I work in a first ring suburb on the north side of a Midwest metropolitan area with a population of just over 3.5 million. Last year, like in many other large cities, we had several #BlackLivesMatter events around the metro. Shortly after one of these protests, a volatile chain of events was started at the high school in our district when a white female student posted on social media something to the effect of "Don't all lives matter?"

We are a small district with one high school and one middle school, separated by athletic fields and a street. We have a non-white student population of 54% at the secondary level but very few staff of color. This social media post erupted a series of reactions and counter reactions that began to polarize the high school along racial lines. The high school staff worked feverishly to get in front of the issue, but many students of color felt their voices and concerns went unheard. Thus, students planned their own walk out events.

As the Principal of the middle school, and informed of the rising tensions at the high school, I did not see the same fault lines developing in our building. The inciting social media post came out on Monday, and some students walked out of the high school on Wednesday to attend a #BlackLivesMatter event, and there were still no noticeable issues at the middle school. Then Thursday evening and Friday morning I begin receiving calls and emails from concerned parents wanting to know what we were going to do about the #BlackLivesMatter protest that was going to happen at the middle school on Friday.

Deeply concerned parents contacted me about their child's learning environment and well-being. Since I had not heard of any such plan, I asked these parents questions to gather more information. I also had the administrative team working simultaneously to collect as much insight as they could from students and families, all before the start of the school day on Friday. We learned that some middle school students heard about the events at the high school, and the inciting social media post, and felt it was unjust that there was no suspension issued to the student who authored the post. Thus, they were circulating a plan on social media to enact a sit-in on Friday while high school students were planning to have a walkout.

That morning I met with the staff to inform them of the student plan, and asked that they actively engage with students throughout the day. Moreover, I encouraged them to be comfortable creating meaning-ful dialogue around issues of injustice, even if it was at the expense of their lesson plans. I also informed them that I would start the day with an announcement reiterating our expectation of a productive and disrup-tion free day, and that we would act against anything that happens inside the school that negatively affects the learning environment. I closed the meeting by letting the staff know that if they had any clearly agitated students who needed an audience, I would clear my schedule and make myself available for any students who needed to talk.

I started the school day with an announcement outlining our expectations and the actions we would take against disruption inside the school. I also said I would be available for students to discuss the reasoning behind my announcement or any related issues. The staff were highly attentive to student needs and valuable discussions happened throughout the day. Some students had strong feelings and many others seemed indifferent; in that regard it may have been a typical day in a middle school. No sit-in or walk out occurred.

Meanwhile, at the high school, the staff and student leaders were working to find common ground. A voluntary assembly occurred in the auditorium prior to the start of the walk out. The students responded well to the opportunity to speak, while the high school staff gained valuable understanding, and no walk out happened.

Back at the middle school, as the day progressed, I found myself spending more time with parents than students. The level of concern parents held, based mostly on what they were getting from social media, took me aback. I continued to field calls about "what I was going to do about the #BlackLivesMatter protest that was going to happen in my school?" Parents began to ask if their kids would be safe. I did not fully understand what threat they perceived was present, since they were in school with the same kids every day. Then came the question that explained what we were really talking about. "I just want to be sure my daughter is going to be safe and not a target, after all she is a lily white, little blonde girl." Shortly after this conversation I had a parent show up, after the scheduled event time, to take his kids out of school for the day. He informed me he was doing so to be sure they were safe, since he heard there was going to be a #BlackLivesMatter protest at the school. In each conversation, I shared what we had learned, what had transpired in each building, and the steps that we were taking to ensure a safe and productive learning environment. The day ended without incident, but when I came in from bus duty the calls continued to roll in.

As life would have it, I had a graduate class that night and had to leave shortly after school to get to class. While I was packing up to leave,

I received a note from my clerical colleague with a parent's name and number and a statement about how upset this parent was, and that she was waiting for a return phone call. I contacted the parent on the way to class and she at once said, "I want to know about the protest that happened at your school today." I asked her where she heard this. She informed me that when she picked her daughter up from school, her daughter told her there had been one and had stories of mass chaos. I realized in that moment that if we were going to rely on adolescents to carry our message we might be in trouble. I decided I would send out a voice and email message to parents to be sure we accurately represent what was planned, what steps the school took, and what actually happened. I was convinced that I had to dispel the rumor that the #BlackLivesMatter organization was involved in the events of the day.

I wrote the message during the dinner break that night, and I asked a black friend and academic colleague to read the message and give me feedback. In other words, I applied the "I asked my black friend" filter. I felt I had struck a very neutral tone and discussed the persistent questions that had come my way throughout the day. I sent the message out that evening around 6 p.m. On Monday I received some feedback from parents that felt the message had assuaged their concerns. I also sought feedback on the message from some colleagues of color to get a perspective beyond my own. Because we have a strong relationship, and they had been involved in different layers of the events of the past week, they felt the message was proper. Then I got an email from a parent of color who expressed offence about the tone of my message, and felt I had denied students their freedom of speech and the right to assemble. We exchanged emails and I invited him to meet with me, but I never regained his trust.

When I got over my own sensitivities of feeling misjudged, I realized that both sides of this story were true. I had acted in a manner that had the intent of ensuring a productive learning environment for the day. However, I also acted in a manner that was pandering to the misplaced fears of some of our white parents. Thus, I created a neutral message that also had a clear tone, which I was simply too tone deaf to hear. I learned that whenever we act responsively to a single perspective, we also close the door for discourse from other perspectives. I wanted to discuss what

I thought was misguided fear, and I stuck to the facts. However, in doing so, I also projected that there was no room for conversation from another perspective. Upon further reflection, I realized I had inadvertently sent a coded message that some of our parents of color were all too familiar with, even if I was not. I now understand that what I really sent was an authoritarian message that clearly informed parents that no real conversations around race are allowed to happen at our school – even though some real conversations were happening. In the end, I not only avoided addressing the real issue with the concerned white parents, I validated their perspectives.

About the Author: *Matthew Boucher spent the first 10 years of his career in education as a social studies teacher in the Minneapolis Public Schools, before leaving the classroom to be a Teacher Advancement Program (TAP) Mentor and building coordinator. He has spent the past 11 years as a building administrator. Since 2008 he has been engaged to leading change at Fridley Middle School where their motto is "everybody learns everyday". He continues to pursue his education as a Doctoral student at the University of St. Thomas.*

Chapter 10

On Being an Inclusive Leader in Hard Political Times

Nancy Barno Reynolds, Ed.D.

eacher preparation is not a job for the faint of heart and we must value the teaching of students in K-12 programs as well as of students in teacher preparation programs, like the ones of which I am in charge. Particularly in tough political times, we must view teaching as the noble profession it is.

Here's the conundrum: in order to teach teachers how to teach, you have to understand what it is to teach, why it's important to teach, and where you position yourself in terms of commitment to your pedagogy. You must, in other words, have hope, passion, and a pedagogy that outlasts political elections, changes in educational fads, and new laws that impact funding for programs you care about. My pedagogy includes a belief in democratic teaching. This means teaching toward particular ideals of democracy which include freedom, equity, and social justice. It demands a lot of me, personally and professionally, but for the past 30 years, it has sustained me in my quest for excellence in education for all students.

Preparing students for inclusive education is not easy – you must lead them through dark alleys of self-discovery, you must teach humility, you must insist on a factual historical foundation upon which to understand what education is, has been, should be – and could be. I was lucky in this respect: I grew up the product of two teacher parents in the sixties and seventies during the Vietnam War, the Women's Liberation Movement, and the Sexual Revolution. My father was the head of the teachers' union at his school and teachers regularly congregated at our house creating picket signs for upcoming strikes, formulating articulate grievances in response to unfair policies, and bolstering each other up to do the important work of a noble profession. We children of public school teachers were poor, but we didn't know it; we sat in the kitchen happily licking Green Stamps to exchange for food, while our mothers mixed powdered milk with cocoa to keep us happy, seated, and relatively quiet. We didn't understand the importance of the activism happening in our living room, but I remember these things that sent me on a trajectory to fight for education and educators.

Our dinner table discussions revolved around inequities in society, inequities in the schoolhouse, inequities in the bedroom and war room, protest, and transformation of *what was* to *what should be*. I understood that what was happening in the world demanded action, but what was happening in schooling was being transformed by my father and his peers. Issues like fair pay for teachers and excellence in education for all students were front and center of my formative years. I knew at the age of four or five that I would become a teacher and that, in my house, this was "the noblest profession". I planned my life around that.

I taught for many years, in private and public schools, raised a family of six, and then earned my doctorate at the age of 47. As I said before, I teach teachers *how to teach*. Because of my background and experiences, I teach through a critical and democratically-based lens, asking constantly, in a Freirean tradition: *Who does this serve? Who is left out?* My goal is to teach my teachers to do the same, and to facilitate the journey of my 18 year old students, blessed with a passion for teaching, to the 22 year old teacher equipped with the skill and the knowledge to teach *well* and *for a purpose*. This involves the partial formula of teaching the dispositions of self-reflection, critical analysis, and evaluation, while honoring and exploring identity. A critical framework is used to teach all courses.

Probably the most popular and important course I teach is my Foundations of Education course: *The American High School: Identity and Difference in Schools*. In this course, we examine American education through major historical struggles for equity involving race, class, identity, gender, religion, sexual identification, and through an array of other barriers to quality education for all peoples - those groups we may call *marginalized*. We examine revolts and protests that lead to changes in law, and the inevitable resistance to policy changes in school which enforce laws protecting civil rights in schooling. Because I am a middle-class, heterosexual, agnostic white woman, I do not represent many of the marginalized communities we discuss in this class. I view it as my responsibility to bring in speakers who represent identities I do not share to talk about their experiences in public school as someone labeled as Black, Latino, Native American, Muslim, Christian, and/or LGBTQ. We also hear the stories of students with disabilities, evolutionists and creationists, and individuals in favor of and opposed to comprehensive sexual health education in public schools. I do this in the hope that each student will identify with a struggle for equity and access and make the connection to the role of education as a vehicle for transformation of *what is* to *what should be*. This is my attempt to create inclusive educators. This passion for excellence in education for all students, I believe, is the greatest thing I can facilitate through my position.

My main job is as the director of three Inclusive Adolescence Education programs (grades 7-12) – *inclusive* being the operative word here. It means planning, implementing, and assessing for a diverse population of students, and insists upon the full inclusion of all students - particularly, students with disabilities who have not been served by public education. However, to an inclusive educator, reaching any student not being served by an educational system that is meant for the public is a sacrosanct responsibility.

As an inclusive educator, I position myself as a person who possesses a mixture of knowledge, talents, and beliefs, as well as "Black Holes" of ignorance, experience, and ability. This evaluation of self is crucial to good teaching, as it invites reflection and demands brutal truth, and finally, concrete action. I must, in other words, commit to a pedagogy that serves all students and first recognize – and change – those things about myself which hinder students' access to excellent education at my own hands.

Right now, these dispositions of good teaching feel under threat, hence my temporary low point of self-doubt. You must forgive. People who feel passionately about excellence in education for all students may occasionally be derailed when confronted with barriers. On a macro-level, we consider the roles of poverty, policy, race and discrimination (for instance) in the attainment of excellence for all. On a meso-level, we examine the roles of culture, tradition, religion, family, community norms, beliefs, attitudes, identity, and even social media. On a micro-level, we consider the role of self in professionalism and craft: our own education, upbringing, abilities and experiences, for instance.

Excellent inclusive educators must study theory, practice, and curriculum design. We must commit to a personal philosophy of education. We must take hard looks at our ideas about multiculturalism, our positioning of self and others, our curriculum and textual choices, and our language use. We must decide to welcome dissent, agree to share power, must admit to our "Black Holes" of ignorance, and we must interrogate our knowledge about identities we don't share. An inclusive educator must decide where he or she is located in their commitment to critical pedagogy and to the valuing of students. Our beliefs and attitudes matter. Our willingness to eat "Humble Pie" matters. Our valuing of identity and difference matter. Our positioning of self and others matters. These things are critical to good teaching.

But today, we must put our money where our mouth is: we must trust that inclusive educators are agents of change. We must remember, embrace, and have faith in the struggles of Educators Past, who persevered through other political and social revolutions. We must remember that our job – providing excellence in education for all students – is for the purposes of a higher good and a sound democracy. In the end, I will assert that teaching may yet indeed be the noblest profession of all.

About the Author: *Dr. Nancy Barno Reynolds is the Director of Inclusive Adolescence Education at Cazenovia College in Central New York. Her work on the use of critical literacies for transformative and democratic teaching* *has been presented at both national and international conferences, and is published in the Journal of Social Sciences Research, New Educational Foundations, Teaching Tolerance, and Idiom.*

Chapter 11

An Experiment in Place-Based Education: Celebrating Family and Community

Jeanne L. Surface

As an applicant for my first principalship in an increasingly diverse rural community, I had formulated three goals that I hoped to pursue. First, I wanted school to be engaging for students. Second, I wanted to be an advocate for diversity and help bridge two cultures newly brought together. Third, I wanted to bring the community into the school and the students into the community. Those goals must have resonated with the school board, because I got the job. The experiences I had over the next five years were unforgettable.

It did not take long to discover that this was a community undergoing rapid change. By the end of my first year, the Latino population had grown from 3% to 30% due to labor needs at a large processing plant. An undercurrent of racism existed, and the two cultures seemed to function separately. I felt compelled to reach out to Latino families and to do everything I could to bring the two cultures together. I wanted them to understand one other but was not sure how to successfully create a bridge between the cultures.

Place-Based Learning

From a university-sponsored network of rural schools, I learned about place-based learning. Once introduced to the concept, it did not take long to see that the three goals I brought to this school could be met with this pedagogy. In place-based learning the curriculum is contextualized in what is familiar and what matters to the students, their community, and its surroundings. The relevance of lessons taps into the child's innate desire to learn.

Place-based pedagogy has roots in the work of John Dewey. More than any other American educator, he worked to overcome the disconnection between the world of the child and his schooling. Dewey was well aware that from the standpoint of a child, the great waste in the school came from the inability to utilize "real life" experience, connecting what they learn to their daily lives. He argued that children have minds that are *drawn to phenomena* rather than to *ideas about phenomena*. (Dewey, 1959, pp. 76-78). Local circumstances can supply the needed ideas. Others since Dewey have argued that using place-based learning enhances the development of children across a range of life circumstances, not just within the realm of traditional school subjects.

The idea of place-based learning was accepted and pursued. Teachers became involved in planning what "could be." The idea of a weeklong "Institute" became the center of our conversations. We had shared readings and discussions at faculty meetings. As the conversations deepened, an experiment began to take shape. The theme was "A Celebration of Family and Place."

The Institute

The weeklong celebration began. Community residents of all ages were very involved in the learning. One group studied the landing at Normandy Beach in World War II with a resident who had been at this historical event. Senior citizens managed the school store so that it could remain open while the students who ran it were involved in their work.

Some students learned to be entrepreneurs. The fifth grade students created a business of making marbled stationary and at the exhibition night sold all of their products within 30 minutes of opening their display. They made $95 after paying back a "small business loan" and they took orders for more stationery. Folk art chickens that were made under the direction of the local carver were displayed and sold.

A professional troubadour was hired for the week. He helped students write oral histories and turn them into songs to honor four very diverse community elders: a woman and three men. The elderly woman was involved in the war effort for WWII and told the story of teaching in a one-room school. One of the men was the founder and CEO of the largest employer in the community. Another man was an accountant and the mayor of the community. This man was physically disabled and put tremendous energy into recording the history of the community. The fourth man was Latino and brought his family to work for the largest employer in the community. His family members were the first people in the community who spoke two languages and did not have white skin. Having the first Latino man and his employer being honored as elders at the same time was a thought-provoking addition to the message of the evening.

Exhibition Night

Exhibition night was truly unforgettable. Students displayed their work for the community. Many conversations took place. At the end of the evening, the performances began. The gymnasium barely had enough chairs for the audience. The exhibition started with ethnic dances. I remember vividly a new immigrant child performing a Mexican hat dance. The audience clapped as he danced, and with the excitement and motivation from the audience, the passion on his face became very apparent, and his moves became even more artistic.

The troubadour and the students ended the evening with the honoring of the community elders. I remember shivering as I heard the dedication, and I could see tears coming from some audience members as a result of this very special tribute. In my own mind, I could see that at least some of the community wrapped their arms around the cultures that were present and grew to respect those who were minorities. I noticed in the weeks that followed, the cultural bridging that happened between the students. The lunch tables were made up of students from both cultures rather than across the room from each other. It was interesting to watch the students in the classrooms working together. Something had changed.

Challenges

Overall, it was an amazing week, but some challenges surfaced. The day before the final event, a parent bounded into my office, angry that their child had to be "at this exhibition night." Students have never been required to be at evening activities in the past, and why did I think this was so important to require them to be at this activity. The fuss with him went on and on. I suspected that his next plan of action was to involve the parents of other students in the complaint. I was correct.

A phone call began with the parent asking me, "Whose stupid idea it was to have this program?" I said, very proudly, knowing that I might as well own up to such a terrible deed, "It was me, sir," I said that I would be happy to visit with him on Monday, but I needed to prepare a few things before the evening event. He said that "he was on his way to my office, and I better be there." I told him very politely that the exhibition was to start in 30 minutes, and I did not feel like I had the time right now to talk to him. I waited for his arrival, but he did not come. I assumed that he gave up on the idea. I was ready to announce the start of a play and left my office. I saw him as I rushed down the hall to the gym. I decided I better respond to this parent. I attempted to defuse his anger, but I realized his goal was to argue with me. I finally said that I sincerely apologized for the inconvenience this night had on his family, and told him that I needed to attend to some details and walked away. The parent stayed at the exhibition for the entire night. His daughter was involved in a musical and some ethnic dances. I wondered if he enjoyed any of it.

The most disturbing challenge of the week involved the troubadour, the oral histories, and song dedicated to these elders. The students were practising for the Friday performance and a man who attended the same church as I do came into the area where the students were practising. I knew how much this man loved music, so I made an assumption that he came to see and hear how the students were progressing toward the performance. Much to my chagrin, that was not his intention at all. I spoke to him for a minute and realized that he was angry. I will never forget what this man who owned a farm said to me. "I am pulling my son out of this waste of school time; he can come home and work in the field for the rest of the week." The student was in the group that created the oral history and wrote the song for the Latino man who was the first member of his ethnic group to join the community. Then the parent said, "no son of mine is going to honor 'a spic.'" I can remember wondering how we could attend the same church and feel so differently about human beings. Besides breaking what I thought was a friendship, I was appalled at his racism. Even more disturbing was the fact that he made this comment in front of 16 students. After this experience, I went to my office, shut my door, and cried.

This week was a learning experience for me. Some teachers embraced it; others did not. Some parents did not support it, though most of them did. The community was very excited to be included in the experience and for the elders of the community, the honor was of great magnitude. Most importantly, the students did not forget the experiences of the week. Community members were very proud of their school and were gracious to be included and honored by young people. There will always be some who want to take away from the beauty of an activity. I've learned to set those experiences aside and remember the impact and joy.

References

Dewey, J. (1959). Dewey on Education. New York, NY: Teachers College Press.

About the Author: *Jeanne L. Surface is an Associate Professor of Educational Leadership at the University of Nebraska, Omaha. She has served as a rural principal in Nebraska and most recently as a Superintendent in a remote rural school district in northwestern Wyoming, next to Yellowstone National Park. Her research interest is rural education and public school law. Jeanne can be contacted at jsurface@unomaha.edu*

Chapter 12

Thomas' Snowsuit: The Unexamined Life of the Principal

Donna Kowalchuk

Have you ever been at a social event and been asked what you do for a living? When I reply I am a principal, generally speaking, the expression on the person's face asking the question, usually reveals some sort of flash back memory and visceral response to what I can only speculate he or she experienced as a child in school. When I jokingly answer with something to relieve the tension, he or she often moves onto either a different topic or to a new conversation. For some time, I have been questioning how the role of the principal is socially constructed in our society.

Recently, while reading with my grandchildren, I started to deconstruct how principals are portrayed in children's literature. Many authors characterize the role of principal as an overbearing and frequently overweight middle-aged Caucasian male who controls teachers and children through fear. I offer *Thomas' Snowsuit*, the infamous book by Robert Munsch (1985). In reading this book and others, I was again prompted to reflect on the stereotype of the principal, asking myself, *"What is the role of a principal?"*

Socrates is often credited with the declaration that "the unexamined life is not worth living." Building on this statement, I would say that the role of the principal is one that teaches how to lead an examined life. The actions needed to do so are the practices of critical thinking and critical reflection. Critical thinking occurs when you question rather than accept all claims. Critical reflection is making meaning out of an experience. Through these actions, students, their families, and educators will be able to examine issues that really matter in their own contexts and in the world beyond.

So how does a person in the role of principal set the conditions to lead others to think and reflect critically? And which action comes first? The first step is to lead by example. This is done by introspectively and critically examining your own journey.

Learning how to think critically may have been part of my experiences as a child. However, in order to understand how I developed critical thinking, I would need to critically reflect on my life experiences. Truly, these actions are simply different sides of the same coin.

From my first teaching assignment in a small rural school, then in a regional high school, followed by a central position, then principalships in four different, diverse and remote schools, I have witnessed the despair and hopelessness in marginalized Aboriginal students for over 20 years. Now, having moved to the largest urban school board in Canada, first as a secondary vice-principal and now as an elementary principal, I have seen the marginalization of immigrant and refugee students due to racism, language and spiritual/cultural discrimination and poverty.

The questions I ask myself, regardless of the context, are about privilege—who has it and, alternatively, who does not; and about power—how is the status quo—the marginalization that exists in public education—perpetuated?

You may be asking yourself, why or how did I come to think like this given that I am a white, privileged female?

My close friends, many of whom are educators, have been trying to understand my need to challenge the status quo for years. They believe one significant factor in developing my passion for critical thinking was born from the decade in which I *'came of age'*— meaning my transition from being a child that accepted how the world was constructed in a certain way, to the realization that what takes place in the world needs a close and critical examination. To be forthright, I may have to concede that they are likely right.

I offer my experience as an example of the close connection between critical thinking and critical reflection. I was a child of the 1960s. Some claim it is the decade that changed America. Canada too was deeply affected by the civil rights and anti-war struggles in the United States. I clearly remember the impact of the assassinations of Kennedy and King. During this decade, I began to personalize how race situated power, and what it meant to be white. At the same time, my worldview was tested by a very personal experience that intensified my interest in equity and social justice, and my consciousness of my privileged white position in Canadian culture. In 1969, "Janet" from a nearby "Indian" reservation, sat in the desk in front of me at school. I observed classmates, teachers, and administrators excluding and punishing Janet for being different — in their words, "a dirty Indian." Then and to this day, I feel shame and guilt for my white privilege and for not following my values and standing up for Janet.

Principal leadership is an intensely personal experience—an iterative process of critical thinking and critical reflection. The questions we ask ourselves about who we are and what we stand for dictate how we lead. Doing so enables each of us to lead authentically.

A passage paraphrased from Stein in *The Art of Racing in the Rain* clearly identifies the importance of critical reflection:

> Inside each of us resides the truth. But sometimes it is hidden in a hall of mirrors. We must shatter the mirrors. We must look into ourselves and root out the distortions until that thing which we know in our hearts is perfect and true, stands before us. Only then will justice be served.

Resistance begins with the assumption that all people have the capacity to produce knowledge and resist domination. By sharing my story, I challenge each of you reading this narrative to similarly critically reflect on your experiences that brought you to the role of principal. It is only through looking inward that we can break down the social biases that exist around the role of the principal. In doing so, we are able not only to free ourselves from the stereotypical boundaries of our role; we are able to increase our personal and professional effectiveness to carry out our responsibility to empower others to do the same.

Critical thinking is not new. Socrates viewed it as central to education. Others view it as being central to a democratic society. If, as I claim, our role as principal is to teach how to lead an examined life, the next time I am questioned about what I do, I will engage in a critical dialogue that, above all, will challenge the dominant conceptions of the role of the principal in education.

And, the next time I read with my lovely grandchildren, I will engage them in questioning whose voice is portrayed in depicting the role of the principal, and whose voice is missing. They can then make their own decisions.

About the Author: *Donna Kowalchuk is first a teacher, and then a principal, whose diverse experiences in public education prompted her to engage in an examination of education policy and leadership through doctorate studies at the University of Toronto. She is devoted to her four grandchildren who teach her daily about the importance of examining one's life and chosen work.*

Chapter 13

Welcome to Working in the Inner City

Paul McGuire

I have been involved in education for 30 years and I have worked in a variety of elementary and secondary schools. I coordinated numerous trips to the Dominican Republic, Mexico and El Salvador with students and teachers to learn more about poverty and social justice. It has only been in the last three years that I had the privilege to work in an economically disadvantaged area in my own backyard.

Over these past three years, I undertook an amazing learning journey that really changed the way I look at my role as an administrator. This occurred by moving to a unique and unfamiliar area in my own city. Characterized by dilapidated housing, little access to parks and recreation, and a high proportion of English as second language families, this neighborhood faces a variety of other challenges that go with establishing a family in a new country.

Working as an administrator in an economically disadvantaged school is like nothing else. It is so fulfilling because there is so much that needs to be done and there are many variables that need consideration. There are also aspects that need a different approach. You cannot thrive in a community like this without a rich network of support. If you are about to enter a high poverty area, make sure you find out who is out there to support your families. You cannot do this by yourself; you will never have sufficient resources.

It is important to state that schools act as an equalizer for kids living in challenging communities. These students are as capable as students living in other parts of the city. We have access to great programming and support materials. Our school is actually one of the only schools in our district where every child from Grades 3 to 6 has a computer issued to them at the beginning of the school year. The Grade 4 to 6 students are required to bring their computer home each night to continue the work they started earlier in the day.

I needed to connect to the community surrounding the school - even before my first official day as principal. The summer before my first year, I visited some of the agencies that were supporting our families. I quickly learned that I was surrounded by a rich assortment of great community resources. One of my most important visits was to the local community health center. This incredible facility offers subsidized childcare services, a mental health intake service, a food and clothing bank, and a whole host of community outreach programs. I really cannot imagine what our work at school would be like if we did not have this incredible community partner. This health center is one of many community partnerships that help us serve our families.

I have brought parents directly to the center to access their services, especially to be linked up for personal counselling. Our families can also receive housing and financial advice and they support parents seeking recreational activities for their kids. Students and teachers deliver important social skills programs with the help from staff from the center. This year, they will be expanding their programming to offer parenting classes right in the school.

It is important to note here that none of this would be possible without the work we have done to build trust amongst the parent community. In many ways, we act as a local community center where parents and children come to us when they need help with family issues, or links to recreation programs. We also run a breakfast and lunch program that really makes a big difference to families struggling to make ends meet.

I am also finding that we can serve some of our families better by meeting them in their own homes. Some families are not always comfortable coming into the school to meet with the principal. Some of the greatest gains we have made in building trust have come from these home visits.

I discovered that the community health center now sponsors a monthly brown bag lunch networking session. These sessions are invaluable; each time I go, I meet someone else who can offer important support to our students and families. The meetings are structured in a way that allows stakeholder community stakeholders to introduce themselves and their services. We all make useful connections to a whole variety of programming that we would never know about if it were not for these open-ended sessions.

Most recently, for example, we were able to enroll our junior students in swimming lessons financed by the neighborhood pool. A great thrill for our kids! The lessons are entirely free and our kids love the opportunity to swim every week. We arranged this opportunity after one brown bag lunch.

We have also developed close relationships with other agencies that provide camps for our students during winter weekends and for ten days in the summer. The camp program - Christie Lake Kids - has been offering these great opportunities to lower income kids for decades. I became aware of their programs through my own children - all three of our children have worked for the summer and inner city programs over the past ten years. Christie Lake offers a number of great inner city programming, and this year, for example, they will be offering after school cooking classes in our school for our students.

Another small agency called Rec Link connects families to recreation opportunities in the community. This agency only has three staff, but they provide invaluable support to our families. In the past week, they have arranged swimming lessons for one of our students and are now working on linking some of our students up to soccer programs in the community. This agency is so important to us that we have offered them office space at our school in the past to make it easier for them to meet up with our parents.

I also found that it is important to get very good at writing grant proposals. Regardless of where you live, there is a long list of grants available for your school. Wherever possible, I worked to develop good, positive relationships with potential funders. Spending a few hours talking to a funder about the unique needs of your school can reap great rewards. Because of this extra effort, we rarely are refused when we apply for financial support.

Over the past two years, we raised over $160 000 for our school. One grant was for $100,000 from the Aviva Community Foundation. Aviva is an insurance company that runs a wonderful campaign each year to support local community initiatives.

With the help of another organization - Evergreen, we developed a proposal for an entirely new yard called 'Asphalt to Oasis'. We garnered support for this program using social media, and in our second attempt we won the national award. Money attracts money. We were able to collect an additional $60,000 to complete the total renovation of our yard.

Finally, attitude is crucial. Sometimes I hear that we are unable to do something because we are situated in a poor neighborhood. The word "poverty" then becomes a wall instead of an opportunity. This kind of attitude leads to inaction. We literally and figuratively cannot afford this. Our students deserve as good an education as any other student in the city. My job as an administrator is to change this negative attitude. Anything is possible, and the principal is the agent of change in the school community.

Changing attitudes can take time, but it is much easier if you take the position that anything is possible with a good support network and some funding. We now believe that we can achieve anything we put our minds to. We can see evidence of this everywhere in our school.

This community has changed me. It is amazing to know that after 27 years in education you can still learn important things. I have learned that even in one of the richest cities in our country, we have terrible poverty. I have also learned, through my principalship and travels to the global south, that poverty manifests itself in many different forms - some more obvious than others. The lack of financial wealth is counterbalanced by the wealth of community support and the sheer energy and good will of our children. I have learned that you need to work as a community to counteract financial poverty and channel strengths. I have learned that there are many people out there who really want to help make a difference; it is often just a matter of asking. Most importantly, I have learned if you want change to happen, you do not wait for someone to do this for you - that simply will not happen.

I feel that here, I can really make a difference, and that the education that we are providing will give these children the tools they will need to prosper. This is a powerful feeling - one that you do not get in every job. I have been in education for thirty years now and I really feel that everything that I have learned in the past has prepared me for this role. This will be my last school and certainly my best experience. This is the best job ever! Be the change.

About the Author: *Paul McGuire is an Elementary School Principal in Ottawa, Ontario, Canada. Paul has a great interest in digital technology for education and making learning visible through various forms of social media. Paul is soon to retire after thirty-one years in education; he is getting ready to climb Mt. Kilimanjaro for a local charity this March. More adventures to follow! You can follow him on Twitter at @mcguirp*

PART III
Leading the Instructional Practice

rincipal leadership development programs often emphasize the instructional leadership role of principals. Instructional leadership is one of many important dimensions of a principal's leadership imperative. Managing the instructional program and leading the instructional program are part of the same continuum. Some may say that managing versus leading represents a false dichotomy. Principals work towards greater precision with each iteration of personal leadership problems of practices based on theories of action. This precision is evidence-informed, and supported by principal learning teams. Principal learning needs are determined by teacher learning needs, which are determined by student learning needs. Principals recognize that their influence on student achievement is indirect. The important work of school improvement, including consideration of student achievement and well-being, occurs when dedicated principals work with talented teachers, and school-based and system-based support personnel. Mobilizing engagement of all stakeholders is required. A deep commitment to honouring the student voice is required.

Chapter 14

Leading for School Improvement: Collecting, Analyzing, and Disseminating Achievement Data to Guide Instructional Practices in Schools

Denver J. Fowler, Ed.D.

Implementing a Data Team

It was summer and I had just accepted a new position as the Assistant Principal at a middle school located in the Midwest. Having already completed some surface level research on the building data for the interview process, I was aware of the report card and the areas that needed attention. During my first week on the job, I met with the principal that I worked with and proposed the idea of creating a data team within our school building. To my delight, my colleague was very receptive to my idea. I envisioned the data team would consist of as many stakeholders as possible. In the end, it would consist of school administrators, teachers, intervention specialists, gifted coordinators, and instructional coaches. The goal for the data team was to gather and organize data. The objective was to provide as much data to the staff as possible in order to inform targeted interventions with all students, close achievement gaps, and to inform instructional practices across the entire school building within all three grade levels (6-8). In August, I sent an email to all staff members asking if anyone was interested in serving on our data team. The response was overwhelming, and in the end we had 13 committed staff members on our data team to start the school year.

Analysis of Data

Shortly after the academic school year began, we held our first data team meeting. After we agreed on our goals, objectives, and vision for the team, the first step was to carefully analyze our most recent state report card. In *Gap Closing/AMO*, we had received a D (66.7%). This component would immediately become an area of focus. Additionally, we decided to focus our efforts on our overall *Achievement (Performance Index and Indicators Met)* component. In addition, we decided to focus on the *Progress (Value-Added)* component. More specifically, we focused on the *Lowest 20% in Achievement* measure. Because the Progress component measures how much students grow each school year, we felt it was an important component to focus on, along with the others. In addition to the focus areas on our state report card, we made it a goal to promote and support the regular analysis of more recent student data such as various benchmark reading assessments and teacher-developed formative assessments – basically any assessment data we could get our hands on. Finally, we decided that we would share as much data with staff as possible, provide detailed methods on how to use the data, and conduct professional development with both the data team and staff when possible. The next step was to collect and disseminate the data. The data team would use *Education Value-Added Assessment System*[1] *(EVAAS)* to collect student data from the state assessments.

---

1   Education Value-Added Assessment System "provides valuable diagnostic information about past practices and reports on students' predicted success probabilities at numerous academic milestones" (SAS EVAAS for K-12, 2015).

Collecting and Dissemination of the Data

Below is a list of data sets (see Table 1) that we gathered through the use of EVAAS. Each data set was shared with staff throughout our school building with the inclusion of a detailed description of what each data set represented, how to use the data to guide targeted interventions, and how to use the data to drive instructional practices within the classroom and grade levels. This data was shared using Excel in order to keep it organized, readily accessible, and easily shared.

Table 1

Summary of Data Sets

Data Set	Description
Data Set 1	This data set included students who were *Not Likely To Be Proficient (NLTBP)* in Math and Reading (Grades 6-8) and Science (Grade 8) on the upcoming state assessments. These were students who were determined NLTBP on upcoming state assessments in Math, Reading, and Science based on their previous performances on state assessments.
Data Set 2	This data set included students who were identified to be in three or more subgroups (i.e., Individualized Education Plan [IEP], Socio Economic Status, Race, Gifted, Limited English Proficiency, Free & Reduced Lunch, etc.) in Grades 6-8. In layman's terms, these students could really hurt (or help) our school building report card data based on their performance on the upcoming state assessments. Essentially, because these students fell under several different subgroups, they can be in multiple relevant subgroups for measures like Value-Added. For example, a student who is identified as gifted in Math and on an IEP, would be in the Gifted-Value-Added measure and that same student would also be included in the Students with Disabilities Value-Added grade. Essentially, their performance on the state assessments carried "more weight" so to speak in either direction with regards to how well they performed.
Data Set 3	This data set included students who were both NLTBP and in three or more subgroups (i.e., Individualized Education Plan, Socio Economic Status, Race, Gifted, Limited English Proficiency, Free & Reduced Lunch, etc.) in Math and Reading (Grades 6-8) and Science (Grade 8).
Data Set 4	This data set included students who were *Not Growing* year to year in Math and Reading in Grades 6-8. Within this data set, we also included what subgroups these students belonged to.

In addition to the four data sets listed above, we also collected and analyzed data from benchmark assessments via STAR[2], BAS[3] and teacher-developed formative assessments throughout the academic school year. We also provided several professional development opportunities outside of the school day and within staff meetings for both data team members and staff. For example, we shared how to analyze and use STAR data to set up interventions and goals for students, how to interpret the scores, shared examples of student growth versus non-growth, presented how to use the student diagnostic report and instructional reading level (IRL) effectively with classroom instruction, shared how to interpret the growth proficiency chart, and how to use the built-in interventions within the STAR software. We also emphasized the importance of discussing STAR data with students and explaining their scores to them in a way that allowed for them to clearly understand their own data, how we used it, and why it was so important for them to do their best on each assessment. This is just one example of professional development that the data team presented to our staff throughout the school year, however, our focus was to provide meaningful professional development throughout the academic school year that could be utilized with classroom instruction.

Using the Data to Guide Instructional Practices

Perhaps the most important element of forming a data team is ensuring that the data collected, analyzed and shared is put to use by your staff. The data from the state assessments (i.e., Data Sets 1-4) were used to create initial intervention groups. This data was also useful in creating a snapshot of our school building and each grade level as it pertains to

---

2   STAR Enterprise "assessments offer expanded skills-based testing, providing even more information to help you better understand student performance and improve instruction" (Renaissance Learning, Inc., 2009).

3   BAS is "the Fountas & Pinnell Benchmark Assessment System (BAS) seamlessly links assessment to instruction along The Continuum of Literacy Learning. This comprehensive system for one-on-one assessment reliability and systematically matches students' instructional and independent reading abilities to the F&P Text Level Gradient."

state achievement. Our staff also found this data helpful as they were able to reference the data sets (list of names) in order to ensure the students in their respective classrooms were growing, and if not, provide necessary intervention/enrichment as needed. The STAR and BAS scores were used in several different formats as well. Our staff used this data to determine instructional and independent reading levels for each student. Because the STAR and BAS assessments are administered throughout the school year, it allowed the data team and staff to identify trends in student growth. ELA teachers used the data to form *Zone Intervention*[4] groups. The focus of this intervention is to close students' reading gaps. Content teachers used this data to determine reading levels and abilities of their students which allowed them to differentiate articles and assignments based on this data. This data also allowed us to determine which seventh grade students would benefit from taking eighth grade *Academic Connections*[5]. Our Science teachers used the data to level articles being used within their instructional units. That is, all students receive articles covering the same content; however, articles can be leveled so that the content is more accessible to students. Our Social Studies teachers used the data to group students into ability groups for instructional units, especially for the *We The People*[6] unit. Each group of students is given a textbook that more closely reflects their reading levels. Our Health teachers use the data to determine appropriate leveled articles as well.

---

4   Zone Intervention is one class period a day set aside for each grade level to pull students for pure intervention (remedial or enrichment) during the school day. This is not to be confused with Study Hall, as students still have Study Hall for one period each school day as well. Study Hall is used more for homework, make-up work, testing, and re-testing, but it also can be used for intervention and enrichment as needed.

5   Academic Connections at Gahanna Middle School South is an ungraded class that appears on a student's schedule outside of Study Hall and Zone Intervention. This class time is used in its entirety for intensive intervention purposes and for closing achievement gaps.

6   "The We The People: The Citizen and the Constitution Program promotes civic competence and responsibility among the nation's upper elementary and secondary students" (Center for Civic Education, 2015). We are the only middle school in the State of Ohio to send a We The People team to the national competition each year in Washington, D.C. where our students participate and compete in simulated congressional hearings.

Being cognizant of student reading levels, our Health teachers located articles on events and issues affecting middle school students across the globe. Overall, by using the data to be aware of students' reading and performance levels, our teachers were able to locate articles and books that make content more accessible to all of our students.

Results

In the end, we received all A's on our report card. We raised our *Gap Closing/AMO* grade from a D (67.7%) to a B (84.5%), the highest in our school district (of 11 school buildings). Additionally, we raised our *Performance Index Score* from 101.5 (84.6%) to 102.4 (85.4%), the highest in the history of our school building. Finally, we raised our *Lowest 20% in Achievement* from a B to an A. In addition, we were the only school building in our district and within Central Ohio with all A's on our state report card, and one of only a few with an A in the *Gifted Measure*. It should also be mentioned that we had a student in our school building score the highest in the state on the eighth grade Math state assessment. These outcomes were certainly an area of satisfaction for all stakeholders involved including students, staff, parents, and community members. Perhaps one of the most important results is unmeasurable, that is, I felt our data team and staff became better at analyzing and using data to drive instructional practices in our school building across all three grade levels (6-8).

The addition of the data team proved to be extremely beneficial to our school building. The following school year there was even more interest from our staff to serve on the data team. Thus, we were able to be more cognizant and strategic as to who was on our data team. We added several more members to the data team and we were even granted several professional development days by our district office in order to allow our data team to meet during the school day (versus before or after). For example, our district purchased a new performance tracking software called PerformancePlus[7]. We spent professional development time teaching the

---

7   PerformancePLUS "provides educators a single point of contact to easily access state, national, and local assessment data" (PerformancePLUS, 2015).

data team how to run reports (create data sets) and share them with their colleagues. We also challenged the data team members to be the "data leaders" in our school building. There were also perks to serving on the data team. For example, our district office granted all data team members special access to student data district-wide (versus only the students in their respective classrooms). In addition, the success we experienced with our data team was contagious as several other school buildings within our district (as well as other surrounding school districts) created data teams the following school year and modeled their teams after ours.

References

Center for Civic Education (2015, June 1). We The People: The Citizen and the Constitution [Website]. Retrieved from http://www.civiced.org/national-finals-2015-about

PerformancePLUS (2015, May 29). PerformancePLUS a PLUS 360 application [Website]. Retrieved from https://guilderlandschools-ny.perfplusk12.com/default.asp

Renaissance Learning, Inc. (2009). *Key questions STAR enterprise can help you answer.* [Brochure]. Gahanna, OH: Author.

SAS EVAAS for K-12. (2015, May 28). Retrieved from http://www.sas.com/en_us/industry/k-12-education/evaas.html

About the Author: *Dr. Denver J. Fowler is currently an Assistant Professor of Educational Leadership at The University of Mississippi within the School of Education. He has over a decade of experience in the PreK-12 educational setting and over seven years of experience in higher education. He was named 2015 State Assistant Principal of the Year in the State of Ohio, and was nominated for the 2015 National Assistant Principal of the Year in the United States.*

Chapter 15

Professional Learning Communities: A Stairs Approach to Increased Student Success

Kevin Reimer

I t was the end of the school day and the gym was full of primary students engaged in a game of skittles bowling. What I envisioned as a fun end of the day activity for about 80 students devolved into a crying fit when kids made up their own game that involved knocking the pins over with their bodies instead of the ball. One could hear tearful pleas to stop all of the noise.

A grade seven volunteer helper came over to talk to me. "This is starting to get out of control, Mr. Reimer." My expectations in the beginning were so high. Of course, as a high school teacher and former middle school vice-principal with no real elementary school training, I was not prepared for all that could and did go wrong. So, now I was standing in a chaotic gym with unhappy and frenetic children, and all I could think was that all I had wanted to do was to give teachers more time to collaborate on student learning.

Let me back up ... it is best that I start at the beginning. Whenever I arrived at a new school, I always liked to ask the staff what is it that they needed from me. I would ask them to bear in mind that I did not have a blank cheque so there were limits to what I could provide for them. However, that always tended to be irrelevant because the answer that I consistently heard was teachers wanted more time to work together. The answer resonated strongly as I had long been a proponent of the Dufour model of Professional Learning Communities (PLC) and was eager to find a way to implement a PLC model in my new assignment.

Back to the office I went, and after many tries, I created a twice-weekly schedule that allowed teachers to meet in grade levels during the school day while I took their students. While teachers followed a PLC model, I worked with support staff and leadership students to provide supervision for the students. As described in the first paragraph, it was at times a challenging and chaotic model that relied on a great deal of organization and commitment on my part. However, for me it was worth the growing pains and the stretching of my skill set and comfort zone so that teachers had the time and space to collaborate effectively. A gym full of restless children on the brink of tantrums was worth the positive results that we could achieve through an effective PLC. Over time, as in most cases in schools, our approach of releasing teachers to meet became a regular part of our routine, and the students began to look forward to their large group time as much as the teachers looked forward to the opportunity to collaborate with colleagues.

Following our initial foray into a PLC model, more schools in my home district began to adopt their own PLC models to create collaborative time for their teaching staff. Over the course of several years, we reached an interesting tipping point in that more than 60% of our schools were involved in creating collaborative time for their teachers. As encouraging as that was, it did come with drawbacks. The biggest drawback, from my perspective, was that while principals and vice-principals were supervising large groups of kids, they were unable to be involved in those collaborative conversations with teachers. This was an important piece of their work as educational leaders. Without going into all the details and the years of effort behind the scenes, the district eventually adopted a bi-weekly early dismissal model for collaborative planning time for teachers to have data-driven discussions about student success. The early dismissal model allowed principals and vice-principals to participate and better support the initiatives and directions that resulted from those meaningful conversations.

For those of you who want to create a PLC approach in your schools and wish to avoid the growing pains that I experienced, I offer the following advice, largely based on the work of Leah Taylor. Leah is an education researcher and organizational coach who greatly assisted our district in the formation and success of our district PLC model. Leah developed our STAIRS approach to create a common framework around our understanding and direction as a PLC district.

Student learning focused
Teacher/educator initiated interventions
Administrator supported and guided
Inquiry based and data-driven
Recognizes and celebrates growth
Shares results school and district-wide

i) Student learning focused

It seems obvious that the intent behind a PLC model is student learning focused. However, the subtle but important shift is that schools move from a teaching-centered model to a learning- centered model. Often in schools, the focus is on programs and pedagogy when in a collaborative model the focus shifts to results-based strategies. As a principal, this can take a considerable amount of time to guide the change in mindset. As experienced school leaders know, changes in school culture and practice only move at the speed of trust. Patience and consistency are the key.

ii) Teacher/educator initiated interventions

One size fits does not fit all. Strategies and approaches must be developed within the school context. There can be a tendency to look at a shiny program or box of resources to address student-learning needs, but often those approaches miss the mark in terms of school context. Developing homegrown strategies and approaches tend to be more successful. What struck me as a school leader in the initial stages of our approach was the messiness of it all. Despite our staff's investment towards understanding collaborative work, the process was messy. There was some creative tension along the way. I learned to embrace rather than avoid the messiness and tension. Over the years, I became to learn that the journeys that led to some of the best programs and results for students started with several wrong steps.

iii) Administrator supported and guided

I prefer the term "school leader" instead of "administrator", but for the sake of the acronym, I will put my feelings aside. The school leader, in conjunction with and support from the system leaders, can play a strong role in the establishment and development of a school-based PLC model. However, the work of the school leader should not be viewed as authoritative or the approach viewed as, "top down". The most effective PLCs that I have been involved in have distributed leadership at their core and rely on the interdependency of the group for their effectiveness. No one person has a greater voice. The work is guided by the shared responsibility for the success of all of the students in the school.

iv) Inquiry based and data-driven

Developing a PLC model around an inquiry question greatly increases the success in terms of achievement and sustainability. Goals and targets are static and once achieved tend to be forgotten about. Inquiry questions establish a greater purpose and create cohesion amongst the group.

As a school principal, one of the most challenging pieces was to have an open conversation about the use of data. While many schools and districts may claim to have PLC processes, if they are not making data-driven decisions, then I would argue that they are not PLCs. At the outset, I encourage people to create homegrown measurement standards to assess the impact of their work. Data also strengthens the social license of schools. A challenge to overcome was the notion amongst parents that more instructional time leads to greater student achievement. To be successful, the community must buy into the belief that decreasing instructional time to increase PLC time has a positive impact on student learning.

v) Recognizes and celebrates growth

Most schools do a good job of ensuring that a positive school culture exists and that all types of growth and achievement are celebrated. In the early days of my PLC leadership journey, I wanted to ensure that I could draw a connection between most of the things that I did as a leader to my commitment to the PLC model. Demonstrating that message in overt ways emphasizes the personal importance that you place on the process. When we launched our district model, another teacher and I decided that we would dress up for Halloween as old school rappers. We went so far as to create fake gold chains that had a large, "Run PLC" medallion on the end of them. That was our way to celebrate and continually emphasize the importance of our work.

vi) Shares results school and district-wide

Share everything in an honest and transparent way. The failures are as important as the successes. We learn and grow as a school community when we share our approaches and our results. A collective willingness to be vulnerable and a belief in shared responsibility for student success develops the capacity to change and grow. The value of sharing materials, tools, technology, connections, and teacher leadership capacity provides a rich inventory of resources for ongoing professional learning for others facing similar student learning challenges. Building an inventory for others to access ensures collaborative work within both the school and the district.

It has been many years since my time in that elementary gym surrounded by upset and frustrated children, but I like to believe that their school experience was profoundly changed as a result of the collaborative commitment that we made as a school community to their learning and success. This process and the success that I have seen confirmed for me that schools absolutely have the capacity to meet children where they are, overcome any deficits that they may have, and positively increase their life chances.

About the Author: *Kevin Reimer has a B.Ed. from the University of British Columbia and a Master's Degree in Educational Leadership from San Diego State University. As a school leader he has worked as an elementary* *and middle school vice-principal and principal. Kevin has led district initiatives and presents regularly on Professional Learning Communities, assessment for learning and creating positive school cultures. In 2013, Kevin was recognized by The Learning Partnership as one of Canada's Outstanding Principals. For a number of years, Kevin has been on the Board of Directors of the British Columbia Principals' and Vice-Principals' Association. Kevin currently serves as the president of the BCPVPA.*

Chapter 16

If Only I Had More Time: Reflections of a School Turnaround Leader

Sarah J. Bailey

There is no way to fully understand and relate to the woes, challenges, rewards, and triumphs associated with school turnaround until you have had the opportunity to personally experience it for yourself. As I reflect over my years as principal of a small elementary school in the Mississippi Delta, the cliché, "hindsight is 20/20" definitely rings true.

I often tell people that I walked into my principal's position at T.R. Sanders with my eyes 'wide shut'. I was 27 years old and just completed my principal preparation program only seven months prior. I was eager to pursue the elementary principal opening in my district. I had so many aspirations and high hopes only to learn the school had received a failing label from the State of Mississippi and was in Federal School Improvement. Not insurmountable, but definitely overwhelming at times.

Within three years, the support of teachers, district administrators, state officials, parents, students, and other staff helped our school move out of state and federal school improvement. We ultimately attained High Reward School status by the US Department of Education. Although the process was extremely rewarding, and I feel like I completed what I was purposed to do at T.R. Sanders, I often reflect and say ... If *only I had more time*. So, I would like to share three key areas aspiring and current turnaround leaders should consider as they endeavor to transform the schools they serve. I refer to them as the three T's: Trust, Teachers, and Transitions.

Establishing and Maintaining the Trust of the Parents and Community

In some school turnaround settings, teacher attrition is a major issue. In fact, if your school receives a School Improvement Grant (SIG), which T.R. Sanders did, releasing staff is a requirement. I was blessed to serve as Principal in my home town. Although a blessing, it was indeed a challenge. Throughout my eight years in Hollandale, I believe the parents I served trusted me and knew I was there to do what was best for students; however, the same did not seem to be true for the teachers. I would have to refute comments like "they are only here to get a cheque" or "they don't care about our kids". In my last year as principal, I had an epiphany as to why my parents had a distrust for the school.

I was doing research for a school improvement project in a leadership course and decided to focus on parent and community engagement. I sorted through school data and looked at the number of parent complaints by grade and the percentage of the teachers with less than 1 year of experience serving those grades. It hit me like a *ton of bricks*.

For over thirty years, the teaching staff primarily remained the same. During the first two years of my tenure, most of the veteran teachers retired. As a result of the teacher shortage and the stalled regional economic engine, we were forced to rely on alternate route teacher certification programs. The majority of the alternatively trained teachers fulfilled their two-year requirement and returned home to teach or pursue other careers. I often referred to it as a *revolving door*. We offered large signing bonuses and incentives but it did not increase the number of applications. I went from no parent complaints my first year to almost thirty in the final year. My parents did not trust the teachers because they did not know them. They did not have time to get to know the person serving as the teacher. Before they could get used to a teacher, three more would come walking through the door.

So I say to you, turnaround principal, as you labor to ensure your CIA (curriculum, instruction, and assessment) are strong, and you have all the people you need on the inside, do not overlook the importance of trusting parents and community members. I needed to address this trust issue strategically, and I did not realize what the heart of the issue was until my last semester as principal. *If only I had more time...*

Training and Empowering Teachers to Lead

When I talk to leaders, they often say that they struggle with delegating (and understandably so). With so much pressure and accountability for results, can a principal afford to take the risk of not getting the task done quickly and accurately the first time? I struggled with delegating as well, but school leadership is not a one-person operation. In larger schools, teacher leaders or department chairs are essential because the staff and student populations are so large. In smaller schools, more specifically struggling schools, teacher leaders are essential as well. Sustainability of school improvement is so important in the turnaround setting, and efforts cannot be sustained without people who *know how and are willing to carry the torch* without being prompted.

I always selected certain teachers to serve as leadership team members, mentors, and instructional coaches. I believe those responsibilities helped to build leadership capacity. Some have gone on to become school administrators, work for the state, or remain in the classroom. What I did not see was them taking leadership initiative in their role; in retrospect, it appears they were completing the task at hand or following my directions and did not feel empowered to lead. My approach needed to be different; it appears I designated rather than delegated. The latter requires I spend a lot more time training and preparing teachers to lead, be reflective, and feel comfortable with innovation.

After resigning from my position as principal to pursue my Ph.D. full-time, I had many teachers tell me, "I learned so much from you," or

"You prepared me for what I am doing now." Although those types of statements make me feel good, I believe developing a group of empowered teacher leaders would have ensured sustainability of the systems implemented, and served as a system of support for the new leader coming on board. In my opinion that would have been more powerful than grooming my successor. *If only I had more time...*

Transitions are Necessary

Initially, you might think the idea of transitions is in reference to a leader recognizing when the time has come to transition to another position, and allow another leader to take the school into the future. While that reality may be true in some situations, I am actually referring to the importance of recognizing when it is time to transition instructionally. When I became principal of T.R. Sanders, the data revealed a misalignment between curriculum, instruction, and assessment. We began to address these areas district-wide by training teachers to differentiate instruction according to readiness, align instruction and assessments to the state standards, and plan effective lessons. Each year we added additional components to improve the effectiveness of our instructional program. By the end of the second year, we saw the results of our systematic approach in the form of student growth.

The need for an instructional transition began to resonate with me as the data began to reveal how great of a job the teachers were doing with developing struggling and average learners; students scoring in the minimum range were at the lowest percentage ever, and more basic students were reaching proficiency. At first glance, this is great; however, as time progressed I noticed a *proficiency plateau;* we were not developing our proficient children at the rate at which our other students were developing. We attempted to address the needs of our proficient learners by providing enrichment periods with instruction and practice on more challenging skills. This was definitely a step in the right direction, but more was needed to support this group of learners. As I coach principals in struggling schools, I help them to come to the same realization when we review student data.

I now recognize that a different type of transition in our instructional program was necessary to move our school to the next level and sustain student growth. This is because our minority, proficient and advanced learners had become the majority. We needed a transition in our instructional practices to transform our classrooms into learning environments designed for the proficient and advanced learner. It was now time to retool teachers and provide training on how to teach and create a classroom conducive to the growth of independent learners, while continuing to meet the needs of students who were not quite ready for grade level content. This would require not only extensive training, but also a transition or shift in the mindset of teachers about the role of the student in the classroom, both of which would require *more time.*

If I had more time, I would strategically address trust, teachers, and transitions for the next two to three years. By doing so, I would be working to ensure parent and community support, sustained leadership, and a school responsive to the needs of every learner, all of which are cornerstones of a turnaround school.

About the Author: *Sarah J. Bailey is an experienced educator with over 5 years of Pre-K-12 school leadership experience and 3 years of state level leadership coaching experience. Sarah is currently pursuing a Doctor of Philosophy in Educational Leadership at The University of Mississippi, and her research interests are school turnaround and leadership for school improvement. Sarah is passionate about school turnaround and school reform and believes that students deserve to have the very best school leaders in charge of their educational futures.*

Chapter 17

The Power to Say YES: Leading in a Virtual Environment

Einav Cabrera, Ph.D.

Being a school leader involves a multitude of facets: knowledge of curricular trends, impactful pedagogy, and, increasingly, emerging technologies. What often determines the longevity of a leader is their ability to engage with the customer in a way that results in a satisfied experience. In schools, students and their parents or guardians could be considered the customers. As a virtual school principal I have found my voice, and the power to say YES, and seek to ensure the school's customers are satisfied.

There is a well-known cartoon caricature that portrays a 1960's parent wagging their finger at their child saying, "What did you do?", and then a 2000 version with that finger now being pointed at the educator. Parents want to create the best learning environment for their child and they expect educators to deliver.

I began my journey as an educator in public high school and then subsequently as a leader in charter schools, where as an instructor and principal, I found myself under multiple umbrellas of oversight: the educational management company, the district, and the state. I struggled with this version of school because of the rigidity of the policies, and thus the decisions I could make as a leader. The district I worked at, for instance, had a behavioral matrix that had to be followed for each event.

That could mean that a 5-year-old child who struck another student might receive the same exact consequence as a middle school student. These policies force your hand to treat all students exactly the same, no matter their need or situation. Yet parents may have a vision for how they want their child's educational path to progress that does not fall in line with the often rigid, brick and mortar school.

In a typical public school, if a parent requested a certain teacher, I had to worry whether every parent would then have a teacher request? After all, that highly requested teacher could only fit so many students in his or her classroom. Not every child can have him or her as their teacher, and how would I meet everyone's needs?

How does the virtual environment change all this you ask? It has allowed me to say YES. The biggest strength of virtual education is that it creates a private relationship between the student, their family, the educational institution, and the teachers serving them. There is no classroom where every student gets to see Abigail's interactions with the teacher. There are no parent volunteers in the classroom who may overhear certain decisions that the teacher makes in the best interest of the student. It is only that student, and their parent, in partnership with the teacher making the decisions.

Each day I get to match up a student with a teacher who motivates them and understands them. All teachers have different strengths; some of mine work really well with struggling learners. They know how to motivate them with their interests and hobbies and believe in them. Other teachers are really skilled at motivating aspiring students, knowing how to encourage them to go even further. As a leader I know my teachers; if a student is not finding the right "fit" with a teacher, I can address the situation by searching for a better "fit."

Students find such flexibility daily in the virtual environment. They can start and end a course at any time during the year as opposed to an August to June calendar.

A student may feel that they need additional time on an assignment to be successful. In a public school, for example, students must have an Individual Education Plan (IEP) or 504 plan to ensure that this additional time is guaranteed. The process to get such plans can often be cumbersome, from meetings with doctors to tests and other analyses, often resulting in a delay before the student receives what they need to be successful. What I really love about virtual learning is that all students get accommodations. Students are afforded unlimited time, multiple attempts to complete tasks and assignments, and the use of resources they may need like a dictionary for an English as a Second Language learner.

In a traditional school, missing 3 weeks would seem like an impossible feat for a student and their school to accommodate. Teachers follow a pretty rigid calendar and the student has a predetermined end date that often shapes the pace they must maintain. For instance, Sheila was an actor who needed a break for 3 weeks. She was filming and would not be able to work for most of November.

In a regular school Sheila would not likely be able to maintain her studies. However, in the virtual environment Sheila is not limited by a rigid calendar. For one, the schedule allows students to take breaks if they need them for different reasons. The emphasis is maintaining a continuous work flow which allows students to demonstrate mastery of the content. Sheila got what she needed, and other students do as well.

The other great asset of being a virtual leader is not needing to make decisions for students based on scheduling restrictions. Just because something doesn't fit on a student's schedule doesn't mean that a resolution can't be found.

Larry was an aspiring valedictorian at his school, but he somehow could not fit AP Calculus into his overloaded schedule. He was especially adroit in math, but the course he meant to take did not fit in the stringent puzzle administrators must often create. As I spoke to his parents, I was so excited to say YES that we can make this work. They were worried that Larry would miss out on an opportunity to advance his math knowledge before applying to MIT in the fall. Taking AP Calculus in the virtual world meant that Larry was able to make it fit for him. There is no scheduled time of day, or even specific days for the class. Larry could work in this course on the weekend if he wanted.

Parents contact me each day with different needs. That is one of the biggest factors that is different in the virtual environment. Here, the principal is accessible. In a brick-and-mortar school, you often hear things such as the principal "is not in right now" or "you'll need to make an appointment." In fact, most times, parents might be shifted to an assistant principal, dean, or guidance counselor for assistance, which from a customer perspective can be discouraging (and can also delay a resolution or solution).

In the virtual environment, the administrative office consists of me alone. Parents see my cell phone number on their child's course page and can call me directly for anything. That is a completely brand new concept for students and families. The first thing I hear from parents is, "Thanks for answering", or "Thanks for calling me back." They are thankful that they can call me directly, and often get me right away or within a few short hours. Accessibility is the first pillar in building great relationships with the customer base.

The virtual school experience is enhanced by the virtual environment's non-school hours. We do not open at 7am and close at 3pm. Our hours are 8am to 8pm, and we are open all year around. Despite these definitions, I make accommodations such as calling parents later or even on the weekend if necessary, as many parents are not available during traditional school times.

As a leader who does not have to deal with such minutiae as transportation, lunch, or discipline. I have more time to focus on instructional concerns. This begins and ends with making sure that every student has a great learning experience in every course they take with us. Resolving conflict is of the utmost priority, and more so it is what continues to create the raving fan: an individual who goes beyond just being a customer to someone who recommends your organization to others and becomes a repeat customer.

The question remains: How do we take the power to say YES in the virtual environment and transfer it to the public, brick and mortar schools? How can we ensure that every student, regardless of his or her race, ethnicity, or sexual orientation, is treated fairly?

How do we make sure that, regardless of whether you live in rural areas, the suburbs, or the inner-city, all students can have an option for a great teacher and any class they might be interested in pursuing?

These facets that have often become norms in the virtual environment can and should be carried forward into the every-day school, and allow for students to get what they need from their educational experience.

About the Author: *Dr. Einav Cabrera works as a principal for Florida Virtual School, one of the biggest, public online school districts in the United States. She began her career as a math instructor in public high school and went on to serve as a principal in charter schools. Einav has a B.S. in psychobiology, as well as a M.Ed. and Ph.D. in Educational Leadership from Florida Atlantic University.*

Chapter 18

Students Give Voice To Their Learning

Em Del Sordo

We often hear about the use of data to inform school-based decisions. Early in my administrative career, I learned that data superimposes a bigger picture onto our school reality. Sadly, I found that the use of quantitative data, EQAO/standardized tests, pass/fail rates, class medians, and trailing data sets have little effect on teacher practice. Teachers can mistrust trailing data sets and often feel "labelled" by them. In turn, the use of data can create a school culture of distrust and angst amongst teachers and administration. It then becomes my task, as a secondary school principal, to find a way to touch teachers' hearts first, before I can ask them to think about data. This is also the juncture where student voice comes into play.

Student voice is *live* data that any teacher can use any time when planning their lessons. The golden question I use, when staff are "stuck" in their practice, is: "Have you asked the kids?" In fact, administration modelling how to use student voice to share the students' *lived* experience seems to be the one entry point into a teacher's heart. Administration modelling demonstrates to staff that we need to rethink how we do business in our educational practice. To do this, I think the most effective pedagogical stance I use is the Instructional Core. It supports student voice in co-creation of learning environments, and is a learning tool that serves as an excellent visual reminder and support.

The Instructional Core is represented by a triangle symbol labelled with three partners of the learning process. They are the: student, teacher, and the curriculum. Asking students what *they* know about curriculum expectation(s) and diagnosing *their* learning gaps guides the teacher in creating authentic learning tasks that speak to the hearts of the student-learner and the teacher-practitioner. As principal, I am working on building this learning culture by having teachers ask and search for student voice. By providing opportunities for the collection of student voice, teachers can determine where students are in their learning trajectory, and thus program and co-design next steps to fill the curriculum gaps. Questions like: "What do we know?", "What do we want to know?", "How are we going to get there?" and "How will you demonstrate your learning?" allow both the teacher-practitioner and the student-learner to co-design student-friendly learning goals and curriculum related success criteria. Student voice allows a teacher to genuinely connect with their students so that he/she can create authentic learning tasks that speak to student interests and passions. Once the teacher collects this valuable diagnostic, he/she can pre-think conditions to co-create a differentiated learning experience that meets the needs of all learners. A by-product of using student voice can be the recognition of a practitioner's passion for the teaching-learning process. By finding success in teaching the curriculum in a way that speaks to connecting with student learning interests and the art of teaching, success is created for all parties.

I invited a number of students to my office and asked them the following questions: "How can I write a chapter for other principals about how we use student voice to help make school-based decisions?" "How do we help teachers incorporate student voice into creating effective learning environments in the classrooms?"

What the students shared with me truly represented the cultural change that we are working on within the school. Student voice gives me direction about how to engage students with the school and how the school can connect with students. I also find their voice touches the hearts of educators. Student voice parallels evidence-based research that many articles and studies promote. So here is what I discovered from my students in writing this chapter. One student commented:

> I feel successful when the teacher creates parameters around what we need to learn and gives us choice to show them our learning. My favorite class is structured around making the curriculum expectations so clear to us that I know exactly what I need to learn to meet the expectation.

As a Principal, I found that creating a professional learning culture with teachers is really about deconstructing the curriculum so that they know exactly what skill-set they need to teach, what it might look like for them and their students, and what body of knowledge they are going use to teach that skillset. I have worked with my staff on building such a professional learning culture by asking them *not to keep binders with pre-prepped lessons,* but rather to have "fun" co-learning with the students by using the curriculum expectations as their guide and map. In some cases, this has shaken a teacher's world because in essence, what I am asking them to do is "let go" of controlling the learning, and instead, begin a new teaching journey where they learn to be co-learners with students. My next step is helping teachers to feel "safe and comfortable" with letting go by posing the golden question: "Have you asked the kids what they need next?"

By using student voice to help with co-creating a learning environment, the teacher places the student on the top apex of the Instructional Core. By diagnosing what the pedagogical next steps might be, the curriculum gaps can be strategically narrowed. It means that the teacher is really no longer creating lessons based on "covering the curriculum" that rely on pre-prepped lessons. Rather, teachers connect with their students and discover what learning gaps exist so that they can use the differentiated instruction to close or narrow those curriculum gaps. One student told me, "Teachers need to beware of their own learning style and not impose it on us as the only way to learn". Once teachers feel safe to let go of controlling the learning in only one way, it allows the teachers and students to truly become "partners" in learning. A grade 12 student told me:

Once teachers create the conditions for learning and show us how to meet curriculum expectations, we create ownership over our own work and we really become engaged in learning and school. This is because they allow us to connect the learning to our world. We learn more from teachers who help create other possibilities or explanations for whatever we are learning. When teachers help us make connections, learning is easier and exciting. That is how we get engaged ... make it about us and our world. Teachers who use Bloom's taxonomy really show us the action-verbs of the expectation and allow us to learn how to become learners.

I often use Bloom's Taxonomy to foster conditions teachers require to reflect on their practice. By using this instructional leadership tool, teachers can often see themselves in the Instructional Core as a critical partner. Bloom's Taxonomy illustrates the movement from lower-order thinking to higher-order thinking with the end goal being to make every classroom a learning environment. Students can see themselves as learners and have the knowledge about learning. Student voice allowed me to consider what my next step might be to collaborate with teachers so that they can let me know what they would need to create the metacognitive learning culture in our school. Student voice warned me that we educators need to beware of the balance needed between structure and creativity. Student voice informed me that students want creativity but they need to learn *how* to. A student told me, "Don't just tell us to create; show us some possibilities and we can then take it from there." Student voice informed me that students want teachers to model strategies for learning, so that they have a starting point for their own learning.

I have asked students to come and share their stories with staff at a staff meeting. The purpose here is that it is another way of building and promoting student voice in the school. Not all students will have the courage to stand before staff and share their experiences so they will also video-record their high school experience and shared their stories with the staff. Some students mentioned that the teachers they had who connected with them and built a relationship were pivotal to their success in school:

> We need our teachers to be persistent and patient with us. We might not know why we behave the way we do, and sometimes we know but can't stop. Teachers who are calm with us and show us that they care about us first are the teachers we will always work harder for.

Student Voice is really about giving the student permission to be curious and growing learners. As a principal, seeking student voice is really about promoting students as viable partners to our school community. If I could have all students graduate feeling that their learning processes were valued and that their voice was promoted and understood, then we are modelling how to be an active and responsible member of society.

About the Author: *Em Del Sordo is a Principal who values all "voices" in leading a school. His current school created a vision statement that speaks to filtering the curriculum through the U.N. GLOBAL GOALS for Sustainable Development through the lens of Human Rights. Em is an Instructor for Ontario Principals' Council Principal Qualification Program, a past VP for Learning Forward Ontario, a Holocaust educator, and a Facing History and Ourselves educator. He believes that once we connect with student and staff interests and passions, then we can connect with the Instructional Core as a measure of student achievement and learning. Most recently, Em was awarded the YMCA Peace Medal.*

Chapter 19

"You are the principal of this school now, and I cannot read."

Liz Davis

D uring the first week as a newly promoted principal I met Brad, a grade two student. Brad approached me and asked me for an appointment to meet. We sat down in my office and I was extremely curious about what he wanted to talk about. When I asked him how I could help him, he looked me straight in the eye and said, "You are the principal of this school now, and I cannot read. I want to know what you are going to do about it." I think it is safe to say that I did not see that one coming. The following is a shortened account of what we did about it and my reflections as a leader and co-learner in this process.

Building a Collaborative Culture

Filled with staff members who cared deeply about what they did, our school team was discouraged by years of working hard without seeing improved student achievement and/or standardized test results. Transitional conversations and feedback made it clear that we needed to develop a deeper understanding of our urgent student learning needs.

For some staff members, this also meant having some challenging conversations around a 'culture of care' that, with the best of intentions, sabotaged our work initially. This was because some staff had low expectations for our students, and assumed that they were unable to work at a standard grade level. I learned that having high expectations for both staff and students, with student work at the center of our conversations, is vital to a culture of improvement.

Another important lesson that I have learned was that the best way to build a collaborative culture is *THROUGH* the work; having student work as the focus of all professional learning. Excellent teacher leaders are critical to this process because they do the work, understand effective instructional and assessment practices, have credibility, and can facilitate discussion and debate about the next level of work. I realized early on that trying to build relationships before starting the work of school improvement was a mistake. *Relationships are built in the muck of doing.* This also leads me to reflect on the importance of professional learning: *SCHOOL TEAMS NEED TIME FOR THIS.* New curriculum, standards, reflective practice, pedagogical changes/adaptations are important parts of our world. School teams need time to plan, teach, reflect, and tweak their practices to improve them.

Dissonance Causes Learning

Initially, I noticed that people complained that change was hard and uncomfortable. I think this is true, but what was more interesting to me as a leader, was the fact that *dissonance causes learning.* Without having a gap in knowledge and practice to fill, we do not tend to shift, reflect and tweak our practices. We have to get out of our comfort zones to improve things for our students. While staff may not initially 'know what they don't know', this changes when they start to experiment with practices that have an impact for their students. I noticed that we needed to shift instructional behaviour before mindsets shifted. I believe most schools and systems that do not reach this level do so because they give up too soon. They do not provide the multiple opportunities to practice new strategies with *specific, timely feedback, reflection and just-in-time coaching.* This would seem to hold true for students as well as staff. As their understanding of effective pedagogy deepened, staff were able to be more effective in collaboratively determining our professional learning. This was an important part of building commitment *to* and accountability *for* the work.

What is the *"Deal"* with Data?

As principals, we work collaboratively with staff to build trusting cultures of teams that are not afraid to experiment, fail, reflect, and renew lessons and experiences for our students. This is only possible if these teams also develop a deep understanding of multiple data forms, as well as a structure for analyzing and reflecting on them collaboratively. It is important to start by understanding what your urgent student learning needs are, and then present research and evidence for discussion, reflection, and debate among staff. I noticed that once staff understood the urgent student learning needs, it was easier to identify their own professional learning needs. This led naturally to administrative team learning needs as well in terms of knowledge, providing and aligning effective resources, and monitoring improvement. Helping staff to understand that our standardized assessment data was NOT everything, but it *was something,* allowed us to dig deeply into why our students were struggling on tasks that most of our Board's students could complete independently. I realized that some of the resistance to this conversation came from a lack of understanding about how helpful the data could be, and a tradition of 'gotcha' approaches to discussing it. When I put this on the table for discussion and reassured staff that 'wherever we were starting was okay,' staff slowly began to embrace the information and these conversations as it helped us arrive at a starting point and then continually monitor our work.

This learning, along with the global data conversation, has made me consider deeply the importance of *building a culture of commitment rather than a culture of compliance.* By this, I mean a commitment to improvement as professionals for our students. I do not believe our families think we should know everything, but when all they see are test results and administrators who do not know how to guide teachers through processes that can support improvement, it is difficult to build public confidence in our systems.

Finally, I realized that data that is collected and not shared is useless for school and system improvement because it does not allow for the building of teacher instructional and assessment capacity or ownership of their instruction. I believe that this does not honour the collective intelligence and commitment of our teachers trying to work as professionals. Simon Sinek calls this the *WHY*, and I realized it is critical as leaders of any organization that we start here so staff understand why changes in practice are necessary. Once we understand the *WHY*, we can collaboratively develop the *HOW* and the *WHAT*.

Act, Assess, Reflect, Renew and Monitor

Educators are professionals and must be able to articulate what they do and why. We reflect on strategies that have worked, resources we need to purchase, ways to make our tasks richer, and how to improve how we interact with our student as partners in their education. Staff had ongoing professional reflection discussions around student work:

- What did we learn?
- Based on our teaching, where do we need to go next?
- What does our student evidence tell us about our student learning?
- How do we know that a high level of learning was achieved?
- What do we need to do for those who have not yet met the standard?

The Final Word

We must continue working together to build culture and capacity as both are needed to create the spaces where we optimize student learning. We must create high expectations for our students and for each other. Principals must be co-learners in this process if they expect staff to be vulnerable enough to admit they may not have all the answers. Cultures of innovation cannot exist without this in place because innovation will not occur if people are afraid to play with new ideas and practices. This means acknowledging publicly when you are not sure of something as a leader. Additionally, understanding that all teachers can teach to a high level with the right support has been crucial to the development of this professional learning community. Part of determining impact is evaluating evidence of improvement and having processes and structures in place to monitor this work. We set an improvement target each year and discuss this regularly. Sounds scary? Not in a professional learning culture that values professional judgment, and is continually working to improve! Accountability is important because we work in a public education system.

Brad is in Grade 7 now and identified with a severe learning disability. He is reading at a junior level, and is learning to use Ontario Education Ministry supported technology to help him be successful. The work we have done as a team is the reason our school is improving, and that Brad is progressing. Is it perfect? No. Is the work complete? No, but we have improved consistently each year and continue to work to sustain the capacity in both students and staff. I find myself reflecting on that conversation six years ago and thinking about what we must continue to do about it for all students. More than anything else, principals are not just educators, principals are learners.

About the Author: *Elizabeth Davis is a Principal in York Region District School Board. She is a passionate advocate for resiliency and school improvement work. She feels fortunate to have been part of 3 collaborative school teams first as a Literacy Mentor Teacher, and then as an administrator working to improve achievement and well-being in underperforming schools. She is the proud parent of two children and lives in Newmarket, Ontario.*

Chapter 20

Positivity and High Expectations

Jean-Francois Boulanger

My narrative starts when I was the Vice-Principal of a kindergarten to grade six school of about 425 students. This was my first experience as a vice-principal. Fortunately, I was joining an experienced principal. We worked well together, and were a good team. I grew professionally during my first year, and hoped to continue this learning for a second year.

On May 5th, I received a phone call from my Superintendent asking me if I wanted to be the new principal at one of our district's urban schools. I could sense the disappointment in her eyes; my Principal and Superintendent had already spoken. After the phone call, we sat down and spoke. Although it appeared difficult for her, she encouraged me to accept the new position.

The things I knew about the school were not positive. There were four principals in the previous year. This was a kindergarten to grade six school educating 92 students. At the end of May, there were only 2 students enrolled in kindergarten. Talks of the school closing were imminent. The rumors in the community were that the school did not have more than a few years before closing. Our closest competing school had close to 600 students. Large-scale assessment scores in reading were at 22 percent, and were at 56 percent for mathematics for both grades 3 and 6.

The outside of the school looked sketchy and I was aware that the school's reputation was not positive. I saw this challenge as an opportunity to make this school great. I knew that I was going to face a few bumps in the road and was willing to take up the challenge right away. I could not wait to get started!

I decided to go meet my new staff members at the beginning of June. I wanted to go early in June because my wife and I were expecting our first child. I showed up to the school and the secretary looked at me as if to say, "Here we go again. Who does he think he is?" Her non-verbal communication appeared to suggest that she saw me as a threat and not an ally. I walked through the school and met staff members individually. The conversations were informal, but I learned a lot from that visit. Some conversations were negative. I was told by some staff that colleagues were disengaged. Moreover, some staff communicated that students were also disengaged and did not have respect for the school. I was told that the school might be closing. I heard that the secretary and the custodians took over the school. I knew then and there that I needed to be present. I needed to be positive and I needed to express my expectations. I saw my first principalship as a challenge, and as an opportunity to make this school great.

Still, in June of the upcoming school year, I asked all the staff members to write a short paragraph of what it meant to them to work at this school. I received something from everyone. The letters, paragraphs or short stories were open, honest, and insightful. It led me to believe that the people working at the school were there because they cared not only about the students, but about what happened to the school. It gave me something to work from.

During that summer, I drew up a plan. I decided that I needed to meet with the secretary to go over my expectations. When we met, I talked about how important it was to make parents, community members and staff members feel welcome. She stopped me in my tracks: "I know what I am doing. I have been a secretary at this school for 6 years. I can't believe you are meeting with me to talk about these things. I have a lot of work ahead of me." I reiterated to her that I was the principal at this school and that my expectations were high. I had more work ahead than what I had originally imagined. This work was going to have to be strategic. I started by taking away some responsibilities and re-working her hours.

The other important concern was the look of the building, framed by my belief that people judged this book by its cover. I invited key people from the school board to walk through the school with me. I explained why it was important to change a few things. All the changes I asked for were done within 2 months. Another victory.

During my conversations with staff, it appeared that they had low expectations for student achievement. I worked positively with staff members to change mindset. I did not tolerate staff being negative or saying negative comments about our students, their families, or the school. Engaging in courageous conversations became an important part of my leadership repertoire. It even came to a point where, in a staff meeting, one teacher said, "I know that you want us to be positive all the time and it sometimes gets on my nerves. I want to tell you facts, and sometimes I will not go see you." I knew that if she was willing to say that in front of peers, she knew I was open and willing to communicate. And she was! We worked together on our school improvement plan to change our instructional practices. In the next few years, I had a chance to welcome to our school speakers such as Garfield Gini-Newman, Marie-France Maisonneuve and Marian Small. These people made us grow as teachers. Within a few years, perception changed and we were a great school for critical thinking. I gave a chance to our staff members to attend conferences, visit other schools and learn together.

Throughout the years, staff members who did not want to be part of the changes left our school, while others joined. We started at 92 students but three years later we were at 150. We had new classrooms, and we almost doubled our staff. All the way through, I was present during PLC's. I followed summative evaluations and I was present in the classrooms to be part of the learning. I got to know the learning habits of students and was there to help where I could.

I asked my Superintendent to give me two years to change the perceptions people had about our school. The first perceptions that needed to be addressed were the ones from the parents. Since they were dealing with rumours of the school closing, parents had little trust in the school and rarely participated in school activities; I decided to reach out to them. One Saturday morning I took a small team and went door-to-door to meet all the parents. That Saturday was great. I had a chance to shake hands with parents, grand-parents, uncle, aunts, brothers and sisters. I not only had a chance to meet them in a different light, but I also now knew where they lived and the situation they were facing. Every chance I got, I spoke to colleagues on how great the school was and that it was no different than other schools in our board. Every school has its challenges. Our school was no different.

I wanted to shed a positive light on our school through media. I took every opportunity to get the word out about what great things were happening inside our four walls. I wrote in school board media, newspapers, school web sites, etc.

I wanted to change the outlook for the students who did not have strong self-esteem, so we started reciting positive mantras every morning.

> I am able to do everything!
>
> I am intelligent!
>
> I will do my best!
>
> I have a positive attitude!
>
> I will give 100%!
>
> I will have exemplary conduct!
>
> I will respect others!
>
> I am part of this family!

I have since left that school to pursue new leadership challenges. I am proud of the fact that we started at 92 students and that by September of 2016, we had more than 200. The school board did not close the school, but decided to invest more than 8 million dollars to rebuild and renovate. Our provincial assessment scores improved. In 2016, large-scale assessment scores in grade 3 were as follows: mathematics 75 percent, reading 88 percent, and writing 83 percent. Large-scale assessment scores in grade 6 were as follow: mathematics 79 percent, reading 89 percent, and writing 84 percent. What an incredible change. And we have maintained these scores for 3 years!

I had asked my Superintendent to give me two years to change perceptions. I think some perceptions are still there but what we managed to accomplish as a school community was incredible! What our school became for students, and who students became, occurred because we believed in them!

About the Author: *Jean-François Boulanger is an experienced principal. He has worked in urban and rural schools. His approach, based on positivity and high expectations, was the main reason why Jean-François was selected as one of Canada's Outstanding Principals in 2014 for his work in reinventing, changing and building a turn-around school. Jean-François is also involved in Principal Qualification Programs in Ontario as a way of giving back and making a difference.*

Chapter 21

The Three "C's" Solution: Communicate, Collaborate, and Cooperate

---

Edward Harris, Ph.D.

"Number 7 of the top-ten teaching and learning issues in education is that educators communicate and share content, applications, and application development. Collaboration is essential for survival and it should occur at all levels with specific reference to professional *development, content sharing, and application development.*"

Educause – Top-Ten Teaching and Learning Issues 2007

Mr. Smith

The principal was in his second year after being an assistant principal in the school district for four years. (Let us call him Mr. Smith.) Mr. Smith's school was located in a challenged, urban neighborhood. Mr. Smith was one of the 25 principals assigned to me as their instructional leadership coach. During our sessions, Mr. Smith and I reviewed student data, attended school-leadership team meetings, and performed dual teacher observations. We attended debriefing sessions where we checked for inter-rater reliability to ensure that our scoring of the evaluations was similar.

During our many conversations, Mr. Smith and I broached a plethora of topics and addressed many difficulties and complications he faced. The students' academic data was dismal. Mr. Smith shared three specific concerns: 1) the discontent of the teachers; 2) the lack of academic effort and drive of the students; and 3) the parents' lack of confidence in the school. Mr. Smith insisted that teachers emphasize Student Learning Objectives (SLO). He instituted an incentive and rewards program for students, and he recruited parents to volunteer in classrooms to improve engagement and involvement. Mr. Smith was distressed that "Nothing he promoted was working."

Mr. Smith said, "Many of the teachers are passively resistant to being held accountable concerning teaching and learning strategies and educator responsibility towards raising student test scores." Mr. Smith was cognizant of the fact that several principals before him were unable to improve the test scores and restore staff morale. The nagging concern for Mr. Smith was how to inspire his teachers to get onboard concerning "his goals" for the school. Mr. Smith asked in a direct manner, "What advice can you give me?"

I realized, as I heard Mr. Smith's question, what he wanted to know was how to develop philosophical unity between building administration and teachers. He wanted to know how to persuade teachers to consistently and purposefully use best practices in teaching and learning, and discover how he and the teachers could work together to uplift students and help them improve academic achievement.

Take a Systems-Based Approach

I understood that Mr. Smith probably could not achieve everything I was about to suggest to him at once. Therefore, I thought it better to help him visualize the big picture then explain it in small pieces as we met each week. I explained to Mr. Smith that a first step might be to move from an attitude of "his goals" for the school to a mindset of "Our (Mr. Smith, the staff, students', and parents') goals for the school. To achieve such a mindset Mr. Smith could communicate, collaborate, and cooperate with teachers, students, and parents to simplify, clarify, and demystify the path forward. I encouraged that he implement the **Academic Engine,** a living entity that changes and morphs as data dictates.

Academic Engine

The Academic Engine is a six-component system for school improvement and revitalization including:

- A Safe and Orderly School Environment
- Guided Learning
- The Presentation Matrix
- Shepherding
- Collaborative Reviews
- Professional Development

I explained that we could discuss ways to implement each component during our weekly sessions. I suggested to Mr. Smith that we begin by discussing ways to implement strategies to ensure a **Safe and Orderly School Environment.** However, before we started, I decided to offer a "big picture" view by briefly defining the other five components of the Academic Engine that we could discuss during future visits.

I defined **Guided Learning** as the component of the Academic Engine that encourages teachers to use the backward design to develop quarterly common assessments and unit tests. Further, the analysis of data, retrieved from the unit tests and quarterly common assessments, could drive recovery and enrichment interventions for students. I defined the **Presentation Matrix** as an organized and sequential way to deliver lessons that all teachers agree to use. The Presentation Matrix centers on time and best practice requirements for the different components of the lesson delivery format (Launch, Discovery, and Closure), and a sequence method to ensure student engagement. I explained **Shepherding,** a form of Looping where groups of students remain with a teacher for two or more years. Teachers would collaborate, cooperate, and communicate in Professional Pairs, students in Cohorts, and parents in Cadres. Each group would adhere to seven Agreements, seven Promises, and seven Commitments respectively.

We discussed the concept of **Collaborative Reviews** where Mr. Smith would meet with individual core curriculum teachers on his staff for 30 minutes monthly. The teachers could identify specific struggling students, discuss their progress, and review the data from unit tests and common assessments. I described **Professional Development** as an opportunity to convert staff meetings into learning sessions and as a way to support teachers and students in their efforts to improve.

Interaction Process Design

Mr. Smith and I began our conversation about creating a Safe and Orderly School Environment with my definition of the **Interaction Process Design,** a four-step guideline for the interaction between staff members, students, and parents.

1) Establish academic and behavioral expectations for students
2) Determine ways to monitor and support the expectations
3) Agree on ways to acknowledge and recognize or redirect students
4) Generate a feedback loop

The Interaction Process Design could solidify the school culture (how we do things around here) and climate (the **values, interests,** and **principles**) of a school. When used at school the Interaction Process Design **protects the learning environment** so that teachers and students feel supported. Educators could encourage parents to embrace the Interaction Process Design at home to engage **Parallel Supervision.** Students should realize that school staff members and parents are on the same page concerning the importance of fostering a Safe and Orderly School Environment. At school, educators could support families by creating a diverse Student Advisory Board for student input, agree to engage in weekly Academic Update calls to parents, establish an after school Academic Lab with paid core curriculum teachers assisted by student tutors, and create an Academic Watch List that identifies struggling students.

Educators could encourage parents to help the student practice for school by injecting similar expectations at home. Parents could establish routine timeframes at home such as definite study times, a specific bedtime, creating a "no recreational technology time zone", and have home departure reviews (Does the student have completed homework, is he or she dressed appropriately, has his or her hygiene routine been completed?).

When staff members, students, and parents regularly collaborate, cooperate, and communicate, success is eminent. When strategies are simplified, clarified and demystified, school improvement and achieving academic and behavioral expectations become much less difficult. The conversations about each component of the Academic Engine must be ongoing because there is much to discuss in each area. Establishing a Safe and Orderly School Environment is the foundation of the Academic Engine.

About the Author: *After serving four years in the U. S. Coast Guard, Dr. Edward Harris taught social studies grades 9 through 12 for ten years (Civics, World History, American History, Sociology, and Contemporary Issues). Ed has been the principal of four high schools; one in Missouri, and three in Illinois that served diverse environments: Urban, high resource communities, rural communities, and a college town. Ed has been recruited as principal to address gang problems, student apathy problems, teacher morale, the achievement gap, and general problems of community disengagement. Ed has also served as Director of Secondary Education and Director of Curriculum and instruction in Missouri and Delaware, charged with doing much of what assistant superintendents and Chief Academic Officers do in larger districts. Ed has also coached 25 to 30 principals over a two year period in Philadelphia Pa.*

Chapter 22

Building a Dream: Extraordinary Staff Empowering Students to be Future Leaders

Aiman Flahat

In late December 2011, I received a call from our Senior Leadership Team informing me of an opportunity to support a school, John Polanyi CI. They said the school had opened its doors just four months prior and was located in Lawrence Heights, one of the highest priority neighbourhoods in Toronto, Ontario. In the last 12 years, two local high schools closed in this neighbourhood due to significantly low enrollment. John Polanyi CI was struggling to move forward with student achievement and student engagement.

Community safety was a key priority and enrollment was less than 300 students in an era of declining secondary enrollment across the city. The challenges were many, but at the center of our dream was hope for a better future and environment. This community needed a school of which they could be proud.

Within a few short weeks of completing an environmental scan of the school community and the neighbourhood, we decided that building a collaborative culture was at the core of creating an environment of high expectations for students, staff, and community. Leadership is about influence, not position, so we immediately focused on listening and working with those who had influence in the school community—students and their parents, staff and union representatives. The objective was to create a culture of shared leadership where voices are heard and experiences are honoured when moving forward with our school community goals. We needed to instill the belief in everyone that it was possible to build a dream.

We discussed vision, and engaged our communications team to create an effective marketing plan; we wanted to take every opportunity to ensure our community knew about all the great things that we were doing. Additionally, we worked with our Equity Department to help identify any existing barriers that would keep students from achieving. In order to truly support student achievement and well-being, we ensured that there was an equity focus in everything that we did. We worked extremely hard to create trust and community through relationship building. We helped shape this culture of trust by demonstrating our willingness as leaders to learn alongside staff; we planned lessons together, visited classes regularly, and gave feedback on instructional strategies. Collaborative leadership through listening, sharing decisions and learning together became the guiding principle of our improvement planning.

The second area of focus was forming and sustaining strong relationships with our parent community, neighbouring schools, senior board officials, and community partners. To do this, we needed to create the conditions that gave our students the opportunity to not only see what is possible for the school, but to see what is possible for them, so that they can say, "Me too... I can do this."

Our passion for relationship building resulted in numerous successful partnerships, including the Integrative Thinking Program at the Rotman School of Management at University of Toronto. This helped shape the thinking of both staff and students. When our school needed supports for our vulnerable students, we partnered with federally-funded programs and post-secondary institutions to recruit full-time social workers, and child and youth workers. When our school needed after-school programming, we partnered with various organizations that brought innovative programs such as the Elite Basketball program. When our students and parent community wanted special programs, we partnered with post-secondary institutions and various organizations that donated technology and other equipment to enhance programming. Our staff was empowered to take innovative, creative approaches when supporting the school community. They became strong advocates for creating conditions that provide excellent opportunities for all of our students. Our strong focus on student achievement and well-being is built on a foundation of leadership for learning, where teachers and students focus on what is possible. This transformational journey allows us to see that things can be better than they are when people are given an opportunity to reach their full potential.

Our learning culture is premised on the Ontario Ministry of Education's Student Success School Support Initiative. It has helped us create an openness to learning and a focus on strong instructional leadership. Our early work, using pre-instructional assessment, co-planning in small teams, co-teaching, observing, and reflecting has increased trust among staff because we were active learners together. We watched student pass rates improve significantly in our applied level courses. Staff took great pride in sharing their learning through the use of Pre-Instructional Assessment tools, the Learning Cycle, and Evidence-Based Instructional Strategies. The success of this work quickly spread throughout the school and was shared with other schools in our area.

With the support of our Superintendent, our work at the district level allowed us to incorporate our successful model when implementing our Family of Schools Instructional Rounds. The goal was to build capacity in the principals and create principal learning networks. I had the opportunity to lead principal learning teams on Board Improvement planning. In the past two years, I have presented this work at the system level, and at the International level with more than 500 educational leaders from more than 15 countries. I am proud of our collaborative culture, the strong relationships we have built with our parents and community partners, and the laser-like focus we have on student achievement and well-being. Our students now see that they have many opportunities if they are willing to work hard.

We have made believers of our staff, students and community! It is possible for students from one of the highest priority neighbourhoods in Toronto to win National and International Awards for developing socially responsible businesses and Global Partnerships, and to raise $47,000 to help build a school in Nicaragua. It is possible for our students to win gold medals at the Toronto Science Fair, to be the City Robotics Champions, to win the Provincial Archery Championship three years in a row, and to win the City Championships in Track and Field and Cricket. It is possible to represent Team Canada and play basketball on a global stage in France, for the Math Team to place in the top 25% in all of Canada, to be a certified Gold Eco School, and to build the largest urban farm in Canada on school property. And it is possible that students are leaving private schools to join the John Polanyi CI community.

I am happy to share with you that at John Polanyi CI, we not only envisioned a dream, we are now living the dream. In less than 5 years, John Polanyi CI has become a thriving community of learners with more than 900 students in attendance. This school is a source of pride to students, parents, staff and the community. We have become a school of choice, and one of the fastest growing schools in Toronto with one of the most diverse school populations in the city. We are extremely proud of the culture of high expectations set by our extraordinary staff who empower our students to be the leaders of tomorrow.

About the Author: *Aiman Flahat is an award-winning educator with more than 23 years of teaching and administrative experience at the secondary school, college and university levels. He was recently awarded with the Toronto District School Board's "Excellence Award" (2014) and a National award: "Canada's Outstanding Principals" (2012) from the prestigious Learning Partnership. He has met with and presented to delegations of educational leaders from more than 18 countries on effective school leadership, school improvement, instructional leadership, supporting newcomer communities, partnership development, and building community schools.*

Chapter 23

Experiential Learning to Promote Student Engagement

Adam Hurley

Education is constantly changing and so should you. I share with you my journey through teaching and administration in hopes that you might recognize the importance of keeping up with the times.

Growing up in a world of rote learning, I came to understand elementary and secondary education as a teacher-led process where students listened and teachers taught. While this process seemed to work for me, I would always see many students around me that did not flourish under this approach. They were often disengaged, lost interest in the class, and even education as a whole.

After these experiences, I came to the realization that education cannot be delivered in a "one-size-fits-all" approach. I made it a personal mission of mine to ensure that my teachers and I provide quality, rich, authentic, individualized, and most importantly, experiential, learning experiences for all students. This shift did not occur until I was teaching for several years; remember I felt that I had learned most effectively when classes were still teacher-led, lecture format. Now I know what you are probably thinking – "As an administrator, how can I change the way some of my senior teachers deliver the curriculum, those who have been doing it the same way for years and are resistant to change?" While this is not easy by a long shot, it is essential to the development and growth of today's students. To do so, we must instill the belief in our staff that experiential learning is not only beneficial and exciting for the student, but also for the teacher. As educators in the 21st century, we must get away from the traditional methods of instruction that we experienced and transform our instruction to prepare our students for success in a dynamic, unpredictable, technologically advanced and connected world.

I still remember the first time that I read about the concept of "experiential learning." It made me reflect on my experiences as a teacher, administrator, and student. It made me wonder why so many educators still do not deliver the curriculum in a way that is engaging, hands-on, and memorable. It made me reflect on my days in university and how all of my experiences were the opposite; traditional teaching with little interaction or engagement in exciting learning experiences. It made me reflect on the benefits that colleges provide in regards to how students learn by doing instead of learning from "being told". Lastly, it opened my eyes to a completely new and exciting realm of education, guiding me on a path to creating engaging, experiential learning opportunities for my students.

To facilitate and ensure that my staff is carrying out experiential learning opportunities on a regular basis, I knew I had to implement some sort of process to see a positive change. When first introducing them to the concept of experiential learning, I asked them to send me a brief report each week outlining these experiences. Not only did this help me to understand how my staff was providing their students with hands-on learning experiences, it also put ownership on them to ensure they were including these experiences in their lessons. Since this initiative began, my staff have been getting out of their classrooms as often as possible – taking the learning experiences outside, providing students with real-life applications, and allowing them to learn through exploration, creativity, and hands-on tasks. It has enhanced the learning experience for students producing an enthusiastic and engaging environment. It has brought the classroom teachings to life, allowing the curriculum to be further understood and digested, and has increased student achievement. The experiential learning focus at my school has helped transform learning goals and curriculum expectations from mere dialogue and text to engaging and innovative learning experiences – after all, learning becomes real when it applies and is related to the students' world. This has led to my math teachers taking their students on the ice and soccer fields to discuss trigonometry and how it relates to sports. My science teachers are leading exploration tasks throughout the ecosystems surrounding our school. My geography teacher is leading a geocaching hunt around Downsview Park, and my business teachers are starting up a school-based store where students run the day-to-day operations and business aspects.

Not only does experiential learning provide an innovative approach to education, it also helps to improve student achievement and engagement. It enables students to view learning as an exciting experience, allows them to see the value of teamwork and is an important strategy for supporting student achievement. The improvements in student achievement, especially amongst students that have otherwise been disengaged or underachieving, have been remarkable throughout the shift in focus at my school. My whole focus on experiential learning is to improve student engagement and to promote lifelong learning. Too often, I have seen students disengaged as a result of the traditional teaching approach; however, since the implementation of an experiential approach, I have seen many of these students become re-engaged and immersed in their learning experiences.

While this change did not occur overnight, it was essential in promoting lifelong learning, improving student achievement, and encouraging self-discovery. I urge all leaders and educators to regularly reflect on your teaching methods, and ask yourselves a few questions on a regular basis: Are my students relating to my lessons? How can I improve student achievement? How can I get my students more actively involved in the learning process? Am I teaching the same way I did several years ago? The last question is possibly the most important and should often be asked. In order to keep up with the needs of our students, we must constantly evolve our teaching and methods of instruction.

While I once viewed education in a "one-size-fits-all" fashion, naively believing that everyone learned as well as I did with the rote learning approach, I now understand the increasing importance of diversification, differentiation, and most importantly, experiential learning. I challenge you to learn from my experience and provide your students and staff with the resources and opportunities to provide the richest, most authentic and hands-on learning experiences possible by getting out into the community and *learning by doing.*

About the Author: *Adam Hurley is the founding Principal of Blyth Academy Downsview Park School for Elite Athletes, a school focused on experiential learning and developing student-athletes through individualized education and elite level athletic training from grades 5-12. His research interests include innovative teaching methods, inclusive leadership practices, and the importance of life skill development.*

Chapter 24

Bringing Extra In

Peggy Hobson

As I joined the professional team at a middle school, it became clear that students were engaged in activities at home or in the community which held their interest, motivated them, and inspired them to return each day after school.

As a school team, we did not initially recognize this extra-curricular engagement nor did we look for connections or curricular outcomes embedded in these activities. The grade level teams and specialist teachers continued to prepare lessons as usual. The invitation for students into the learning process was missing; there was a disconnect between practice and student learning reality.

There was a need to adjust traditional educational practices. Aligning programs with intentional student involvement could create a possibility-rich learning environment. There were many diverse paths to achievement of educational goals. Keeping students engaged, involved, and intrigued would help us development positive, sensitive, informed, capable, and engaged individuals. "School" continued with a traditional base of what we knew despite advances in, and strategic embedding of, new ways to create and learn. Disconnect.

My objective with this school team was to implement at least one transitional change each year. Shift. The main outcome of trying something different was the dialogue. Almost parallel to my start at the middle school was the installation of a wireless network. In addition to the excitement, there was fear from adults. Dialogue with adults led us to propose a charter to inform our community about embedding the wireless possibilities as an integral part of the learning environment. We worked toward implementing a 'Bring Your Own Device' policy. (BYOD). The charter was never written. We realized that all expectations did not have to be dictated. Many stakeholders were already deeply involved in the conversation. Learning. Connection. Encouragement to use these new applications and possibilities did not need a charter to make sense of the progression. .

Students engaged in possibilities and were motivated by the opportunities. Respect increased and students felt heard. This learning made sense to them. The learning environment shifted categorically. The possibilities for connection were growing as rapidly as the students' ability to identify the opportunities.

Disconnect remained however. The shift was difficult for many adults. They grappled with the thinking that a teacher needed to know more than the students. Worksheets, textbook assignments, and traditional methods were fall back strategies. As BYOD increased, adults became apprehensive about the result. It meant students might have access to knowledge that adults did not, or the growing suspicion that students were using devices inappropriately.

Students came with their knowledge of devices. They knew which ones to use for what purpose, or they asked, or they figured it out collaboratively. They came with video editing skills, gaming ability, awareness of how to quickly find requisite information, skills with coding and a renewed enthusiasm for learning. The students continually showed they were part of a learning team. They took risks. They failed and tried again. They shared their learning. They were willing and excited to prove, help, teach, and learn about meaningful use of devices. At the time of the wireless installation, we invited children in all grade levels to be participants as Student Technology Leaders. The only prerequisite was their wish to be part of this group. They met together. They met with teachers. They helped teachers navigate through problem solving with devices. They presented at staff meetings. A powerful quote from a Student Technology Leader as he addressed the staff still resonates today: "Teachers will guide us and tell us which topics we are to learn; we will decide how to demonstrate our learning". Connection.

Students joined us in the dialogue about digital citizenship. They were forthcoming with information about proper use. They reported other students' negative behaviour with devices and a conversation followed. Parents and community members engaged in the process. In no time at all, adults realized the students had significant information and experience to share, regardless of age. To try to keep devices out of the learning environment pushed students to do more secretly. The conversation was where it need to be: on the table, not beneath it.

I was unable to visualize a difference between a class of students using a recommended device from a class of students each using the same textbook. 'Open to page 43 and do the first ten questions' versus 'open the app and follow the first ten instructions.' Devices offered a learning freedom not recognized by traditional delivery. It would be irresponsible to limit this to a device-powered textbook experience. Students came to school with their device of choice or no device at all. The school offered sign-out devices from the Media Center. Students chose when to use a device, as well as what device would be proper for the activity or to show learning. Students also chose to create with no device at all. Multi-level learning engaged students with the mechanics of outcomes and knowledge acquisition, including research and app usage skills. Teachers helped students in their research strategies through direct teaching of search and select methods, citing sources, and strategies to seek correct information. We were all learning together. Shift.

As we began to level the "playing field" in educational delivery and move students to center stage, the learning environment needed a shift. Students needed to have input in their program. One of my goals was (and still is) to erase lines on the timetable. Enter FLEX time. Was it possible to adjust the timetable to have blocks of flexible time? Intent combined with intense reconfiguration, and by September the timetable indeed had a half day FLEX block per grade level. All classes were scheduled to be with their homeroom teacher for that specified time. Each grade level had a different half day. The teacher librarian could join teams during their block. Other teachers with available time were invited into a block. Options surfaced.

During FLEX time homeroom teachers could help with student choice. Students, knowing what work needed to be completed, could individually choose the order of completion. This meant the classrooms turned into workshops. Students made decisions and the teacher could circulate, remediate, teach a small group, answer questions, or offer guidance. The embedding of variety developed, and then meaningful connections and trust relationships developed.

Another strategy for this FLEX time was to use the half day for an activity or field trip, taking the class or the grade level out of the school. As the students were with their homeroom teacher for that time, no specialist classes were missed. All programs were equally important. As teachers became familiar with the possibilities, FLEX time became a place for students to work in different areas of the school. Teachers, during their once a cycle team meeting, designed the next FLEX block. Perhaps a teacher noted there were some students in math having trouble with a concept. That teacher would take the students from the other homerooms to facilitate a workshop on the identified outcome. Other teachers would focus on other areas for either remediation or extension. Students could be assigned to a group during one FLEX, or perhaps choose an activity of personal interest during another block.

As problem-based learning and inquiry delivery took center stage, FLEX became a terrific structure for students to pursue essential question research. FLEX became an unexpected way to "bring extra in", and have students work on an area of special interest or personal passion. The more teachers became comfortable with freeing up this time, the more they became adept at recognizing when students could name their own learning. Students achieved outcomes through personal, authentic engagement. These outcomes were not covered in a traditional uniform classroom delivery model. Students shared their learning plans and made decisions on where and how they chose to work during FLEX. Community members or community areas became resources instead of separate from the school. Students were meaningfully enrolling themselves in the process and in their learning. They were involved. Connected.

As FLEX developed in positive ways, we looked to our next timetable change. We adjusted the eight-period school day to enable the addition of a ninth period. Every morning, students began their day with an active start or a morning meeting. Morning meetings became part of the fibre of the school. Classes circle-up with their chairs, intentionally greet one another, play a game and engage in meaningful dialogue and learning about each other's perspectives. Alternatively, an active start allowed all school participants time for exploration of preferred choices or involvement in a sports activity. We had to tread carefully at the beginning as there was always a genuine need for added rehearsal or team practice time. Teachers did not schedule activities with a designated group. Instead of a team basketball practice, a basketball game for anyone was an option. Teachers or students could play. Choices were available to everyone. Choices. Meaning. Engagement. Passion. Connection.

Active start became the way to start every day. Everyone in the school looked forward to this time. There was choice, relationship building, fitness, meaning and fresh air. Curricular outcomes were met in many ways. Outcomes were not tracked. There were other priorities. Engagement.

Another area that inspired me was the influencing of professional development. Professional development is fundamental to what we do. It is necessary to keep up to date with educational practices and current brain research. There were advancing strategies for teachers to apply to help students in their learning connections and positive self-concept development. We embedded much of our professional development traditionally. Sit and get. Sometimes it is the most effective way to impart information. Sometimes it is not.

We were involved in our professional growth and supported by the division. We watched the "Did You Know" YouTube videos and learned there were more students in India on the Honour Roll than there were students in North America. We learned we were trying to get students ready for employment that was not invented yet. We heard Sir Ken Robinson's concern that schools were killing creativity. We wrote twenty-first century skills lists and intentionally tried out a few. We had difficulty changing our content delivery practices. Students were wanting to work with us but that translated to "in spite of us". Disconnect.

Looking to set up a different model of professional development, I facilitated the implementation of an "Open House" plan at the middle school. This plan originated due to the number of external school teams asking for visits to dialogue with our staff about the current, innovative delivery of information, involvement of students as leaders, BYOD, digital citizenship, video production, active start, morning meetings, MakerSpace, and FLEX time. The preliminary concept was to schedule open house days for which visiting teams would register, instead of scheduling visits randomly.

The first year, we scheduled one open house for each of the ten school year months. All ten filled quickly by a variety of other school or college teams looking for new ideas. The outline of the day began with the timetable. Visitors showed the area(s) in which they were interested in learning more. We shared this information with the middle school staff. Teachers then let us know which period they were working with students on one of the focus topics. At times a teacher would choose to schedule a prep period with the guests to allow a professional conversation with the visiting team. We consistently scheduled at least one period with the Student Leaders. Their voices mattered most in the bridging of the disconnect. Students lead visitors through our MakerSpace, showing RaspberryPi, robots in action, our 3D printer, or leading the visitors in playing with the devices themselves. Joy.

In this professional development plan, relationship and connection were the foundation and dialogue was the key. The visiting teams spent time engaged in their chosen topic(s) of interest. The participating school team members each gave one period to help with the demonstration or the dialogue and proceeded with a regular school day. The interruption to the learning environment was minimal, and enriching. Professionals and students worked collaboratively to advance 21st century education through debate, discussion, and strategy sharing.

Schools were expected to submit a school plan each year. To introduce a shift in this area, in line with the other initiatives, the team at the middle school developed a strategic plan, condensed to one page for ease of reference for all school participants. The staff asked that we develop a framework that did not need to change every year. The school had several initiatives in place and established connections in the community. Using the initials of the school name and the plan to engage all stakeholders, the areas of Humanity, Growth, Innovation, and Sustainability were chosen. Instead of developing leadership teams under each heading to further the school plan, individuals or teams were asked to come forward with their initiative(s). Their first responsibility would be to find which area(s) their project or passion addressed. Students, staff, and community members are now an integral part of every section of the school plan. The participants own it. It is celebrated often as we share progress, successes and next steps through news, video, and at regular assemblies. Leading through intentional invitation to all participants was powerful and resulted in multiple participant, high-level engagement. Connection. Trust. Meaning.

The strategic plan blossomed with multiple focus areas embedded in current educational trends. MakerSpace, mindfulness, inquiry, infusion of technology, genius hour, progressive assessment strategies, global initiatives, and increasing student voice were a few of the significant areas. Motivated by children involved in initiatives, creative endeavours or community outreach, we continued to push illusory boundaries.

Disruptive innovations (3D printing, self-driving cars, climate change, information access, video capture) were all changing the very world in which we live; this is the new reality. We infused the education system with a great deal of recent, progressive information and so despite the many challenges to change, it was hard to believe we were moving so slowly. Disconnect. Change embeds the very process of learning with the risks attached. Risk taking increases engagement, resilience, and deep learning.

My focus will be to continue developing a learning environment which connects students and educators. The priorities will be identifying curricular outcomes met through the student's own inquiry process of creating, researching, relating, and developing and having disconnected students develop into connected individuals. To develop this new skill set, we (or the students themselves) need to demonstrate outcomes achieved after the completion of a self-initiated project. The intention is to replace setting an outcome at the outset and to have all students work on that outcome as a collective. This sounds like an accomplishment. Some students are more than ready: Are we able to bring that extra in?

About the Author: *Peggy Hobson is a recipient of The Learning Partnership's (TLP) Outstanding Principals Award 2015 and the Manitoba Association of Education Technology Leader's (MAETL) recognition for outstanding leadership in technology. She is passionate about infusing student voice, developing global and digital citizenship and embedding technology into education. Peggy has worked in public education at all levels for over 40 years. She is very fond of the middle years. Peggy and her partner, Les, live just outside Winnipeg, Manitoba. She has six children and a small herd of grandchildren who provide enough material for a novel or two. She enjoys gardening (especially mowing as it provides pondering time), kayaking and photography.*

PART IV
Leadership And Adversity

P rincipal leadership offers the privilege of navigating daily opportunities and challenges. At the end of the day, principals hope to return home to loved ones, confident that they have done their absolute best in the service of public education. And then the phone rings, the door knocks, or your intuition lets you know that something is seriously wrong. Leadership and adversity can go hand in hand. Suicide, catastrophic illness, extreme violence, sexual assault, substance abuse, and abhorrently unethical behaviour will confront every principal at some point in their leadership tenure. These challenges typically come without prior warning. Principals are often expected to demonstrate strength, emotional intelligence, calm, and stability in situations of adversity. Relationships, respect, and resiliency are keys. Faith and strength of character are required when faced with adversity.

Chapter 25

Student Death

Sheila Eller, Ed.D.

Student Death

As a principal for over 20 years, I have faced many challenges and emotional experiences. None of these past experiences could prepare me for what I was about to face this year: the death of one of my students. As I reflect on the experience, I'll share some background about the situation, how I responded to the situation, what I have learned as a result, and advice for my principal colleagues to consider if they face such an emotional situation.

Background

I knew the student, Anna (I changed her name for this article), for five years. I first met Anna when I was her elementary principal. I had since moved into a middle school in the district. Anna had a lung transplant when she was in 5th grade. During that year, we worked with the family to help her stay connected with her friends and keep up with her school work. Anna's parents were worried about exposing her to germs and possible illnesses due to the anti-rejection drugs that she was taking related to her transplant. Anna, on the other hand, was strong and committed in relation to her recovery. She wanted to come to school and be with her friends. I knew I needed to connect with Anna's parents and build a trusting relationship in order to help her stay connected with our school and her friends.

Anna moved with me to the middle school when I became the principal there. I had an immediate connection with her. I talked with Anna and understood that she wanted to be like all of the other 6th grade students, to be with her friends, and learn. My relationship with Anna grew. I found that she was wise and strong beyond her years. She knew what she had to do in order to stay strong. It would be up to us as adults to find a way to stay strong ourselves.

During her 6th grade year, Anna's parents and I worked together to make school a normal part of her life. We kept in constant communication. I let them know how things were going for Anna in school, and they kept me up-to-date on issues related to her health. Whenever Anna was unable to attend school (because of periodic setbacks in her condition), staff members would go out of their way to keep in touch with her and help her stay connected. Teachers would go to Anna's and do home bound teaching. I would periodically take her over some lunch from a local restaurant; this gave me a chance to take messages the teachers and the students wrote for her, take her school work, and build my relationship with her parents. In spite of periodically missing some days during her 6th grade year, we were able to help her stay connected. I could see that the students and teachers had made a strong connection with Anna.

The Sudden Change in Anna's Health

During their periodic visits to the specialty health clinic (in another state), Anna's parents received updates related to her health. Things seemed to be progressing along well for a quite a while. Then in the summer before her grade seven year, I received the call I was dreading: during their most recent visit to the clinic, the doctors noticed that Anna was beginning to reject the lung that had been transplanted over a year ago. The doctors were hoping that the drugs they were administering could help Anna ward-off this rejection, but that wasn't the case. Because of the nature of the illness, Anna was planning to have another transplant. She would gradually get weaker and weaker until she eventually passed away.

I was devastated by the news and immediately wanted to reach out to Anna's parents. I asked if it was okay if I came over to talk with them. When I was there, I just listened and tried to comfort them. I asked them if it was okay if I shared the situation with Anna's teachers. They said yes, and Anna added that she wanted her friends and the other 7th grade students to know what was happening. She was determined to try to stay in school and keep in touch with the classmates who meant so much to her.

We developed a plan for Anna to keep in touch, and also to keep up on her school work. I kept in regular contact with Anna and her family as her situation worsened. I was keeping in touch with Anna's family by phone and social media. Then one Sunday afternoon, Anna's mom called me to let me know that Anna had passed away. Even though we had become close over the years, it was still hard for me to find the right words to say to her. We cried together and talked about the family's (and Anna's) wishes for how we communicated the news to the school community. It was evident that they wanted everyone to know about Anna's passing and the profound influence she had on everyone during her fight to live through this difficult situation.

Strategies to Help the School Community with the Situation

Since it was a Sunday evening, I decided to send an email to all the teachers to let them know that Anna had passed away. I asked the staff to come together for a staff meeting at 7:15 AM on Monday where I would share with them our plans to help the rest of the school community deal with Anna's passing. I also talked to the school psychologist to let him or her know about the situation. The psychologist made arrangements for counselors to be available for staff and students to talk with about Anna's passing as well.

I informed my superintendent and district office personnel about Anna's passing. I asked the school secretary to make arrangements for guest teachers to be available at the school to cover classes for teachers who felt too upset to teach, or who wanted to talk with small groups of students. I wanted to provide the resources people would need to deal with their emotions on this very hard day.

When I arrived at the school on Monday morning, I knew this would be one of my hardest staff meetings to conduct. I also knew I had to stay strong to help the rest of the school community. At the 7:15 AM staff meeting, I told the teachers that we were meeting so they could express their emotions, and for us to develop the plan to help the rest of the school community in their grief for Anna's passing. I shared details related to Anna's journey and asked staff members to share their experiences and memories of Anna. Many teachers shared positive stories about Anna and her strength in dealing with her health issues. I asked the school psychologist to share information related to the grief process, what the teachers might experience, and what they might see in working with their students and families.

I also shared a statement that I had prepared with Anna's family to be shared with all the students. We decided that the statement would be read during the first hour of the day. I also told staff that we had six guest teachers who could teach for them if they wanted time to meet with a counselor or students. We also shared with staff to let the students know that we had counselors available for any student who wanted to visit. We set aside three rooms where students could meet and write a special letter or card to Anna. We discussed who Anna's closest friends were so the staff could watch over them and help them through this difficult situation.

The first hour at the school was very somber. Each staff member greeted their students at the front door or classroom door (which was very important to help the students feel the caring the staff had for them). As the first hour progressed, my assistant principal, the school psychologist and I walked around the school and checked on everyone. As we noticed that people were having difficulties, we were able to provide comfort for them. For example, not all of the teachers were able to get through reading the announcement about Anna's passing so we stepped in and read this announcement. We also helped to guide the discussion with students about Anna's passing. Many teachers and students took advantage of the counselors who were available to talk, spend some time in the open rooms writing cards and letters to Anna, and found ways to comfort and support each other during this hard time. At the end of the day, we were all exhausted but felt a sense of support and community. This is the legacy that we knew Anna wanted to leave with us. We knew this is what she would have wanted.

My Learning

Once a few weeks passed, I was able to reflect on the experience, what I learned, and how it changed me as a principal. First, I was reminded about the importance of emotions in our schools. Beyond the technical aspects of managing the grieving process (such as setting up substitute teachers, providing open rooms for thought and reflection, etc.) was the importance we placed on helping people work through their emotions. I knew the staff really cared about Anna, but I saw a new level of caring during this experience. I have many new teachers who have never been through this type of situation before. I learned that they needed extra support in order to provide support to their students and families.

I also learned the importance of working with Anna's parents and helping to gather their wishes in relation to her passing. I found that our school was able to help them as they dealt with the very emotional experience of losing a child. I never really thought about the influence we had in relation to our families. This experience helped me to keep that influence in perspective.

I learned from some of the strategies we employed during the first couple of days after Anna's passing. For example, staff members told me that they really appreciated the opportunity to meet in the early morning to be able to come together as a school family before they met with the students. They felt good about the ability to deal with their own emotions and hear about the resources available to them and the students. It was also an important lesson for me to allow the students their own ways to express their love for Anna. For example, some students decided to decorate her locker. Other students wanted to make posters about Anna to post around the school. It was important for me to provide students with freedom they needed to work through their emotions in their own way. All of these and the other resources we provided were designed to be focused on the emotional aspects related to Anna's passing. In the end, we feel that we were able to help everyone express their emotions while celebrating the impact Anna had on each of their lives.

The death of a student is something that can have a profound impact on a school, the staff, and the students. It is something that we all wish would never happen, but my experience has helped make me a better principal and person.

About the Author: *Dr. Sheila Eller has had experience in almost every education level during her leadership and teaching career. She is currently a middle school principal in Minnesota, and has served as a principal in the Fairfax County Public Schools in Virginia, as well as in schools in Minnesota and Illinois. She has also served as a university professor in Illinois. Sheila supports schools through her work in the areas of teacher evaluation, working with difficult and resistant staff, school turnaround and transformation, climate and culture building, effective teaching strategies, energizing staff meetings, school improvement and other important topics to build effective schools. She is a regular presenter at national and regional conferences, providing practical and proven strategies for success.*

Chapter 26

Integrity in the Face of Adversity

Justin Guerin

It is safe to say that people enter the education field for a variety of reasons, yet one could argue the mindsets are relatively similar along a shared inspiration to change the world, one child at a time. Every first time teacher excitedly approaches the school year with visions of exceptionality cut straight from a Hollywood film, with an engaged and enthusiastic classroom where student learning and growth is awe-inspiring. For administrators, the mindset is often the same, just on a larger scale.

When I left the classroom to take my first administrative position, I firmly believed my passion, energy, and work-ethic would enable me to not only inspire students, but also the teachers throughout the school building. I felt I knew what type of planning, instructional methods, and relationships could be used to promote a positive learning environment centered on student learning. I was confident my leadership preparation program had provided me with the knowledge, skills, and network to serve as a successful administrator. Nevertheless, this is not a typical chapter about leadership methodology, but rather a conversation about the reality, which all administrators will confront at some point in their careers, that sometimes things will go wrong. The key for a successful school leader is not the ability to anticipate every potential issue, or expertly remedy every problematic situation; rather, the most important aspect of a quality administrator is the ability to react appropriately and with integrity to each and every issue that arises. By doing so, a successful administrator demonstrates a temperament which will build trust amongst the school's faculty, and promote a high quality professional environment.

Strength in the face of tragedy

While I hope it never happens to any of you, there are unfortunately many instances of senseless violence impacting schools across the country in recent years, and as a school leader, how you react will impact on how your school will cope with the situation. Our school experienced a horrific and shocking tragedy one cold November morning. Our district was made up of just two schools; an Elementary School and the High School where I was serving as the Assistant Principal. When I arrived that Friday morning, I was made aware that our Elementary School Principal and her young son had been murdered the night before. The details were still mostly unknown, and unfortunately, as is often the case in the event of a crisis, rumors of varying degrees of truth and rationality would fly around our small community for weeks to come. In that moment, the mindset of our leadership team had to immediately shift, from a typical Friday schedule and preparing to host a home playoff football game that evening, to providing a stable, calming environment that would allow all members of our school community the opportunity to process and grieve. My principal and I sat at the front desk all day, fielding calls from parents who had seen rumors of armed gunmen on school buses posted on Facebook, or news media personnel from across the area asking for comments. In that situation, our goal was simply to help everyone get through the day in the best possible way. Being an administrator became more about being a comforter and friend than anything else.

Things would only get tougher in the weeks to come as the community tried to cope with the tragic events. In order to help bring stability to the heartbroken faculty of the elementary school, our superintendent decided to send the High School Principal to the Elementary School for the remainder of the year. As a first-year assistant principal with only a few short months to my administrative resume, I was afraid. My boss, mentor, and friend was now across town, and I had the responsibility of providing leadership to a faculty who was still just getting to know me. During this difficult time, it was critical for me to be open and transparent to build trust with the faculty, while also being positive and supportive every day. Rather than complaining about things we could not control, we focused on working hard and celebrating the small victories we experienced throughout the year. While that community still winces at the thought of that fateful day even now, together we were able to survive the year and move forward, which is what our beloved colleague would have wanted us to do.

Sometimes there is simply nothing you can do

In spite of these stories, my most difficult experience as an administrator was yet to come. After two years as an assistant principal, our head principal of twelve years accepted another job offer and, while we were happy for him to get the opportunity, it left a huge void to fill on our campus. Additionally, our superintendent retired and was being replaced with someone new from outside of the district. After a lot of thought and reflection, I applied for the principal position and was promoted as of July 1st. Of all the things which concerned me about becoming a head principal and filling the shoes of my mentor, the one thing I never expected was to experience conflict with the new superintendent.

The day I was offered the position, I began making preliminary calls to fill the now-open assistant principal position at the request of the superintendent. But the next morning, I was told we "had to make a move" on a candidate from the superintendent's former district, and that his principal had been notified as well as all of our school board members. When I raised some questions about the candidate after conducting an interview, my position was threatened, as I had not officially signed a contract yet. This was just the beginning of a downhill slide that would end with my termination on September 14th of that same year. To this moment, I will state I believe the superintendent's actions to be unethical and inappropriate. I committed no felonious crimes, I never put a student or teacher in harm's way, nor did I jeopardize the educational environment in any way; I simply thought a people-first approach to leadership was the most effective course of action, and quite frankly, the superintendent disagreed. In the following months, I would appeal the decision to the School Board, and later the local Chancery Court, both of which would eventually rule against me after more than a year of legal proceedings.

In spite of the situation, which has no doubt significantly altered me as a professional, I still have some firm beliefs about successful school leadership to share. Throughout my appeal process, I had several opportunities to behave unethically. After all, I had the support of the entire faculty and community and could have easily spoken out on social media to incite even more outrage. On a personal level, however, I felt the most important thing I could do was model professionalism and leadership throughout the process. I wanted my students to see how to respond with class and grace in spite of what may seem unfair. I wanted my faculty to know that I did everything I could to put them in a position to be successful, even at the expense of my own employment. I wanted the community to know that I still believed in the school and that the people serving there each day could be successful.

Life as a school administrator is very difficult. Long hours, high-stakes decision-making, and pressure from every aspect of the school environment are every day realities. It is in these moments of difficulty that a successful administrator shines as a beacon of strength, equity, and professionalism. Even on a good day as a school leader, things will go wrong. You will sometimes have control and be able to remedy the issue, but, sometimes, there will be little to nothing you can do, with one exception. Always, at any given moment, you can choose to react with integrity and professionalism in spite of what is happening around you. You may not be able to "fix" the issue, but the manner in which you choose to handle each situation you face will impact your school and the people in it. It is never easy, (I still wake up in a house two blocks away from the school that terminated me) but successful school leaders find a way to exercise ethical leadership principles, regardless of the time, place, or problem at hand.

About the Author: *Justin Guerin is from El Dorado, Arkansas and earned a B.A. in Secondary Social Studies Education from the University of Louisiana, Monroe. From there he relocated to Oxford, Mississippi and earned a M.A. in Curriculum & Instruction, as well as an Ed.S. in Educational Leadership from The University of Mississippi. He has served as a teacher and administrator in several districts across North Mississippi. Currently, he is serving as a Graduate Assistant at The University of Mississippi while finishing a Ph.D. in Educational Leadership.*

Chapter 27

Learning to Lead Through Adversity

Christopher Allen, Ed.D.

My first principalship took place at an international school in Ho Chi Minh City, Vietnam. I made the jump from being a head of department in one school, to becoming the high school principal of another, overseeing 36 teachers and almost 300 students. It was a relatively new K-12 school, and there was also a new Head of School, Steve, coming in as well. He was the person who actually hired me, and he would act as my mentor as I made the transition from the classroom and middle management to becoming a full time administrator. That was the plan anyway...

You see, it isn't easy going from being "one of us" to "one of them" when you move into a leadership role. You can read books, take classes, or any number of other things to try to prepare yourself. But nothing truly prepares you except experience. I did not even have the experience most people have before becoming a principal of being an assistant principal. So while I was excited about the opportunity presented to me, I was also nervous and unsure of myself. This is why I was so eager to get to the school and begin working with my new boss. We both had roots in the state of Georgia, and my wife and I had actually gone to his house for dinner one evening to get to know each other better, and to begin planning during the summer before we both moved to Vietnam.

It was at this dinner that one of the first red flags was raised for both of us about our new adventure. The school had just been suspended by one of the major recruitment agencies for continued inappropriate HR practices towards its teachers. But Steve and I were confident that this was a remnant of the "old guard," and that once we arrived, things would change for the better. There were already several positive changes taking place, and there was a feeling of hope coming from students, parents, and teachers about the upcoming school year.

The first few weeks of preparation, induction, and orientation went well for both the new staff and the returning teachers. There was still tension between the Western administrators (myself included), and some of the local Vietnamese managers in different departments. But it seemed the owners of the school (a Vietnamese husband and wife team) had decided that changes needed to be made to help take the school where they wanted it to go. They were finally loosening the purse strings in a few areas, and were allowing Steve to do things, such as create a transparent operating budget, which no previous Western administrator had been allowed to do. The positive feelings came to a crescendo the Friday before the first day of school, as teachers, administrators, and support staff from each of the three divisions (elementary, middle school, and high school) came together for a team bonding "sports day." Games were played, food and drinks were consumed, and smiles were on the faces of everyone. I still remember a teacher coming up to us towards the end of the day and saying "This is the best staff morale has ever been at the school. I can't wait for school to start on Monday!"

Now I'm not going to say that everything had been smooth sailing for me up to that point. I was still trying to find my way as a principal, and I tried to make my mark in my division, which included trying to create more consistency between departments in relation to assessments and grading. I had recently taken a course on assessment, and was eager to try out many of the things I had learned in "my division of the school." Things such as not giving grades for homework assignments, allowing students to reassess work they had done poorly on, and limiting the different category types, each with a different weighting on the final grade that teachers were giving to their assessments. These were quite drastic changes for many of the teachers though, which understandably led to pushback. But with Steve's support, I was able to handle most things being thrown at me so far.

When I arrived home from the sports day, my secretary called me frantically on the phone. "You need to check your email right now," she said.

"But why? It's the Friday before school starts. It's time to relax" I replied.

"Check it right now" she insisted. So I did. In my inbox was a message from one of the Vietnamese managers telling the middle school principal and I to change our class timetable because she didn't like our lunch schedule. "This is absurd," I thought, and tried calling Steve to see what was going on. I called several times and sent a number of text messages and emails to him, hoping he could clear up the confusion. Around 30 minutes later he called me..."Well, I'm out," he said. It seems he and the owners had decided to part ways, and he would no longer be the Head of School.

Unbeknownst to any of us, there had been a power play made by the Vietnamese managers, who were old family friends of the owners, and they were now back in control. I was frozen. What do I do now? The person who had hired me, the man who was supporting and mentoring me, was gone. Not only that, but I was seen by everyone as "Steve's guy," which placed the bull's eye squarely on me now! The first thing I did was call several of the "informal leaders" in the high school. Every organization has people who, while not necessarily listed as part of the leadership team on the organizational flow chart, are definitely influential people within the organization, and people you, as a leader, need to get on your side in order to make things happen. I told them what had happened and asked them to spread the word to the rest of the faculty.

Over the next hour I received a number of calls from confused teachers asking if the news was true, and what were we going to do about it. Before I knew it, an impromptu faculty meeting was taking place in my tiny two bedroom apartment. Teachers were stunned, sad, and above all, angry. There were calls to go on strike. Some teachers said they didn't need this, and wanted to pack up and leave the country. I had no idea what was happening with the elementary and middle school divisions, but I knew I had a crisis on my hands, and I needed to deal with it as best as possible. "I know you are angry about all of this. I am too. But the kids are expecting for school to start on Monday, and they are expecting teachers to be there to teach them. I'm not going to let them down. I will be there on Monday, and I hope you all will be there too."

And do you know what? Of the three divisions, mine was the only one that had 100% teacher attendance on the first day of school. I knew what I had to do. I needed to put the focus on the students. I needed to protect my staff. I needed to make things as "normal" as possible for everyone else, no matter what I had to deal with behind the scenes. It was the most difficult year of my life. In that one school year I had a total of 5 different Heads of School. Immediately after Steve left, the manager who had sent the email to the middle school principal and I became our supervisor. She only lasted a month though before immigrating to Canada with her family.

Next was my former counselor, who had orchestrated his own Machiavellian coup to make himself Head of School. This was the darkest period during the year, as he led through fear and intimidation. It took all of my energy to try to redirect his anger and hatred away from my teachers, helping to shield them so they could focus on teaching the students in our care. Thankfully, by late spring he too was gone, replaced with the polar opposite personality that helped to stabilize the school through the last few months. Finally, as the year came to a close, another family friend of the owners was placed in the highest leadership position in the school. She was young and inexperienced, just like me, and she did a good job straddling the local and expat line, which allowed us to finish the school year successfully.

Through it all, I tried to lead by example. No matter what my feelings were in private, publicly I tried to stay strong, providing calm through the terrible storm. Every day I went into work after Steve left, I expected the locks to be changed on my office door and someone to be there to tell me that my services were no longer needed. Every day I walked on egg shells when trying to deal with the owners, their family friends who still exerted enormous power throughout the school, and with the ever changing cast of characters "leading me." I did not have the mentor I sorely needed, and I had to learn the hard way. I made mistakes along the way, but I always tried to do what was best for the students. If you keep the focus on that, it is difficult for anyone to argue with decisions that you make.

I did learn a lot that school year. Much of it was what not to do, which is an equally important lesson for any leader. But the most important thing I learned through it all is that people look to the leader to help them get through the tough times. If the leader is scared, then everyone else will be scared too. If the leader is calm, then everyone else will calm down as well. I'm sure this was a lesson I read about in books, or heard in classes I had taken. But nothing truly prepared me for it, and the experience I gained in that one year has helped shape my view of being a learning leader in a school. While I hope to never go through another school year like that again, I also do not regret the choice I made to accept the position as principal in the school. Know that you will face tough times in your life, but you have the strength to overcome them. Do not be afraid to take risks, but always bring the focus back to the students and do what is best for them.

About the Author: *Dr. Christopher Allen is currently the High School Principal of the American School of Kinshasa (TASOK). He has held teaching and leadership positions in schools in the USA, China, Brazil, Vietnam, and the Democratic Republic of Congo. He holds a BA in History, an MA in Curriculum & Instruction, and an Ed.D. in Educational Leadership and Organizational Leadership.*

Chapter 28

Leading Through Tragedy

Christopher E. McCants

Young, energetic, happy-go-lucky, full of life, and gone too soon are just a few adjectives and phrases to describe —"Chi-Chi".

I can still remember the first week of school having this young, athletic, sixth grader approaching me and saying," Mr. McCants, you know my older brothers." And me asking, "Who are your brothers?" When he told me who they were, I could definitel y see the family resemblance. "Oh yeah, I do know your brothers. Let me know if they ever give you a hard time, and I will take care of them for you." We both laughed, and he said, "Yes sir." Although he had an athletic build, he was still a small framed boy compared to his brothers and some sixth graders. His brothers were very athletic and were stand-outs in the sports they played in high school. His brothers were good guys. He was also a good guy and young, at eleven years old, to be in the sixth grade.

It would only take a short time for Chi-Chi's personality to shine. His smile would light up a dark room, and the white-rimmed glasses that he would occasionally wear to make a fashion statement set him apart from other students. Whenever I passed him in the hallway, he made sure we would fist-bump. I would ask him every now and then if his brothers were treating him nicely. He'd smile and say, "Yes sir, they're alright."

He was average academically, and even though he wasn't a behavioral problem, he was still your typical sixth grade boy. When his teachers emailed his mom to let her know that he seemed to be getting a little lax about his studies, they told me that when she showed up to his class, without him knowing, you would have thought he'd seen a ghost. She was an involved parent.

Tuesday, March 15, 2016 will be a day that is forever etched into my memory. The morning started off well, until I was told by my assistant principal at about 7:30 that one of our students tried to commit suicide the night before by hanging himself. She said the outcome looked grim. Being a person of prayer, I immediately began talking to the Lord, while listening to her, as well. When she told me who it was, the name didn't ring a bell at first, but then I looked up his picture and said, "That's Chi-Chi". I called his grandmother to get a prognosis. She said there was a lot of swelling on his brain, but they were remaining prayerful and hopeful. I told her that I would come to the hospital after my 9:00 meeting to check on him.

My principals' meeting ended at about 11:00 and I left the district office's parking lot and headed to the hospital. I had arrived at the hospital about 11:30. When I stepped off the elevator, I received a phone call from my assistant principal, asking if I'd gotten to the hospital yet. I told her yes. That's when she told me that he'd just passed away. "What? What do you mean?" I asked as I kept walking towards the doors that led to the rooms. I unintentionally hung up on her, trying to quickly wrap my mind around what I thought I had heard.

As I hurried through the hospital doors in shock, I told the nurse who I was there to see. She quickly confirmed what I thought I had heard from my A.P. He had just passed away. The nurses were torn up about it themselves. I then asked to see his family. I hugged his mom and told her that we'd be there for them. I then left so the family could have their time alone. I was numb ... in disbelief.

I knew that breaking the news to the faculty and staff that afternoon was going to be just as hard. I was a first year principal and barely keeping my head above water with trying to operate a building, listen to teacher and parent complaints, making sure students were complying, etc... How in the world am I going to do this? What will I say? I was very strong at the beginning of my meeting with them, saying to myself, "McCants, you've got to keep it together—you're the leader—-you can't breakdown."

But by the end of me talking to them, I couldn't hold it together any longer. They were sad, and we all cried together, yet knew we had to be there for our students the next day. I think by allowing myself to be vulnerable in front of my staff and crying with them, it definitely allowed them to see a different side of me—the human side.

We all knew the following day would be even more difficult for our school as the news of his death was beginning to spread like wildfire. That afternoon, I met with our assistant superintendent and some members of the district's crisis team, and we devised a plan for the crisis team. This team was made up of Guidance Counselors and School Psychologists from throughout the district. We made sure we had areas in the school available for students and teachers to express their emotions. I made sure we had bottled water, plenty of tissue, and snacks available for the team (or students).

By that evening, students and adults on social media had it publicized that he'd committed suicide because he was being bullied at school (administration never received any reports from him, his parents, or teachers about this). One person on social media said that he was depressed because his girlfriend had broken up with him. Okay, but he was eleven. He would have had plenty of girlfriends within the next five years of his life because he was a handsome young man. This notion didn't sit well with me because of this student's personality. He was so outgoing and seemed happy. Did I miss something? Had he given me any warning signs? It troubled me deeply to think that things could be so bad in this little guy's world that the only solution for him would be to check-out of it.

The next day was very difficult for our students and faculty. We began by taking visibly sobbing students to the library where the crisis team was prepared to receive them. We used office areas and corners of empty classrooms to console students. I kept watch to make sure students were able to express their grief, but that they were also at a point where they could go back to class. This was difficult because I didn't want it to appear as if I was being insensitive, but I knew some students, if given the opportunity, would take advantage of this situation to get out of completing assignments or being in class. I knew I had to do it. We still had to move on. Teachers pretty much went along with their scheduled lessons, but remained sensitive to their students' needs.

To assist "Chi-Chi's" team teachers, I had teacher assistants periodically go into their classrooms to give them breaks throughout the day so they could collect themselves. The next couple of days were difficult for us, but we got through them.

As the days passed, his mother and step-father reported that he had been playing a challenge game, and accidentally hung himself. While this conclusion wasn't any better, it helped me compartmentalize his death a little better in my mind.

Social media has changed the way people communicate. It has prematurely exposed children to dark, dangerous pockets of society that they can't cognitively comprehend at their ages. Since the ice-bucket challenge, I've seen a spike in the number of "social challenges" that have hit the internet each week, each one a little more daring than the last, and all for internet fame and a quick thrill.

I encourage parents to become investigators like my mom was. Technology affords kids the opportunity to have so much at their fingertips nowadays that it would behoove us all to monitor what they are accessing on the internet. I pray that there be some type of regulations placed on what people can post to the internet. Why not? The government can place regulations on other things that are less important than a human life, so why not on dangerous challenges being posted on the internet?

This experience has taken me to another level in leadership as I now realize what I am capable of as a leader. How I was able to lead a faculty and staff of about seventy people, and 635 fifth and sixth grade students through this process now seems like an out-of-body experience. No course or seminar could ever prepare anyone for losing a student. I think this experience helped my teachers trust me a little more as their new leader, and also see that I am human. I have feelings too.

About the Author: *Christopher E. McCants is a native of Florence, SC and is the youngest of three children. After completing Wilson High School, Chris continued his educational aspirations at North Greenville University,* *earning a Bachelor of Arts degree; Troy University, earning a Master of Education degree; and Furman University, earning a Master of Arts degree in School Leadership. Chris has taught 6th and 7th grade ELA for a number of years. He had served as an assistant principal for several years, before becoming the principal at Beech Springs Intermediate School in 2015. He feels strongly about making sure students are successful and feel successful. He is also passionate about mentoring. He is a member of numerous educators' organizations, and sits on the board of directors and advisory board for several non-profit organizations. He is also a member of Kappa Alpha Psi Fraternity, Inc.*

PART V
It's All About The People

Relationships, relationships, relationships! Relationships can be fostered, forged or forfeited with every interpersonal interaction. Nurturing talent and fostering relationships remains the essential umbrella competency of the principal role. Relationships are heavily nuanced through individual and collective reflective practice. Emotional intelligence, tenacity, joy, dedication, and humility are required. Who were your role models as you navigated the career trajectory from aspiring to novice to experienced principal? To whom are you a role model? Principal leadership represents the deep commitment to the process of learning; an ongoing, daily, individual, reciprocal, and collaborative reflective practice in the service of others. People may not remember the content taught, but they will almost certainly remember how respectfully they were approached, listened to, considered, treated, and understood.

Chapter 29

The Importance of Non-Technical Skills for Effective Leadership

Michael S. Trevisan, Ph.D.

I have always maintained that the way the message is given is as important, if not more so, than the message itself. Said another way, how I communicate with people is essential to motivating people to productively act on initiatives I set forth in the organization. Not to overstate it, this has been a key aspect of my career as a leader; however, I do think the people who work for me would likely attribute this quality to my leadership. I am not a school principal nor have I ever been one. I am a dean of a college of education. Our college is a modern college of education with a wide variety of programs that one would typically associate, and not associate, with a college of education. To be sure, the college does educate and train teachers and school leaders. In fact, a mentor of mine suggested that a good teacher preparation program and solid K-12 administrator training program is the "one-two punch" of a successful college of education, regardless of the other programs that might be housed within the college. My experience bears this out. While teacher preparation is the historical rationale for the existence of my college, preparing K-12 leaders, principals and superintendents, is the hallmark of the college. My college has educated and trained hundreds of strong school principals and superintendents who have gone on to have exemplary careers. My college has also produced influential K-12 leaders in the state and has done so for more than 50 years.

I have worked with dozens of school principals over my 30-plus year career, both as a faculty member and a college administrator. Sometimes I have worked closely with them over extended periods. This has afforded me the opportunity to observe a wide variety of leadership styles, individuals and demographic groups, as well as school leaders from other countries. My observations are hardly scientific. My experience and intuition tell me, however, that my conclusions about the importance of non-technical skills for effective leadership are true. Ask yourself: Do you know or know of a school administrator with a top-down administrative style or an abrasive or even abrupt personality? If you have, I will bet they were not an administrator for long, or they struggled and needed to move from position to position in order to survive. In short, they were not very effective.

The people who work in our organizations look to us as leaders to gauge their individual, organizational, and professional well-being. How am I doing? Am I perceived to have value? Does he or she like me? These are all questions that people in our organizations ask themselves, particularly when we as leaders cross paths with them, for whatever reason. I maintain that I can get more productivity out of my employees by treating them with respect and showing them that I care. The effective school principals that I have worked with and that I have learned from maintained this same core principle with the people who worked in their buildings.

The *Professional Standards for Educational Leaders 2016* (referred to here as the *Standards*) are expectations that most administrator training programs in the United States are obliged to adhere to for the professional education, training, and development of K-12 school principals. All K-12 professional school administrator organizations in the United States endorse these expectations. The *Standards* promote and set the expectations for technical aspects of being a school principal. Development of mission, vision and core values for the school; appropriate curriculum and instruction; sound use of student assessment data;

and evaluation of strategic initiatives are all examples of what I call the technical aspects of being an effective school principal.

The *Standards* also maintain the non-technical aspects of being an effective leader. Sometimes referred to as soft skills or professional skills in some professions, these include communication and collegiality. In fact, two words, communication and collegiality, are used throughout the *Standards*. Moreover, while performing the technical aspects of being a school principal are absolutely essential for being a successful building leader, the fuel for achieving success are the non-technical aspects of effective leadership: communication and collegiality.

Clarity in communication is critical to the success of building initiatives, particularly when teachers or other building staff have specific roles to play. Clear expectations, communicated with respect, sometimes multiple times and in multiple ways, help motivate individuals to step up and provide work and support that is essential to the success of the initiative. Clear and supportive communication can motivate individuals to want to participate, but also to reach for new heights in their performance.

Of course, communication can occur in a variety of different ways that include in-person, telephone, email, and formal correspondence; and thus, the kind of communication used differs. Communication in person affords the opportunity to learn from non-verbal cues allowing for adjustments in communication promote the idea that we, as building leaders, have the opportunity to be heard. On the other hand, email communication is devoid of non-verbal cues. We as leaders must sometimes give a good deal of attention and thought to our choice of words as we work to get our message across. Regardless, clear communication with a respectful tone is essential in whatever medium of communication we choose.

The effective school principals that I worked with and observed over the years viewed every instance of communication as an opportunity as leader to send a message about the worth and importance of each individual with whom he or she works. Each communication has a different context; for example, one-on-one communication with a teacher about dealing with a challenging student or communication with the entire building staff regarding the implementation of a new reading program.

Each communication however, when done well, has the real benefit of adding energy to school building cohesion, as well as the school building initiatives thought to be important for the students and families served.

As a colleague, the principal has much to add to building cohesion. While the principal cannot control all interactions among other individuals, the building principal, by definition, comes into contact with all employees, often multiple times within a week. Thus, he or she has the opportunity to set a tone of collegiality among all in the building. Strong interpersonal skills, a good understanding of personal boundaries, and a willingness to spend time with people even when it is inconvenient, are some of the attributes of collegiality for strong school principals that I have worked with and observed during the last thirty years.

Some may say that what I have articulated here is obvious. Any good school principal knows that communication and collegiality are important. In part, I could not agree more. The problem and challenge, I maintain, is that the importance of understanding non-technical skills for effective leadership is paramount. There are many who have not embraced this idea. Moreover, everyone should embrace clear communication and acting collegially. Given the decline in overall civility in the United States, these qualities are more important than ever. The school principal (or college dean) has the moral imperative to set the tone for communication and collegiality. An effective, well-functioning school organization will be the likely result, and an organization that is poised to reach new heights for the students and families it serves.

About the Author: *Dr. Mike Trevisan is the Dean of the College of Education at Washington State University and Professor of Educational Psychology. Over a 30+ year career, Mike has had the privilege of working with dozens of K-12 administrators across several states concerning a variety of education and policy issues. He is well published, particularly in the measurement and evaluation fields, and frequently provides workshops and consultations to school districts, and state and federal agencies. Mike is proud of the positive climate he has engendered in the college by advocating for, and promoting the development of, nontechnical skills.*

Chapter 30

A Sacred Duty

Nathan Warner

S acred. This is the word that comes to my mind when I think about the role of a principal. It is not an orthodox way of thinking about the principal role, and I do not mean it as a religious statement. However, considering the vast array of responsibilities principals assume, it is not hard to see how principals influence the lives of the children, families, and communities where they serve. One cannot help but to be impressed with the importance of the position. The principal role carries a unique responsibility and respect that sets it apart from other positions. To be entrusted with the educational, emotional, and physical safety of hundreds of individuals in key formational times of their lives each day is nothing short of incredible. The work of the principal is a sacred duty.

Each day I am present when 550 students exit their bus and begin walking into the school building. As they walk past me, I am often struck by my interactions with them. Each student who walks in brings his or her own personality, experiences, talents, and current or past problems. Some of them go out of their way to be seen and greeted by me. Some of them move away, not wanting interaction with me. Some of them even pretend to not see me in hopes that I reach out to them. I am there giving smiles, silent waves, high fives, fist bumps, asking a new student how their first week is going, reminding them about their behavior in 5th period, asking about a sick grandmother, and complimenting about a performance in last night's game. The interactions might look different from student to student, but there is something deeper happening here.

The purpose for me to be stationed where students exit buses and come into school is to establish and maintain order and safety as students enter the building. However, to me, this is a ritual that symbolizes something greater. My presence there communicates something very simple, but of utmost importance: "I see you. I'm glad you're here. I care for you." The students, at some level, understand this as well. They often use this time to communicate their successes on a recent test, a problem they are having with another student or a teacher, or some issue they are having at home. This ritual allows us to celebrate, strategize, grieve, or plan together. These interactions can be the determining factor whether a student has a successful day or not. These are moments when my students' worth is communicated to them and where I establish myself as a person of trust and accountability for their excellence; all this happens in the first five minutes before the students even enter the building! Sometimes sacredness is measured by the weight and potential impact of a moment. Any encounter where a student can walk away from us with their unique identity and belonging affirmed and celebrated is a significant interaction.

In this age of accountability, there is constant pressure to improve standardized test scores. We analyze data and discuss test scores in an attempt to effectively group students to promote and improve future test scores. We implement researched-based strategies targeted at students' academic needs. We chart their data and hold teachers responsible for implementing research-based best practices in their classrooms. We move forward in a prescribed cycle of collecting, analyzing, and responding to data. The accompanying planning, paperwork, emails, and documentation of these activities is impressive to say the least. As the instructional leader, the principal is tasked with leading all these efforts. Principals are in the business of school improvement, and that business often rules the day. We must do this work. I get this. However, there is a danger here to reduce students to a number: a quantifiable measurement of our success or failure in order to reward or punish conformity to various standards set forth by state government. We can get lost in our data, systems, and improvement plans. The danger here is we can allow *our students* to get lost in these efforts.

When we see our work as principals as sacred, it can transcend the systematic, assessment and accountability-driven culture in which we exist. Seeing the role of principal as sacred allows us to "zoom out" to see the whole person of our students. We are able to see their trauma, their intense needs, their uniqueness, and their talents. We are opened up to celebrate and grieve with them. We can have interactions with them that are characterized by care and empathy. We are able to see the whole child, in all of their successes and shortcomings, and respond in a way that dignifies the person they are and communicates their worth and potential to grow.

Now, more than ever, students need educators who see the sacredness of their position. Students need educators whose belief in the profession transcends the pressure to improve test scores at the cost of meaningful experiences and conversations. Do they need to know how to analyze three different texts and synthesize the information into an argumentative essay that defends their point of view? Yes, but they need something deeper as well.

Our students need to know how to give and receive acceptance of others. They need to develop the skills to function in a society that sometimes sees their differences before seeing their character. They need to know how to impact their communities to make them places of educated, accepting citizens who understand how to function in a democratic society. Students need to know that despite their greatest challenges and failures, they are valuable, and with hard work, grow to have a positive impact in this world. They need to understand their great importance to this world.

The five minutes of interaction after the buses arrive is hardly enough time to accomplish all of our goals. However, success is found in the hundreds of interactions we have each day with students, teachers, parents, and the community. We can lead our schools toward a more holistic approach to our students' education. We should expand our ideas of school improvement and professional development to be more inclusive, as well as mindful of the social-emotional learning our students need and the culture our schools are developing. Let us develop and implement programs that focus on social-emotional learning. Let us have honest and open dialogue about hard topics and learn to value diversity in society. Let us rethink disciplinary practices to be restorative to students who are acting out, and often calling out for help. Let us focus on relationship building with students and community as a way to facilitate deeper learning and higher achievement. Let us see the *whole* of the children we educate.

Principals must be the ones to lead these efforts. It is our sacred duty.

About the Author: *Nathan Warner is an assistant principal at Trotwood Madison Middle School in Trotwood, Ohio. He has served as a K-12 curriculum supervisor, worked for Ohio Department of Education's Race to the Top team as Regional Specialist for Southwest Ohio, and taught grades 6-8 in English Language Arts and Social Studies at Trotwood Madison Middle School. He received his M.A. in Education at The University of Dayton, and is currently in the Miami University of Ohio's doctoral program for educational leadership.*

Chapter 31

"Trust is not freely given; it must be earned, and the price is humility and vulnerability."

Micah J. Doramus

O f the lessons I have learned over my career I do not think it was lesson number one, but it was definitely in the top three: surround yourself with a great team. It has taken me a long while of trial and error, with many bumps and bruises, to finally understand the key components of a great team.

As a green administrator, I envisioned surrounding myself with educators that shared my philosophy, my vision, my mission, and my desire for a school of the future. I imagined surrounding myself with people I trusted to have my back. I imagined people that I could easily communicate with, and would easily understand where we were headed. I expected people that accepted the full responsibility of ensuring students received a high quality education. What I did not anticipate, and what no one shared with me, was that the team was already in place. I was the new kid on the block, and I was already surrounded. It wasn't necessarily friendly territory.

I remember my first year seeking administrative placement. I prepared tirelessly: I researched the schools, talked with people from the school community, and tried to identify what I thought each school needed in a new administrator. I interviewed fourteen times for various positions in the local area. After the thirteenth, I steeled myself for a return to my classroom. I made my peace.

It was at the encouragement of a mentor that I put myself out there one last time. I do not exactly know what changed in my approach. I would *like* to say it was some epiphany about who I was and what I wanted, but in reality it was much subtler than that.

Rather than focusing on what I thought the school needed in an assistant principal, my focus shifted to what I could bring to the school: my experience in educational technology, my understanding of school safety and security in a post-Columbine world, and my passion for educating students living in poverty. It just so happened those were exactly the areas of expertise that the administrative team was looking to fill. And just like that, I fit the missing piece in someone else's team.

Over the subsequent years, I began to see leadership through a new lens and the lesson finally clicked. Leadership is not about surrounding myself with people that share *my* anything. Leadership is about surrounding myself with people that sharpen me, and I them, as we work toward a common goal. Together we share a united philosophy, vision, mission, and a desire for the school of the future, focused on what is best for kids. Remember, as a new principal, the organization picked me to fill a need. I did not pick my team. It was in place before I got there. But the core of our success has been the people I work with joining in my efforts to build a strong team based on our individual strengths.

While we collectively may not have the most experience as a leadership team, I firmly believe ours is one of the strongest teams I have had the privilege of joining - let alone leading. We did not choose each other, but together, through trust, communication, and accountability, we choose to be the best we can to support our school, our staff, and our students.

This year, has been the hardest start to a school year ... EVER ... in my career as an educator. There are myriad reasons. None worth noting here. Suffice it to say, we have been picking and crawling our way up a mountain, where one misstep could cost us weeks of effort, if not see us tumble down to the base. At the very least we would have to begin the journey again, assuming we were to survive the fall.

About a month ago my resolve wavered. I blamed myself for the lack of progress we were making with our staff culture. I worried that I was not supporting my staff leaders enough in mentoring teachers under their care. I was tired: emotionally, mentally, and physically. At our weekly administrative meeting, I owned it all. I shared my thoughts and feelings with the team and asked for one thing. It was not grace or forgiveness. It was not patience. It was accountability.

I asked my team of new administrators to help hold me to my word, to my dreams for what our school could be, to the promises I had informally made to them as their mentor. It was a huge risk to peel back the layers of my pride and insecurities. It was scary to open myself up to the difficult conversation I was sure that would come next.

But the difficult conversation didn't come. Instead, a real conversation came. Each of my team members shared how difficult the year had been for them. They shared the challenges they felt, like not being able to break through to their students, or their mentees. They expressed gratitude for my steady guidance in the difficult times. They honored my vulnerability. They offered support. They renewed my faith in myself. They sharpened me, and in turn our entire team was strengthened.

In the weeks since, we have shifted from an emphasis on reaction to problems to an emphasis on proactive leadership. We still have to deal with the daily grind of school management, but it does not dictate or hijack our meetings any longer. We have had extensive, real dialogue about philosophy, mission, and vision. We have had tough conversations about teacher performance, student learning, needed development, and many other critical long term goals that we want to work towards. We know that no matter the situation, we can trust any member of our team to help each of us reach our goals.

For me, the point where I recognized the true power of our leadership team came in the past two weeks. One of my administrators came to me and shared some struggles. Again, the details don't matter. We talked. We came up with a plan. And we went back to work knowing that we had each other's backs.

A few days later, another administrator came to me needing to step away from a situation in order to maintain perspective and preserve a positive relationship with a student. I stepped in gladly, honoring the request, ensuring that the student received a balanced opportunity, but more importantly ensuring that the student did not lose an advocate that felt too close to the situation.

It is easy to build trust when things go well, when the mission and vision are clear. The true test is what happens when things fall apart, when the mission and vision are clouded or unseen.

Trust is not freely given; it must be earned, and the price is humility and vulnerability. Even among leaders.

About the Author: *Micah J. Doramus has served in school administration since 2006 in elementary, middle, and high schools in Boise, Idaho and the surrounding area. His focus in school leadership is organizational/ systems effectiveness and building leadership capacity through intentional change. He is the current President of the Idaho Middle Level Association and works with that organization to increase developmental awareness and effectiveness of instruction and learning for students ages 11-15 years.*

Chapter 32

Reconciliation Through Education

Lori Pritchard

Recently in Canada, the Truth and Reconciliation Commission (TRC) released its final report, *Honouring the Truth, Reconciling for the Future* (2016), documenting the stories of residential school survivors as a starting point for reconciliation. As expected, the release of the TRC and its 94 calls to action, along with a statement by Justice Murray Sinclair (2015) that "education is the key to reconciliation," has led school leaders across the country to consider our role in the truth and reconciliation process. My own understanding of reconciliation through education requires that we come together to learn the truth, and then work together to heal. Therefore, reconciliation cannot happen without relationship building.

In K-12 education systems today, our First Nations, Métis and Inuit students typically account for the highest drop-out rates, and lowest high school completion rates. Research, wise practice, and my twenty-plus years of experience in Indigenous education, has shown me that establishing meaningful relationships and working *with* First Nations, Métis and Inuit community members is not only critical for the success of our Indigenous students, but also for the success of Indigenous education for all students, teachers, and leaders. For reconciliation through education to occur, there is nothing more important.

As a teacher and leader in Indigenous education, often I find myself in familiar and repetitive conversations with teachers and school leaders who want to engage with the community, but do not know where to start. Frequently, they express their discomfort, unknowing, and fear in approaching First Nations, Métis or Inuit Elders and community members to help them to include Indigenous voice, and ways of knowing and being, into their teaching and leadership practice. Teachers and leaders have shared with me that they are afraid of saying or doing the wrong thing, and do not want to appear ignorant, disrespectful, or even racist. They are not alone. Through my conversations with other leaders in Indigenous education across Canada, United States, New Zealand, Australia, and Peru, I found this discomfort to be a common denominator with regards to why so many non-Indigenous teachers and school leaders do not engage in leading Indigenous education learning in their schools and school districts. As a leader in Indigenous education, I have worked tirelessly to mentor and support my colleagues to find the courage to move past their apprehensions, and to enter relationship building with a willingness to be vulnerable and to learn. To encourage and support them, I begin with sharing my own story of being in that place of unknowing, discomfort, and fear while needing to establish and nurture new relationships with local Elders and community members.

My leadership story began in 2001 when I first moved from Treaty 6 territory (Saskatoon, Saskatchewan) to Treaty 7 territory (Calgary, Alberta). Being born and raised in Saskatoon, and beginning my teaching career working with Cree, Saulteaux, Dakota, and Métis peoples, blessed me with a lifetime of family and community relationships, which supported my role as an Indigenous educator and leader in Treaty 6 territory. During my decision-making process to move to Treaty 7 territory, I assumed that being an Indigenous educator and leader would translate easily from one territory to the next. However, I learned quickly that my relationships with local Blackfoot, Tsuut'ina, Stoney Nakoda, and Métis peoples would not come more easily simply because I too am Indigenous.

Fortunately, my experience with the Calgary Board of Education (CBE) offering leadership in Indigenous education did provide me with some access to the local community. I was lucky to join an existing team of CBE Indigenous community leaders, and was the recipient of many invitations to join community meetings and celebrations on behalf of the CBE. Even so, there I was, in Treaty 7 territory, appointed to offer leadership in Indigenous education, without one single meaningful relationship to rely on for guidance and support. I was on my own, anxious, and afraid to take the lead in establishing new relationships in an unfamiliar place. However, I could not let my fear keep me from this critical element for success, so I gathered my courage and designed a plan to respectfully step into the community. The following recommendations represent a snapshot of my plan, and the lessons that I have learned and carry with me, as I continue to meet and nurture new relationships in and beyond Treaty 7 territory.

Make one new friend. When I first moved to Calgary I did not know anybody, so my plan to build relationships in Treaty 7 territory began with making one new friend. I needed to find somebody that I could trust to learn from and become my guide. About one month after moving to Calgary, I attended a community learning session where Piikani Elder Leonard Bastien was speaking about Blackfoot history and worldview. My first impression of Elder Leonard was that he was kind, patient, funny, and brilliant. I knew instantly that I wanted to make him my one new friend. As he was sharing his stories with the small audience, he must have sensed my anxiety about being new to Calgary. During the break, he walked over to introduce himself and to ask how I was doing. I shared with him that I was new to Calgary. He responded with a simple nod, and then shared a joke. We laughed together, and it was in that moment that I knew we would be friends.

For the fifteen years that have followed, the teachings that I received from Elder Leonard have helped to shape my practice as a school and system leader. He offered cultural guidance to me while I was the principal at Piitoayis (Eagle Lodge) Family School and led our students, staff, and families through ceremony and learning that brought us together as a community of learners. He has been an important member of our CBE Elder Advisory Council, guiding our CBE leaders to learn and be responsive to the needs of our Indigenous students and families. Elder Leonard offers a safe place for me to ask questions about Blackfoot worldview, and for me to make mistakes without judgment. He has been a trusted teacher and guide, and I will be forever grateful that he is my friend.

Know the land. Know the people. Know the stories. As a leader in Indigenous education working to establish relationships with the local community, it was not enough for me to just know that I was in Calgary, or in traditional Treaty 7 territory. My plan needed to include seeking learning opportunities that would help me to know the land, know the people, and know the oral stories that have lived here for thousands of years. Taking part in community and professional learning opportunities and researching Indigenous history were important. When I first moved here, I thought that Treaty 7 only included three Blackfoot Nations; it was only through my own research that I learned that the Tsuut'ina and Stoney Nakoda Nations are also a part of Treaty 7.

During my knowledge seeking process, many Elders and knowledge keepers from our Treaty 7 Nations shared stories about Nose Hill Park, which is situated in the center of NW Calgary. Essentially, Nose Hill was used as a vantage point for First Nations peoples to find buffalo herds, water sources, and approaching allies or enemies. Nose Hill is also a sacred place, home to many traditional medicines. Listening to Elders share about Nose Hill and spending time there, I was at once drawn to the land and its stories. Whether a coincidence or not, many years ago I bought a house with a view of, and immediate access to, Nose Hill. More recently, I was appointed principal at a school just a few minutes from Nose Hill; it was an obvious choice to open the school year by telling some of the Nose Hill stories that have been shared with me. Because of these stories, my staff and students also want to spend time at Nose Hill learning from Elders. This makes me happy.

Visit. Listen. Listen. Listen. Being visible in the community, attending events, professional learning, and volunteering increased my access to people. I attended everything, including community meetings, pow-wows, round dances, feasts, ceremonies, and conferences. I joined committees, volunteered, and even took a beading class. Making time to be with the community allowed me to meet and visit with Elders, knowledge keepers, cultural resource people, agency representatives, students, and families. My visits with community were always focused on listening to everything that they had to share with me. I entered each new relationship as a learner. When approaching an Elder to ask for advice, or to know more about worldviews, language, or community relations, I would always present some sacred tobacco and a gift. Each time, I listened with my heart. I rarely kept notes and I never interrupted. I remember leaving those moments thinking for days about what Elders and others had shared with me, making sure that I understood. Then I would use those teachings to enhance my leadership practice as I continued to establish new relationships in Treaty 7 territory. My times spent with Elder Leonard, in ceremony or having lunch at his favorite diner, are profound learning moments that I will never forget. I treated, and continue to treat, each of these moments as a gift. The opportunity to sit with and learn from Elder Leonard and other knowledge carriers is a privilege. In the Indigenous community, the Elders are our scholars. They carry the knowledge and wisdom of our communities, to ensure that Indigenous ways of knowing and being are shared and passed on to the youth.

Nurture and care for the relationship. Relationships with members of the Indigenous community need to go beyond inviting an Elder to pray, a drummer to sing, or a dancer to dance. As I set out to build relationships in Treaty 7 territory, I knew that I would need to commit to nurturing and caring for long-term friendships. My years of experience working with Elders has taught me that inviting a member of the Indigenous community to visit my school or district, and then sending them on their way following an "event" is not relationship building. Rather, surface level participation. Reciprocity is a relationship principle that I have embedded into my leadership practice when working with Elder Leonard and others. As such, I will call them often for no reason other than to ask how they are doing, invite them out for coffee, lunch, or to a school/district event as a guest without any expectation. Replying to requests from the community and accepting invitations to attend community meetings, ceremonies, and celebrations are critical. Reciprocity also includes listening to community generated ideas and creating opportunities for Elders and others to be leaders in our work with Indigenous students.

My leadership story of relationship building in Treaty 7 territory has been inspired by the many friendships that I have built since moving to Calgary fifteen years ago. My hope is that, by reading my story, other school and system leaders will learn that being with and working with Indigenous communities across Canada often needs courage, learning, listening, and love. I hope for others to be encouraged and courageous in their own efforts to seek and build relationships with Elders and members of the Indigenous community, inviting them to be a part of their leadership practice.

All My Relations. (This statement is commonly used in the Indigenous community and signifies that we are all related and interconnected.)

Reference

Justice Murray Sinclair http://www.cbc.ca/news/politics/truth-and-reconciliation-chair-urges-canada-to- adopt-un-declaration-on-indigenous-peoples-1.3096225

About the Author: *Lori Pritchard (B.Ed., M.Ed.) is an Indigenous (Métis) educator and leader. She is currently the principal at Sir John A. Macdonald School with the Calgary Board of Education, and previously provided district-wide leadership in Indigenous Education. Lori is also an instructor with the Aboriginal Relations Leadership Training Program at the University of Calgary, and a sessional lecturer at Mount Royal University. She is an active member of Calgary's urban Indigenous population, serving as a Board member of the Pathways Community Services Association and volunteering at community events.*

Chapter 33

People First, then Percentages

Larry Dake, Ed.D.

"We feel like we're a sinking ship." This is how the Speech Pathologist described the school to me when I met her on my first day as Principal. As the new building leader in a large, suburban, and increasingly-diverse elementary school, it was clear to me that the school's culture had to improve before anything else could get better. I was hired from a neighboring district, and brought a reputation for using data skillfully to improve test scores. In my previous role – district-level data coordinator – I facilitated a K-12 improvement plan that resulted in common assessments being delivered across grade-levels and an associated rise in student learning and test scores. Upon my hire, my new Superintendent made it very clear to me that the same was expected in my new role. But, upon meeting the staff in late August, it was clear that people had to come first, and then perhaps percentages could follow.

The school building itself, as well as the community, had undergone large changes over the last fifteen years. In 2000, the building was founded when two smaller schools were merged by the district. A 25-year veteran Principal led that change; moreover, he was the Principal of one of the former schools. Although almost fifteen years had passed, remnants of that "us versus them" mentality, that often occurs when two schools become one, remained. Compounding that challenge, the beloved, veteran Principal retired in 2010 and his successor was tasked with "tightening up" many of the school's policies and systems. No longer were parents allowed to walk their children to Kindergarten on the first day. PTA meetings took on a more formal tone. Some of these changes were reflective of the times; unfortunately, the schoolhouse can't be as open in the 2010s as it was in the 1980s. Regardless of their intent, the community perceived the changes negatively and associated them with the successor Principal.

At the same time, the community's demographics were undergoing dramatic shifts. While an affluent part of town still existed, the school increasingly took on a "haves and have nots" feel. The school encompassed a part of town called "Little Italy," where thousands of Italian immigrants had settled in the 1900s to work in nearby factories. Those factories were gone, and so were many of the people who had lived there for generations. In their place came an extremely transient and diverse population from the New York City area. Poverty increased from 18% in 2006 to 41% in 2013. Additionally, many of the new students and their families had little emotional connection to the school due to their transience. Most importantly, many of the instructional and cultural strategies that worked in the 1990s no longer proved effective in the 2010s. It didn't help that the new school was located in the affluent part of town.

It was upon this backdrop that a 33-year old administrator with nine years in education became the Principal. I had some roots in the community; my wife and her family went to one of the original schools, and the aforementioned beloved 25-year Principal was her Principal in the late 1980s. Test scores had dropped and the community had largely disengaged with the school. To make matters worse, the school's staff projected a sense of hopelessness. The "sinking ship" comment was echoed in many ways by other staff. I heard comments referring to "those kids not being able to learn" and "those parents" who didn't value education, and countless other similar phrases. Complicating matters was the fact that the school was recently labeled "School in Need of Improvement," and scars remained from the state-led review that took place the previous year. In the past, the school had been a community jewel; scores were high, poverty was low, and morale was positive. I was tasked with getting the school "off the list," raising test scores, and bringing recalcitrant staff "into line."

Having consumed Dale Carnegie's "How to Win Friends and Influence People" over the last few years, I decided to start by building relationships and trust. It was quickly apparent that staff would only trust their Principal if it was proven that I wasn't "out to get them." Therefore, I started out with two very intentional tasks: I walked the building every morning before school started and said "good morning" to every staff member I saw, and I started praising each and every positive I encountered during the school day. Over the next months, staff started opening up about their challenges and their ideas. Once I sensed that the staff trusted my intentions, I started visiting classrooms more regularly. That led to more intentional praise, but also more "have you ever thought about..." or "have you ever watched Mrs. Walker teach writing" conversations. My goal wasn't to change teacher practice – after all, as a 33-year old I hadn't been alive for as long as some of my staff had been teaching. Rather, the goal was to build trust, get to know the kids, and help staff see that they themselves had the skills to reach this changing population.

This strategy extended to non-instructional staff as well. I worked hand-in-hand with our lunch monitors, for example. It became very clear that student problems at recess were having instructional implications. For example, if students were sent to the office during recess, they often missed part of their afternoon instruction. My Assistant Principal and I cleared our schedules every day from 11:30am to 1:30pm so we could be in the cafeteria and on the playground. We modeled how we wanted our Monitors to interact with the students – especially those who exhibited challenging behaviors. Moreover, we started to intentionally organize playground activities. 4th and 5th graders started a kickball league, for example. Not everyone played, but 50 students in each grade did, which cleared congestion on the playground. As Principal, I oversaw and organized the league myself so I could defuse any conflicts and reinforce good sportsmanship. Not only did we see far fewer behavioral referrals, fewer students were going to the nurse at recess. The result was that far fewer students missed their afternoon instruction due to health office visits or behavioral referrals.

It all took time, but by my second year the building had a very different feel. And something else happened quickly that I didn't fully anticipate – test scores rose dramatically. Our 4th Grade Math scores rose from 21% to 36% (and up to 49% the following year). By the end of my second year, the school was removed from the state's "in need of improvement" list. After the third year, our 3rd grade ELA and Math scores rivaled those of the most affluent district in the region – 66% of our 3rd graders were proficient in ELA at that point! I always thought we would improve our data, I just didn't think it would result from a focus on people and not percentages. By the middle of my second year, we had instituted more data-driven models; because they knew it wasn't a personal attack (as many teachers perceive data-driven instruction), most teachers embraced it. Not all did – there's no doubt about it. But with some staff, it's more of a long-game – some of the most recalcitrant teachers have lived through five, seven, or ten Principals. They've seen initiatives come and go. I always tried to frame these challenges from their perspective, not mine.

Then, my phone rang. The Assistant Superintendent was retiring the next June, and I was offered the position. Although I wasn't ready to leave, I didn't think it was an opportunity I could refuse. Even as I write this I feel some guilt about that decision. While I was advancing my career, I was leaving behind a building that had come a very long way in a short time. As I said to them on my last day, "it would be a bigger problem if you all left and I stayed, because you're the ones who are teaching the students." Upon leaving, however, I knew I could look back and be proud of the building's journey over the last three years.

About the Author: *Dr. Larry Dake is the Assistant Superintendent in the Union-Endicott Central School District in Endicott, NY. Previously, he served as a K-5 Principal in Union-Endicott and as a teacher and administrator in the Vestal Central School District in nearby Vestal, NY. In 2014, he earned a Doctorate in Educational Theory and Practice from Binghamton University and currently serves as an adjunct instructor in their Educational Leadership program. He resides in Endwell, NY with his wife Kelly and three young children.*

Chapter 34

Lessons Learned Living and Leading in a Cross-Cultural Context

Darlene Nuqingaq

Sometimes it seems like just yesterday that I first moved to a small Inuit community on the southern tip of Baffin Island, Nunavut. At the time - it was August of 1987 - this isolated hamlet, accessible only by boat, small twin otter plane, or snowmobile in the winter, had a population of about 250 Inuktitut speaking people. Hired to teach the grades three and four class, I was these little eight and nine-year-old children's first English speaking teacher, and, at the time, I knew very little Inuktitut. This made for some very interesting learning experiences for all of us. Little did I know that I was embarking on a thirty-year journey of many firsts: my first time living alone, and my first time experiencing what it feels like to be in the minority and not be able to speak the majority's language. However, I survived in this 'foreign' and cross-cultural context because my Inuit colleagues (and one in particular) took the time to mentor me, welcome me into the community, and show me the 'Inuit way.'

Educational leadership interested me, so in 1990 I attended the Northwest Territories Principal Certification Program in Yellowknife. This was a transition time for the program, as it moved from being led by professionals from a southern-based institution to long-time northern educational leaders reflecting on culturally appropriate leadership. I later became principal of a small neighbourhood elementary school, and then principal of a city-wide middle school in Iqaluit, Nunavut. I joined the leadership team for the Nunavut-specific Educational Leadership Program, and became co-principal and then coordinator of this program for many years. During this time, I reflected often on the characteristics of an effective educational leader for Nunavut Schools. These are some of the lessons I learned.

To Listen

It is important as an educational leader to take the time to listen. Over the years living in the north, I have seen many newcomers come with an agenda to fix or make things better, without taking the time to truly seek out and listen to the people who have lived here all their lives. It is difficult to prioritize this important task when we have a long 'to do' list to carry out. However, it is essential that we not rush into action without truly listening to our staff, our students, their parents, elders, and community members so that we can gain an understanding and a respect for the cultural and historical context in which we are entrusted to lead.

To Learn

Take time to learn the culture and history of the community in which you will lead. It will help you to understand the parents' and community's perception of schooling, and any resistance or reluctance to come into the school building; feelings perhaps due to the experience of residential schooling, or another historical or personal event.

Take time to learn the language. Learn how to greet people in their first language. It will help you to appreciate their journey to learn English as a Second Language.

Try to learn to see things from another's viewpoint. Take time to reflect on your own hegemony and place in privilege and power. As leaders, it is important to learn when to take the lead and when it is proper or necessary to step back and let others lead. I have learned this important lesson from observing my Inuit colleagues and elders. There is a time to lead and a time to observe others leadership. One example I have experienced is planning a school-wide camp. I can take the leadership in ordering supplies, and hiring resource people with input from my staff, however at camp it is more appropriate for cultural resource people to lead the camp program. Shared leadership is a valued aspect of traditional Inuit leadership.

To Like

When it is 50 below and cold and dark outside, it can be hard to find anything to like, but once dressed for the weather you soon notice the beauty of the sky, the stars, and the dancing of the northern lights. As educational leaders, we need to be prepared to face many situations. Self-care will help provide the fuel we need to weather turmoil. There will be some people who will be difficult to work with; we need to strive to find something to like about each person. It is in finding and appreciating their unique gift that we will eventually gain their warmth.

To Laugh

Inuit (and most children in fact) value an open face, a face that smiles and is welcoming. A face that is too serious appears closed. Inuit refer to this kind of face as 'Annu.' Luckily a colleague, early in my leadership career, told me that I look angry when I am thinking. Because of this, over the years I have worked to make my face appear more relaxed, open, and inviting, without doing a forced smile which does not look believable. As leaders, it is important to be aware of our body language so that we are not sending mixed or contradictory messages to others.

Spending time building relationships and positive memories with others is important for educational leaders personally and professionally. It is important for leaders to share their passion with others and to be a person, not just a principal. Looking back on my career, I know that my volunteer work teaching an extra-curricular fiddle club and school choir, as well as organizing an annual week long summer music camp for 125 plus Iqaluit youth, has made my life as a principal much easier and more rewarding. The relationships and respect gained from my volunteer work has transferred into my professional work as an educational leader.

To Linger

Daily personal and professional demands of being a leader can be overwhelming. It is necessary to take the time to connect with other people and to 'linger' in the staffroom, or at the local store, or at a community event. It is important for others to see you value life outside the school.

Being together as a community is an important Inuit value. The community feasts, dances, and games events are fun to attend and a great way to mingle with parents, elders, and community members on neutral ground. Community members appreciate seeing their school leaders taking part in these events.

To Lead by Example

When I was first starting my education career in the Arctic, many people took the time to mentor me. Now as an experienced educational leader I need to 'pay this help forward' and take the time to mentor and support emerging leaders through my professional and volunteer work.

I also need to be a servant leader. I need to show that no job is beneath me. If it needs to be done, then do it. Others will be more apt to follow and respect a leader who is willing to do the hard work too. The school is a community, and for a community to succeed everyone needs to work together.

To Live

This last lesson is one that is the hardest to learn for a workaholic like myself. However, it is important to take time to establish a healthy work-life balance. When you ask an Inuk child what they want to be when they grow up, it is hard for them to answer because a job does not define a person. It is your relationships to others that defines a person. For the Inuit, being a mother/father, aunt/uncle, sister/brother, friend, and so on, is far more important than the job title.

So my advice to educational leaders anywhere is to take the time to listen, learn, like, laugh, linger, lead by example, and live your life to the fullest!

About the Author: *Darlene Nuqingaq is an experienced Nunavut educational leader and one of Canada's Outstanding Principals. She is a passionate and dedicated leader who strongly advocates for the well-being of her students, staff, and community. Whether she is coordinating a summer music camp for children or co-leading a leadership program for educators, she willingly gives of her time and talent to provide a high quality program and positive learning environment for all involved.*

Chapter 35

Relationships Matter

Ronald Davis

After 34 years as an educator, with almost half of those being a school level administrator, the most enduring truth that I can share is that relationships matter. While I am sure this is not news to fellow educators in general, and administrators in particular, time and time again my day-to-day experience has borne this out. When I first started teaching in 1981, and also after becoming an assistant principal in 2000, I learned that building relationships and acknowledging the people, not the "stuff," was the key that makes a school work.

Interestingly, I can remember my first assistant principal interview and the only question I can recall was, "What do parents want most from administrators?" My answer was, "Most times parents want to be heard."

Now some may disagree, but I believe the first step in school success is to listen - really listen. Not listen to defend, or listen to finish a conversation, or listen to promote a point of view, listen to understand - no more and no less. I have done all kinds of listening, especially the kinds of listening I have described earlier, and I can tell you the best outcomes have happened when I listened to understand. I can remember getting my first school in 2004 and engaging in a summer of listening first, before I tried to do budgets or create schedules or write handbooks or anything like that. Despite the wave of expectations a novice principal has, I felt it was important to build relationships with staff, parents, and others in the community. I wanted to hear the "story" of my new school from the people who lived it and helped create it. About 90% of the staff took me up on the offer, as did many parents and community members. As you can imagine, the points were as varied as the people; I cannot say that I did not go down a few "rabbit holes" at first, but nothing happens in God's world by mistake, so even my mistakes led to better outcomes eventually.

I learned to be clear about my vision and explicit about my expectations. I tried never to forget that sitting in front of my desk, or at the table at a meeting, or in a student desk was a heart, mind, and soul. To be clear, some may not agree with that approach. Considering the high-stakes environment of accountability/testing education in American has become, this approach certainly is not the most efficient way to show growth, but it was what worked for me. I wish I could say that every year we had the best test scores, but that would not be true. We always kept the main thing, the main thing. You fill in the blank. After moving to a much larger school in 2007, I learned that the power of relationships seemed more important and concentrated only because of the sheer number of people who needed a connection. The kinds of life events that are beyond the instructional mandate of a school were not unique to me I am sure. Illnesses, trauma, financial hardship, and even death, were not unique to my situation; I can only emphasize that the relationships we shared helped us weather those storms. I retired about 16 months ago and wI will carry the lessons I learned about relationships with me for a lifetime.

About the Author: *Ronald Davis is a lifelong educator of over 34 years and has worked as a school level administrator for almost half that time. Retired since 2015, he now works in an advisory role to support other school administrators.*

Chapter 36

'You can't boil jam at the clothesline."

Susan E. Murray

How many of you often begin a staff meeting or event with a thoughtful quote? Perhaps you have one posted close to your desk or as a tagline in your email. Often, simple words of wisdom or sage advice are thoughts from a favorite movie, book, or mentor. They guide and inspire us by the simplicity of the statement, not the depth of the meaning behind it.

I will share three of my favorite quotations with you. They provide a quick reminder about the work that we do as leaders, along with an opportunity for daily reflection and motivation. As I mentioned, while simple thoughts, it is the depth of meaning behind them that guide me in my decision-making, my daily action, and my vision for success.

"The key to this business is personal relationships."

At the beginning of the movie *Jerry McGuire*, a wise mentor says, "The key to this business is personal relationships." One of the key messages of this movie was that only through developing strong relationships can we be successful, both professionally and personally. It may be suggested that the foundation of the development of human capital is grounded on this premise. While the best school systems may have multiple policies, procedures, and practices in place to enhance the learning for both staff and students, it is truly the power of the relationships within the systems that impact learning and development.

What are the critical relationships for a school principal? While the connection with students is of paramount importance, closely followed by teachers, parents, and the broader school community, I would like to focus instead on the power of the principal's relationships with other school leaders.

As a leader, we are counted on to solve problems: the playground tussle, the parent-teacher conflict, student achievement results, and the perpetual parking lot congestion. We wear the title of "Leader" and all eyes are on us to fix, to solve, and to make a difference. A daunting task, since we often do not want to lose face. In my first principalship, I quickly realized I could not solve everything on my own; however, I did not want to appear incompetent, particularly to my staff and supervisor. Luckily, I quickly figured out, through both formal and informal structures, the power of personal connections with my fellow principals. The quick phone call, the coffee date, the senior level meetings – all of these provided valuable opportunities to connect, to share ideas and plans, to support one another, and to find common voice. In my conversations with leaders in education and business, they all recognize the power of these connections for their personal and professional development.

Professionally, we recognize the value of formal structures such as conferences, district meetings, professional development days, and collegial circles at both the local and national level. These structures engage us in professional dialogue and provide desired leadership development opportunities that link to our key work in schools. Likewise, these opportunities allow us to connect more deeply with our colleagues and develop networks for support, growth, and guidance. In my career, I have been lucky to have developed such relationships, both locally and across Canada, through my involvement with the Canadian Association of Principals and The Learning Partnership - valuable organizations that support and develop leadership.

That may seem rather obvious, but in my work with new and emerging leaders, they often hesitate to reach out to senior colleagues for advice and support. As school leaders, we need to ensure that we reach out to new colleagues, perhaps providing a safe-trust relationship as they navigate their new roles. At a senior level, we need to ensure that our leadership development programs, structures, and policies contain opportunities for mentorship, ongoing support, and networking. These relationships are essential for our personal and professional growth, and are synonymous with those that we create and model in our own school communities.

"You can't boil jam at the clothesline."

I doubt if you can do an Internet search on this quote - it is from Madeline, an old woman who used to take care of me when I was a little girl. Madeline was famous for her sayings and while, at 10 years old, I did not appreciate her wisdom, I frequently think of her words in my daily work. As a leader, we are many things to many people. We teach, we lead, we design, we solve problems, and we bring joy. Because our leadership is valued, our calendars quickly fill with meetings, and more; we sit on committees, attend social gatherings, represent at public events and march in the Santa Claus Parade. All great opportunities to highlight your work and connect with others. "Busy" is the buzzword, and our 24-hour connectivity ensures that we are constantly on alert and being pulled in many directions - kind of like a clothesline on a windy day!

Have you ever made old-fashioned jam? The kind that requires careful measurement, constant stirring and observation so that when it reaches the setting point you remove it from the heat? The timing and stirring is critical to success, even with the best ingredients. You need to stay with it until it is done.

What needs your constant attention now? Your improvement plan? Your student success initiatives? A teacher that is struggling, or a student that is presenting with behavioral challenges? As leaders, something will always require careful attention. We need to provide structure and care. Most importantly, we need to be visible.

As such, we need to prioritize carefully the expectations of others along with those that we have for ourselves. It is okay to say "No" when you realize that the constant committee work, emails, and events are taking you from what is important. You may also need to ask the question,

"What am I avoiding?" It is that careful balance and observation of defining your priorities that will make an impact and create desired change.

"Bold steps will define you."

It is a little strange to share my daily mantra, but I guess that speaks to the power and meaning behind it. It is one of those deeply personal statements that come to mind when you are faced with a decision or a wicked problem. I learned it from a wise mentor when I was faced with a bold decision many years ago, and it has since lead me on new journeys and experiences.

As a woman leader, the term "bold" could be considered derogatory. For many, "bold" implies a sense of rudeness or brashness. For me, it implies strength, risk-taking, and wisdom. My guiding quote means not settling, making strong choices, using your voice, and positioning for a better outcome. As a leader, how do you use your knowledge and power to create change? How do you step out of your safety zone to grow your organization? How do you know, on a personal and professional level, that it's time for you to challenge yourself and make a change?

There is comfort in the everyday experiences; the daily routines, the predictable events, and even the unpredictable moments create a sense of safety. Is that not what we want to create so that our students have a safe and secure learning environment? I have worked with amazing school leaders who are constant, bold advocates for their students and teachers. It is through their boldness that teacher allocations increase, resources are attained, and curriculum is enriched.

Are you one of those leaders? Are you using your position and voice to make a difference at your school? Are you taking the risks needed to create a learning environment that meets the needs of all students? If not, why not? What defines you? Many of us have the privilege of serving in multiple leadership roles, whether at the school or district level. Ideally, we leave our mark, a legacy of leadership, in the communities and schools that we serve. It is never too early, or too late, to think about that. When you leave or retire from the profession, what will your legacy be? What will define you? It is hard to think about ourselves as leaders. Our learning and professional development steers us towards serving and leading others - as it should. Yet, to really be a leader is to truly grasp your strengths, flaws, passions, and insecurities. The complexities of our work do not often allow us the time to reflect deeply. Often, the simple thoughts from friends, mentors, movies or literature can provide a gentle mantra to both ground and motivate us. The ones I share bring me joy and keep me focused on my work as a leader. What simple words motivate you?

About the Author: *Susan E. Murray (M.Ed., M.Sc.) has over 25 years' experience as a principal, district leader, and educator. Her work and doctoral research focuses on leaders and leadership development in both education and broader organizational contexts. She now teaches leadership studies at Memorial University in Newfoundland, as well as executive programs for educational leaders at the Rotman School of Management, University of Toronto. Find out more about Susan at www.clearpathleadership.com*

Chapter 37

It Is People, Not Programs

Dennis Neal

At some point in my twenty-five years in public education, I realized through experience at many levels, at all types of schools, one of the only absolute truths in our profession. Are you ready? It is so simple, so obvious, and yet so often missed in a myriad of so-called 'new' initiatives, monitoring systems, and flavor-of-the-month instructional strategies that seemly consume all of our time only to produce marginal, if any, improvement. I have been around so long that I am now subjected to going through the latest educational panacea, only to discover that it was done before under a different name, but now with a new expert attached to it as an endorsement.

Here is the big secret, the forest that is so often missed due to any number of random trees in the way. It is people, not programs that produce results. That is it. Period. Any money, time, or resources spent on anything other than recruiting, developing, and supporting personnel is not giving you the greatest return on your investment. Bell schedules, organizational structure, curriculum, or individual philosophy have their own relative impact, but they do not compare to the impact that a talented, committed, motivated teacher can have on a student.

I see many modern administrators lose sight of this truth because they prioritize their monitoring systems, checklists, and compliance reports in the day-to-day rigors of school life. We are inundated with what seems like an endless list of other people's "top priority initiatives."

We are accountable for successfully implementing, monitoring, and documenting. If you allow it, this then becomes your priority and what is truly a top priority begins to fade away.

Often relegated to being an afterthought, we ignore our most important asset: the people. As leaders, we deal with laborious evaluation systems, redundant monitoring processes, cheerleading moms, booster club drama, and so much more. There is no substitute for, or larger factor in your school's success than, the quality of the teacher in the classroom. Block scheduling, academies, year round school, virtual school; they all pale in comparison to the impact your personnel have on moving student achievement levels. The beautiful forest of student achievement is lost behind the multitude of well-intentioned, but relatively insignificant, trees.

If people are the key that unlocks a hidden treasure bounty of student learning gains, how do we as administrators recruit, develop, and retain these talented difference makers and maximize their potential? It starts with the hiring process. When I interview candidates, I am looking for the right person as a whole; not necessarily the most credentialed or experienced. You see, effective teaching is not a mystery. I can show you how to be an effective teacher, how to plan, how to arrange your classroom, teach the instructional strategies, etc. I cannot, however, teach you to have a genuine love for young people, empathy, a love of learning, a good work effort, or to be coachable. What I am looking for is not common, nor can it be taught. I am speaking of the natural teacher who innately possesses qualities which allow them to develop into a master teacher; one who can change lives and increase student achievement when other efforts have failed to produce results.

How do I go about finding the kind of teachers I want in my building? It is a three-part approach. I am looking at the heart, the head, and the hands. What I mean by this is I am looking first to determine if they are the kind of person I would want to teach my own kids. Do they have character, a love of learning, and an overall positive attitude? Then I look at their credentials. Do they possess the certification and credentials for the position? Lastly, I try to ascertain if they have the work ethic, the drive, the motivation to face the challenges we know are ahead of them as a teacher, and would be willing to do the hard work required to overcome those challenges. Questions I might typically ask a candidate may seem out of place for an interview. I may ask if they consider themselves relentless. I may ask what they are passionate about. I may ask them to tell me the qualities of the best teachers they ever had. I am looking to determine the person and potential. If they meet all three criteria - heart, head, and hands - then I feel they have potential, but if any one of those is missing then there will be an imbalance. That is the mindset you need to have. I don't want to ever hire someone and think to myself, "I just hired a mediocre teacher." I want to be excited that I just added a potential superstar. Our students deserve only the best.

So now, the question asked is, once they are hired how do you maximize their potential? Develop them as professionals? Make them feel valued in the organization? That too is a relatively simple, but often overlooked, key to your success ... relationships, relationships, relationships. If you want your teachers to go above and beyond then you have to build positive, trusting, supportive, professional relationships with them. This process takes time, and some effort on the part of the administrator. Writing hand-written notes of encouragement or thanks, asking about family and personal interests, having casual conversations that are not a part of a formal evaluation, spotlighting teacher best practices, giving them autonomy on a project; these all help to build a positive, professional relationship that sends the message of genuine concern and respect. Just like with our students, once your teachers feel that you are supporting them, and genuinely care about their success, they will be motivated to their very best - and usually exceed your expectations.

It takes time and effort, but, again, if you want to see real positive change in your building, the investment in hiring, developing, and supporting the very best teachers will provide you with the greatest return on your investment, bar none.

About the Author: *Dennis Neal is currently the principal of Leesburg High School in Lake County, Florida. A native Floridian, he has been in education twenty-five years with administrative experience at all levels, as well as being an adjunct professor, certified trainer in classroom management, and guest lecturer. Whenever possible he is near, on, or in the water.*

Chapter 38

Get Out of the Office!

Diane Roberts

As a school Principal, it is so easy to get caught up in the paperwork, the emails, the meetings, and the reporting, that before you know it you have spent the day (or many days!) in your office. The school seems to be humming along without you because you have very capable staff and well-established routines for students. They will survive; besides, you have all those reports from central office to finish.

The culture of a school is shaped by the people who work and learn there, and the principal has a lead role in shaping this culture. What those people believe in and are working toward together can thrive or fall apart depending on the influence and guidance of the principal. The paperwork can wait until after school because the people in your building need you when they are in your building. Staff, students, and parents need to know you are available to support student learning and teaching practices. The students need to know that they are part of a place where the school leader cares about them and is ensuring that they are getting the best teachers in front of them and the best education provided to them. The parents need to know that they are included and that the success of their kids matters. Finally, the principal's presence in the hallways and classrooms allows you to be on top of, and proactive about, security and safety concerns.

When I first became a principal, I vowed to be present both in classrooms and all around the school. I found that some teachers were not used to my ongoing presence in their rooms and when I entered a classroom I was met with a, "Class, the principal is here. Do you need someone, Mrs. Roberts?" They soon grew used to me not actually needing anyone, and welcomed my visits and the help that I could offer to students. I found that these visits would lead to conversations with teachers after class about their lessons or learning activities. Being in touch with the learning in the classroom helps me to see what the professional learning needs of my teachers are when planning staff learning days. These visits also help me to see when a teacher is struggling with a class or with students, and it can lead to conversations with that teacher about possible solutions. Approaching teachers with an attitude of curiosity and a desire to learn from them is a non-threatening way to build the trust needed to be a helpful leader. Phrases like, "I am curious about why you chose that particular learning activity" or "Tell me more about Johnny" can open doors to conversations better than telling teachers what you would do. As well, if you ever have a disgruntled parent with a grudge or complaint against a teacher, especially an unfounded one, being in the classroom on a regular basis enables you to vouch for, and support, your teacher. For example, "Mrs. Smith, I am in your son's class every other day: I have observed the teaching and learning that happens and I can attest to the professionalism of this teacher." Additionally, by being a constant presence in classrooms, you can often head off complaints before they happen. After all, you are helping your teachers to be the best they can be by regularly having those supportive, professional conversations about student learning.

When students know the principal, and the principal knows them, they feel like they belong. I start my days on bus supervision, where I greet students as they arrive. I strive to learn the names of all of my students. I am by no means perfect in this, but I have a few tricks; using their names when I speak to them, making family connections (Joe is Charlie's brother), and studying my principal's photo album provided by the photographer. I sometimes test myself by trying to see how many kids I can greet in the hall by name before I get to one I do not know. In my current school we have over 400 students, so this is no small feat; it is worth it though because I know that this is an easy way to build relationships with students. Recently, I was touring a new family through my school and, as we walked through the halls, I acknowledged students by name. They asked if I knew all the students' names; I admitted that I was not all the way there, but that this is something that I am striving for because all the children in my school are important to me. When I see students in the community they are so excited to see the principal. I know part of this is the fact that the principal can be like the rock star of an elementary school, but I also know it is because I know their names.

As the school principal, it is important not to underestimate your impact on parents and the community. Whether you wish to be seen this way or not, the principal is someone who parents often turn to for help and advice with their child or with their child's teacher. Building relationships with parents often happens in the school or at school events. It is important to get to know your parents, though you likely will not get to know them as well as you know your staff and students. Fortunately, you can use many of the same strategies for building trust that you use with staff and students; gett to know names and show a genuine interest in getting to know a little bit about them - for example ask questions about where they work or what they have planned for the weekend. Parents want to know that you, as principal, care about student learning, and can show that you are present and visible in the school by sharing with them all the great things that are happening. Social media is a great tool for this; I use Twitter and Facebook to connect with parents by sharing photos and video of what I am seeing in classrooms and at school events. I try to share at least one thing a day that I see in classrooms (usually more). Whether it is a video of students learning Hip Hop with a guest instructor from a local studio, the Kindergarten students sponge painting pictures of apples, or grade three students completing word sorts in literacy time, the parents - and the public - like to see the day-to-day goings-on, as well as the special events that happen in our school. Recently, I have experimented with Facebook Live videos to do a tour of the school before the first day in September. I am planning on using this at other times to give our community a peek into our busy learning world. Of course, it's important to keep privacy laws in mind.

The safety and security of the people in your school must be a top priority of the principal. When the principal is a presence in the school hallways, you tend to have your thumb on the pulse of the school. You know if the adults walking in your halls are parent volunteers or strangers who have not checked in at the office. You know if there are students who are fooling around in the washrooms or are having a melt-down in the hallway. When you are out of your office and walking through your building, you know what's going on; this is important because you can proactively deal with problems. Your staff sees that you are in control and are aware of everything from small incidents with students to larger threats to the overall safety and security of everyone in your school.

The paperwork, the emails, and the reports can wait. Those things will always be there, and you will get them done. You would not be a principal if someone had not already seen that you can be organized and meet deadlines. To support your teachers, to let your students know you care, to communicate with parents, and to ensure that safety and security are top of mind, you MUST get out of your office and be present in your building. They can survive without you doing so, but you will not be able to move your school forward. Find times in your day where you schedule yourself to be out of your office and stick to it like you would with an important central office meeting. If you believe that school culture starts with the principal and you work every day to build relationships with the people in and out of your building, everything else will fall into place. Put people ahead of paper.

About the Author: *Diane Roberts is the Principal of a dual-track French Immersion/English K-5 elementary school in Red Deer, Alberta. She has been an educator for over twenty years and is in her seventh year as a school administrator. She holds Bachelor's degrees in Arts and Education from the University of Lethbridge as well as a Master's degree in Educational Leadership from the University of Calgary. Diane is bilingual, with French as her second language, and has a passion for French Immersion education.*

PART VI
The Challenge of Change

T he only constant in the principal's role is change. Volumes and volumes of books have been written about change. David Bowie sang about *Changes* in 1971 and his wisdom still rings true today. Change presents principals with significant opportunities and challenges. Change initiatives, while well-intentioned, do not always result in desired outcomes. The implementation of a successful change initiative requires a disciplined application – and honouring - of each step in the change process. While change is often presented as a linear process for simplicity purposes, it is a highly, non-linear, iterative process with numerous feedback loops. Successful principals operationalize change through a process of influence. Leadership theories inform practice, and vice-versa.

Chapter 39

Second Year, Have No Fear

John LaFleur, Ph.D.

The change process is incredibly complicated and ominous for some people. Making changes to a school adds an additional layer of emotional turmoil, as parents and students could see themselves as lab rats for someone's 'stepping stone' grand experiment. The chosen change process has to be strategic as to its purpose and supported by sound processes. This contribution suggests one possible means to student-centered successful ends.

You have spent a lot of time and effort securing the position of principal by going through what can be a very daunting process. This probably included the tasks of applying, researching, preparing for presentation, interviewing, and, finally, feeling satisfaction by accepting the offered position. However, the reality of what the job truly involves is only beginning to shed light on "the work".

I spent my first year establishing a culture of honesty. We spent several staff meetings confronting the brutal facts of our achievement data and graduation rate. Each data point was below the State average and we were the second lowest scoring union high school district in Wisconsin. This was not an easy process, and several egos were bruised along the way, but the point got across; we needed to change what we had been doing. We continued the conversation by examining our classroom assessments and level of questioning. All roads led to change.

I was the first principal in the high school to come from outside of the district in approximately 15 years. During that time there was no explicit examination of data, evaluation of programs or initiatives, and, to be blunt, no confronting the brutal facts. Enter a new principal with a doctorate that focused on evaluation. I eventually located longitudinal ACT Test results, Advanced Placement scores, and a copy of the school's budget. My review of this data showed no use of the budget to support student learning. There was no strategic plan for either the district or the school level. The building and the district were a 9-12 union high school which means that all of the K-8 schools that feed students into our building are run independently of one another, and of us. Creating the new culture was going to mean I was going to have to be very careful, very honest, and I was going to need to euphemistically wear a Kevlar vest to be able to take salvos from those that were not going to want any change to their well-established world.

As I stated before, the data I found was not favorable at all. We were below the State average in both graduation rate and ACT Test composite scores. We had a chasm in our special education gap closing measures. We held individual meetings with our department chairs in order to support them in creating a professional learning community. We wanted them to operate differently so we needed to help them understand their role, with our undivided attention to assist in this process. A few months into this structural change, we changed again to begin meeting with single departments at times that all of the teachers could be better supported in examining student data. We also added STAR testing for our 9th and 10th grade students so we knew what their progress was in algebra, geometry, and literacy. Now we had data, and now we began real conversations. We also began meeting weekly with our freshman team, which had a common prep period, so we could monitor our "new" student's progress and help create a more comprehensive transition process.

None of this was easy. This is the time you channel your inner 'Navy SEAL' and tell yourself you do not care how high the 'suck meter' is reading, this is what you signed up for and this is your opportunity to help lead the changes the kids deserve. You have to check your ego at the door and first confront the brutal facts with your associate principals and your director of teaching and learning. Neither of these teammates had ever seen this data. That is another opportunity given to you by the previous chair holders - and you have to look at it from that perspective. You cannot take the tact of some of our US presidents and run down the previous administration. You are the principal and you have to own it if you expect anyone else to help the organization move forward. Fortunately, for me, I previously taught at a high performing high school and spent 12 years as an associate principal. There, I worked with a principal who did not let much rattle him and just kept chipping away at the improvement process.

I worked with the directors in the district office to give me some flexibility in the budget and was able to move $10,000 into professional development. I was able to use connections at my previous district to choose a consultant to come in and provide a third-party audit of our students' classroom experiences. We were also able to gather 20 staff members together to consult about the brutal facts of our high school's performance data. Additionally, we went after the master schedule and made student-centered changes to improve instruction. Because the feedback from the special education teachers was that they did not have any scheduled time with their students, we were able to affect positive change for our most vulnerable population. These were big moves in the first seven months I was on the job, moves that I continuously spelled out as part of our "why."

From the first staff meeting to the last meeting, I focused every discussion around the mission statement, because it was our reason for existence at this school. It was developed during the time where 90% of the current staff were present. Our mission statement and our poor data were our "why." If we were supposed to be helping prepare our students for college, career or the military, and we were supposed to be functioning as a professional learning community, then we better act and live that mission. We were not, and that was why we had to change.

The gist of year one: take a hard look at the current state, know and live your "why," develop the relationships with those who can help you have the greatest impact, develop strong processes to help maintain your building's focus, and then develop an action plan involving the entire staff.

In transitioning into year two, where the real work towards showing progress begins, I addressed the school board and explained what I was going to do, engaged in the same training that my staff was and also sought out information to try and avoid the being pulled away from the target. I had been trained as an AVID District Director in my previous district, and I led a dozen staff members to the summer institute. The key leaders in the tier one classroom instruction efforts, along with our consultant, gathered together twice during the summer to establish a common understanding and a common language. Finally, I attended The Global Leadership Summit sponsored by the Willow Creek Association. This conference featured John Maxwell, Patrick Lencioni, Alan Mullaly, Chris McChesney, and Bill Hybels among others. They were the golden ticket for me. Mullaly had been the CEO of Ford Motor Company and he focused on the power of confronting brutal facts. Lencioni described the three characteristics of a great teammate, and McChesney spelled out the process I needed to implement, taken from his book *The 4 Disciplines of Execution*. These speakers encapsulated what was going on in my head, but was struggling to articulate to my administrative team and my staff. Once I wrote all of my process thoughts on a white board, I met with each of the APs individually to explain it and their role within the plan; I also met with both the assistant superintendent and the superintendent and gave the same process plan explanation. Now everyone of the leadership team knew what I was going to do, and how they could help support the plan.

You cannot take on the uphill task of school improvement by yourself. You have to utilize a team, and you have to establish those strong processes. The speakers I heard at the conference validated my efforts and galvanized my process for accomplishing the milestones along the road to continuous improvement. I was fortunate enough to have toured the Under Armour corporate headquarters in the fall and witnessed a winning corporate culture. What I saw on that tour was what the speakers described. I was able to articulate the type of staff members that I wanted in order to get things going in the right direction. I wanted people who were going to be humble, hungry, and smart. Being humble in this case means thinking of others more than yourself, being hungry means doing more than what is asked, and being smart means being able to read the room and know what your students need now. Far too often we were just pounding through the curriculum without having student learning.

As a side note: do not ever be afraid to contact your mentors, as they will always help you zero in on the target if you just walk across the room and talk to them. Here are some of the statements that resonated with me:

> "What you permit, you promote." (Dr. Robert Rammer)
>
> "It's all about student learning." (Dr. Dennis Bussen)
>
> "Be 'ware of kings bearing gifts." (Dr. David Lodes)
>
> "Everyone has a box called time and you can only put 24 hours in it. Limit the contents of that box to what's important to you." (Coach Tom Taraska)

In closing, dear principal, you have read briefly how one school is going about building their "bus." You have to put the gas (passion) into the tank in order to get - and keep - it going, whether uphill, through rough terrain, or places where the roads do not show up on your GPS. You must make the implicit explicit when you explain the why, and, upon establishing your cadence of accountability, know that what you permit, you promote.

About the Author: *Dr. John LaFleur has 23 years in education, all at the high school level: 12 of those years as an associate principal and 2 as principal. Masters of Educational Administration from the University of Wisconsin - Madison and Doctorate from Cardinal Stritch University (Ph. D). Dissertation - A Program Evaluation of the Association of Wisconsin School Administrators New Building-Level Leader Mentoring Program Using Dr. Michael Scriven's Key Evaluation Checklist.*

Chapter 40

Turn Around

Thomas Seaton, Ed.D.

L eaders who are late in their career can change; it happened to me. I share this journey with you in the hope that you may see that the nature of our work and life is about change.

I have been a principal for twenty years in four elementary schools in the private and public sectors. It has been my desire to be the lead change-agent, to ensure that our kids will find liberation through education and live the lives they deserve. Sounds like a pretty noble and worthy goal, don't you think? In my time as principal, I have experienced a great deal of success and I have received distinguished ratings. Until now.

Two years ago, after a successful turnaround effort at my last school, I was asked to move to another school. Hearing this request, I asked, "Is this the school that you are most concerned about?" "Yes." "Then I'll go." My supervisor said, "This will be your legacy: you will be known as the principal who turned schools around in our district."

With district endorsement, I was to "turn this school around." The turnaround model I have previously implemented is formulaic, and success was based largely on standardized assessment scores. I knew what to do. We began the school year with a three-day academy, at which time we "shared the brutal truth" regarding student assessment performance and instructional practices. I had a reputation that preceded me; my new staff members were nervous. Our message set the tone for what was to come.

Many factors converged to create what I now refer to as the "perfect storm for failure." Perhaps it is fair to say that *we (local and district)* failed; we did not read the billboards advertising that failure was waiting at the next turn.

Under new district leadership in recent years, we embarked upon the "reinventing of education." Instruction has changed drastically, assessment practices are evolving and we no longer rank schools based on their scores. We do not *value* any assessment that does not prepare students to utilize twenty first century skills for problem-solving. Teacher training through coaching and the evolution of instructional strategies were rolling out simultaneously. Teachers and leaders in *high performing* schools were questioning their work, let alone those in our struggling schools.

Moreover, in the middle of this perfect storm, we moved forward in a turnaround model that was obsolete. We did not *evaluate* whether it was obsolete; we trudged forward. Is not that what we do in a storm: stay the course?

I now see that the *causes* of the turbulence are not as important as the *effect*. As the staff push-back reached epic proportions, I felt unable to lead, was questioned about my leadership, and told, "Stop what you are doing and fix it now." I began to doubt my abilities and myself. There is nothing quite like losing one's confidence. The diplomas on the wall in my office, which I have since removed, do not save us when what used to work does not work. Turnaround models do not always consider history, culture and politics, which are all elements to be understood. I told myself that a turnaround effort is *supposed* to be difficult; we were challenging the status quo and needed to persevere.

Our organization began to challenge a different kind of status quo. We challenged the status quo of American education, which has not changed much in two hundred years. Our district turnaround model trumped the status quo of the building turnaround model. The traditional turnaround model was focused on test scores. Our district turnaround model focused on reinventing education. What a stark contrast. It was chaotic.

If we put *kids first,* how can we lose? It was with great pride I would declare, "I am not here for adults, I am here for kids." My desire to stand up to the societal forces that keep opportunities *from* children of poverty and second language learners compelled me to "take no prisoners" and "fight the good fight." We cannot lose a single minute. The status quo of public education tries to choke the fight out of me, which makes me more determined to "be there" for kids, not adults. Kids *have benefited as* a result of my leadership. Passion can render us unable to see the "forest for the trees."

Now it is a new day in my district, in my building and in education. I put all my "eggs in the basket" of "kid care," but I did not consider the "caregivers." Systemic change includes all members of the organization; I see that now. I see many aspects of leadership differently now.

Like it or not, the turnaround plan was about *me,* not my school. My way was no longer "the way."

I have also learned, painfully, how "our inside becomes our outside" in the workplace. The more public the role, the more prominent the revelation of who we are. Plagued by doubt and a complete loss of confidence, I became a manager. I did not talk about kids or instruction beyond a district-prepared presentation. The phrase "assessment data" ceased to exist and I oversaw the running of a school. Our entire organization was in such a positive free fall of new learning that we all questioned if we were grasping the new messaging connected to reinventing education. No small task to be sure.

However, my chaos seemed profoundly deeper: life stealing, not life giving. I felt the responsibility to ensure that students *would succeed.* However, I did not know how to advise and reignite a sense of well-being or joy in the workplace. I have been a "nose to the grindstone, get me the results that would let me sleep at night," kind of leader. How does the leader measure success or progress with a blank dashboard? How does the leader *lead* when the conditions for deep and powerful learning have changed? How does the leader *lead* when the change effort is about the leader and the building at the same time?

I continue to walk through the tunnel of understanding; now I see the parallels between my life and the lives of my colleagues. Hard to believe so late in my career, right? I see that we *all* want our kids to know success and live fulfilled lives, but my way of leading, even in the name of desire for kids' success, did not make it easier for staff to do their work. While I believe that I have inspired many by my devotion to our kids' success, I now see that I added a layer of anxiety on my staff as they question if they have what it takes to ensure kids' success. How does a leader understand and communicate that we all care differently, and that is all right? How does the leader allow the "insides of each person" to be outside, inside the same school?

My supervisor asked me if I could be comfortable with being a principal who was "good enough" at his work. My first thought was, "Would we choose an oncologist who is "good enough?" Can a leader be gentle with oneself as "good enough?"

Our work as educators has a cumulative effect; we seldom know if we were "good" or "good enough." When we have that chance encounter with a former student who has found success, we know. This is not a daily occurrence.

"Good enough" is a two-edged sword; perhaps it offers breathing space in a difficult profession. However, "good enough" can stalk us when we hope our "good enough" model is, in fact, "good enough" for our kids. If we aspire to a "good enough" mindset, we have to band together as a village and prepare students in a "good enough" way so they find their way.

The most significant lessons I learned connect to my failure, and to turning oneself around. In the classroom we now promote failure and perseverance, and the lessons they teach us. In the workplace, are we good at all or "good enough" at allowing the leader to fail? Do we celebrate teachers when they feel they have failed? What does the celebration of failure look like?

Regarding turning oneself around, it is helpful to understand that as lifelong learners it is to our benefit, and ultimately to the benefit of all stakeholders, that we remain open to turning ourselves around on our life journey. Lives depend on it.

Regarding celebrating my failure, that is still a hard one for me. I know I was *destined* to take on this assignment, but not for the reasons I originally considered important. My supervisor has shared that my transformation has been inspiring, and while I appreciate that acknowledgment, I urge leaders everywhere to know their inside before it becomes their outside in the workplace.

As for legacies, I now believe they are highly overrated. I see now that I have always been failing at my work. I would not have it any other way!

About the Author: *Dr. Tom Seaton has been an elementary school principal in suburban Chicago for the past twenty years. His leadership focus has been the application of the turnaround model for school improvement in high poverty, ELL schools. Tom's dissertation (2007) explored Transformational Leadership among principals in NCLB Blue Ribbon Schools.*

Chapter 41

Look, Listen, Change!

Marylène Perron

"The secret of change is to focus all your energy, not on fighting the old, but on building the new" –Socrates

Good things take time to cultivate. In the fast paced world we live in, it can be challenging for principals to invest in building relationships with everyone walking through the entrance door. From personal experience in my current position, relationships are crucial in accomplishing long-lasting change.

The year prior to my arrival at Parkdale Elementary School reshaped the life of the school. It changed from being a dual-track school offering French Immersion and English Core Education to offering English Core only. Many teachers transferred to other schools, while others received assignments at Parkdale. Furthermore, due to a neighboring school's closure, 50 new students were set to start the year at the same time I was. Needless to say, the school community was in turmoil. Everyone was holding on to what they had lost: friends, colleagues, and traditions. The healing process had clearly only begun; pain was still present and visible. A new school culture needed to be created and everyone had to, somehow, set aside the past and move toward the future.

Following the first contact with my new school community, it became obvious to me that my goal would be to instill a sense of pride, purpose, and power to everyone in the building. I spent the entire summer vacation puzzled about what I had seen during my visit. I decided to set aside any preconceived ideas and to start with a clean slate. Curiosity guided my steps. For example, as I was introduced to members of the school community, I asked as many questions as I possibly could. I soon discovered everyone's narratives. Quickly, a common thread appeared. All conversations included a variation of "when I was at the other school..." or "at Parkdale, we have always done it this way." Those statements helped me understand how deeply ingrained the past was. I made a conscious effort not to focus on the surrounding negativity. Frankly, it was time to replace regrets with excitement. In retrospect, it is clear that empathic listening was one of the keys to establishing successful relationships.

Creating a welcoming environment was also at the top of my list of the things to do. The initial step I took was to develop an atmosphere of approachability. My approach was to model what the concept meant. To that end, I tried to be as visible as possible, taking any opportunity I could to be out of the office and part of the daily life of the school. Such moments included running in the gym with grade 6 students, singing with the Pre-Ks, and reading daily messages with Kindergartens. I also extended my presence by greeting the students coming off the bus in the morning and talking to parents bringing their children in. Teachers would stop me in the hallway and I took the time to listen. My presence was being noticed and acknowledged. I was everywhere I could be and made sure staff, parents and students knew I was an easy person to reach. Although it took a lot of my time, the personal connections I built were an investment lasting to this day.

As a teacher, I used to set the stage by developing strong relationships with my students. Every September, time was dedicated to activities that allowed me to connect with them. Connection is also a powerful tool for a principal because it offers the possibility of bringing people together and uniting them. With this idea in mind, I prepared a plan of action by seeking, above all, balance between change and status quo. With just the right dosage of push and pull, I believed I could move the school slowly while making sure all felt included. Moreover, it was crucial that my interventions focused on the similarities rather than on the differences. For example, I soon found out that dismissal was extremely chaotic. Students would line up according to their bus number and wait for a teacher to walk the groups one by one to the bus. As you can well imagine, by the end of the day, students were not always displaying their best behavior. It often took more than 15 minutes before busses were ready to go. I started questioning different staff members about the procedures. I soon found out that the group of teachers from Parkdale wanted to keep the status quo while the teachers new to Parkdale wanted to dismiss the way it was done at their previous school. At a staff meeting, I brought the issue up and we discussed the pros and cons of the two systems. One teacher made a strong argument about student safety and everyone agreed on that aspect. Keeping this one common element in mind, we came up with a different way of dismissing students. A group of teachers, with members from the two schools, got together to put the new procedure in writing; it included maps, instructions, and schedules. All were in approval. Together, we were able to innovate; that is, to tweak the old in order to find new answers to problems. To achieve such results, building connections with everyone involved with Parkdale was crucial.

First impressions are important. Both parents and students look for their school to offer impact - a lasting impression. By making a few small changes such as changing blinds and chairs in the entrance, an area that was inviting to parents and visitors was provided. Gradually, murals were painted by graduating students to add life to the entrance and hallways. The paint colors of the walls were changed to softer, pastel colors lighting up the school. Though these things are superficial, it did have a positive effect on staff, students, and visitors. This welcoming attitude has slowly been developed in turn by the members of staff who also take the time to greet visitors as they are walking in the hallway. Many visitors comment on how welcomed they feel when they come to Parkdale. They feel treated like family. Over time, this welcoming feeling was extended to the classroom. Every day, I blocked some time in my agenda to visit classrooms. I found teachers were looking forward to them. Although the main purpose of the visits was to assure that teachers were delivering quality education to the students, they became central to the change process in the school. The more I visited, the more visible I was. My presence was perceived as supportive rather than threatening. I provided support and resources. To this day, what surprises me the most is how easily teachers allowed me in their classroom and how eager they were to establish a dialogue about pedagogy. As pedagogical leader, I learned that it was crucial to create a safe space for discussion to take place. Ideas are meant be shared and debated without apprehension. Trust is an essential part of the change process and, ultimately, of team-building.

Now, almost five years later, I understand that my job will never be done. Change is an on-going process. It must be supported by a school culture based on trust, approachability, and openness. Those values need to be promoted constantly. Any time a new staff member walks through the front door, the process carried out during the first year must be repeated for their benefit. For individuals to be part of the team, they must understand, believe and enact the core values of the school. This can only be achieved by building and maintaining strong relationships with all.

About the Author: *Marylène Perron is the lead learner of Parkdale Elementary School in Montreal, Quebec. She believes that her role is to multiply leadership and help everyone be better at what they do. Her educational background includes a B.Ed. in Teaching Second Languages from McGill, and a M.Ed. in Administration. She is currently completing her D.Ed. in Administration at University of Montreal. She was chosen as one of Canada's Outstanding Principals for 2016. When away from school, she is often found camping and hiking in the middle of nowhere.*

Chapter 42

Using Formative Assessment Strategies to Enhance School Climate

John B. Bond, Ed.D.

F ormative assessment is widely implemented in the classroom to provide both teachers and students timely feedback about learning. A growing body of applications of formative practice has emerged over the last few decades that is based upon research (Black and Wiliam, 1998; Bond, Denton, and Ellis, 2015; Bond and Ellis, 2013; Dignath and Büttner, 2008). Formative assessment is also an effective approach for school leaders to apply regarding enhancing school climate and culture. A mammoth body of scholarly theory and research exists regarding formative assessment focused on the classroom. In this chapter how the same formative approach can be used by school principals is reviewed and discussed.

How Can Principals Apply Formative Assessment?

Effective use of formative assessment is much more than just giving a faculty member an exit slip or short survey. As important as the actual information collected is how it collected and followed-up on. Implemented with skill and savviness, a formative assessment cycle can enhance trust in a leader - a key factor in school climate and culture. And, of course, it is a powerfully effective tool in unveiling and resolving problems that can erode school climate.

Monitoring Climate

Successful principals have radar about the climate and culture in the school they serve. It is an essential practice that occurs on an ongoing basis as a principal goes about his or her daily tasks. Much of this is intuitive and subjective based on interactions, experiences, and in-the-moment judgments. Theorist Donald Schön (1987) referred to such professional behavior as "knowing in practice" as we reflect upon our professional behavior. However, while Schön's work emphasizes the mental reflection on such things as school climate, there are practical and tangible strategies that can be employed regarding school climate and culture. Wise leaders embrace both approaches: the internal reflection-in-action (Schön, 1983; 1987), and the external feedback strategies.

As with the reflective assessment strategies used in the classroom, (Ellis, 2001) there are simple and effective feedback strategies that leaders can use when their intuition tells them it is the right time. How these are employed, however, is just as important as the actual tool.

Anonymous Feedback

First of all, it is essential that principals ensure anonymity when requesting feedback or input from staff. This accomplishes two important things. First, it invites genuine feedback without fear of retaliation. A principal who makes this a safe experience builds trust and respect. Second, a principal models humility and courage when she or he asks for anonymous feedback. Teachers and other staff members usually understand the risks involved for the leader with anonymous feedback, and typically respect and admire such courage. While some may take advantage of the opportunity to vent frustrations, the unveiling of such concerns leads to healthy discussion and reflection by a staff. When one hesitates to make the feedback or input anonymous there is cause for some deep reflection, for while seemingly threatening, it is actually a path toward improved relationships and building trust.

Small Scale

While there are many online tools for surveying groups anonymously, these can be lengthy and thus discourage busy professionals from completing them. Return rates are often low and this can be problematic when "outlier" data drives the results and subsequent perceptions. Online surveys are also impersonal and do not provide the opportunity for the in-person engagement between a principal and those she or he serves. Rather than an annual comprehensive climate survey, employing small-scale feedback experiences through a school year offers a formative approach to seeking timely feedback and input. For example, a principal might ask for teacher input at the end of staff meeting regarding a specific issue, such as student behavior, testing procedures, dealing with a scheduling problem, engaging with challenging parents, or special education inclusion—to name a few. Small scale feedback should be simple and concise—one issue only, hand-written on a half-sheet of paper or index card, requiring only a few minutes to complete. Asking a staff member to collect the exit slips as the principal leaves the meeting early emphasizes the intent of anonymity.

Staying Ahead of Problems

Formative strategies are especially useful when issues among a staff are brewing just below the surface. Wise principals intuitively know that the pressure must be released while the problem is small to avoid bigger challenges down the road. For example, such unrelated problems as playground or passing time misbehavior, teacher voice on program decisions, scheduling of classes, or parent engagement can be addressed one issue at a time. If left unattended, though, multiple concerns are sometimes lumped together and packaged as evidence that the principal is irresponsible or ineffective. Savvy leaders know that perceptions are made and judgments formed with or without accurate information.

This should serve as added motivation for principals to regularly "check the temperature" regarding school climate so that the concerns can be addressed while still manageable. Inviting those most involved—teachers, playground supervisors, coaches, bus drivers, etc.—to provide timely input on how to resolve an issue avoids the path to bigger problems and possible crises.

When a principal takes the initiative to seek input she or he owns the issue and is in control of the process. It pre-empts others from taking control of the situation. The principal's nightmare of the union unexpectedly conducting a climate survey occasionally occurs when a leader has ignored or is oblivious to the signs of discontent. While the problems and concerns at issue can be extremely challenging to resolve, it is by far simpler when a principal takes initiative to understand and unravel them. We have all heard tales about, or observed from a distance, a case where a principal's leadership capital evaporated. Wise principals swallow their pride before this happens and deal with potential problems while they are small. Formative assessment offers an effective approach to do so.

Modeling for Those You Lead

A principal's character is just as, or more, important than their knowledge and skills. This point, of course, can be argued; ideally they are all of equal importance. Yet, in times of climate upheaval, it is character that gets a principal through a crisis. When a principal stands in front of those she or he leads and asks for suggestions on how to better serve their needs, it is powerful modeling of both courage and humility. Jim Collins (2001) in the book *Good to Great* described a great leader as someone who is equally committed and humble. Few would disagree about the importance of these traits. In a school most constituencies want a gentle and collaborative leader, and, at the same time, one who can step up when strong leadership is needed. So, how can a leader's character be modeled in the midst of a growing problem?

Transparency is Powerful

When a staff has provided anonymous feedback to a principal it is imperative that this data be shared with them. Kept confidential by the principal can exacerbate a problem, for once issues are called to attention there is an obligation to act upon them. Sharing the anonymous feedback avoids this pitfall, and done with skill is itself a climate-building step. When a principal shares the results in-person, it is a unique opportunity to model character, display humility, and exemplify courage. Doing so makes transparent both the actual feedback from the staff and the personal character of the principal. Both are of high importance.

Handwritten, Not Digital

An advantage of handwritten, rather than digital, feedback is that a principal can use the actual documents—the index cards, as mentioned above—to review the data in-person in front of those who gave the input. The actual feedback slips should then be shared with all who provided input. This can easily be done by routing them during the staff meeting, and also making them available after the meeting. Keeping this data on paper is an intentional strategy to reduce the opportunity for in-house "dirty laundry" being shared beyond those directly involved. E-mail and, especially, social media are usually not productive avenues for resolving issues of school climate. While digital tools simplify and expedite communication, they present risks when a principal is trying to resolve a complicated climate problem.

Follow-through is Essential

Open discussion with staff members regarding the concerns and suggestions offered is the beginning of a plan of action. This must be followed up with action steps that are also visible to all. Periodic progress updates show a staff that their input was taken seriously. Being done in a cyclical fashion allows initial outcomes to inform and guide subsequent actions (Ferraro, 2000). Ideally, the plan grows out of teacher input and its outcomes are owned by staff members and supported by the principal.

Keeping the issue alive through discussion and proactive steps is the final stage of this process. Obviously, trying to put the problem to rest before it has been thoroughly processed can be a fatal error. Wise principals let the perceptions of the staff guide them on when to consider the problem resolved.

Concluding Remarks

Formative assessment strategies are useful tools for principals, just as they are for teachers in the classroom. This is especially true regarding monitoring and enhancing school climate and culture. When principals use small-scale feedback strategies to gather anonymous input from teachers and staff members, it is in itself trust-building. When principals humbly seek the input of those they serve, it models an openness and transparency that both empowers teachers and enhances the principal's leadership platform.

Enhancing school climate is a complex and challenging endeavor. Over time, principals accumulate effective strategies, tactics, and tools as their knowledge grows and professional artistry matures (Schön, 1987). Similar to how a teacher uses formative assessment in the classroom to guide instruction, principals can apply the same approach to enhance school climate. It is a versatile tool with little, if any, downside.

References

Black, P., & Wiliam, D. (1998). Inside the black box. *Phi Delta Kappan, 80*(2), 139–148. Retrieved from http://www.pdkintl.org/utilities/archives.htm

Bond, J.B., Denton, D.W., & Ellis, A.K. (2015). Impact of reflective assessment on student learning. *International Dialogues on Education, 2*(2), 172-184. ISSN 2198-5944 172.

Bond, J.B., & Ellis, A.K. (2013). The effects of metacognitive reflective assessment on fifth and sixth graders' mathematics achievement. *School Science and Mathematics, 113*(5), 227- 234.

Collins, J. (2001). *Good to great: Why some companies make the leap...and others don't.* New York: HarperCollins Publishers, Inc.

Dignath, C., & Büttner, G. (2008). Components of fostering self-regulated learning among   students: A meta-analysis on intervention studies at primary and secondary school level. *Metacognition and Learning,* 3(3), 231–264. doi: 10.007/s11409-008-9029-x.

Ellis, A. K. (2001). *Teaching, learning, & assessment together.* Larchmont, NY: Eye on Education, Inc.

Ellis, A.K., Denton, D.W, & Bond, J.B. (2014). An analysis of research on metacognitive   teaching strategies. *Procedia - Social and Behavioral Sciences,* 116(2014), 4015-4024.

Ferraro, J.M. (2000). Reflective practice and professional development. ERIC Digest. Retrieved   from http://www.ericdigests.org/2001-3/reflective. htm2

Schön, D.A. (1983). *The reflective practitioner: How professionals think in action.* New York: Basic Books.

Schön, D. A. (1987). *Educating the reflective practitioner.* San Francisco: Jossey-Bass.

About the Author: *Dr. John B. Bond is a Professor of Educational Leadership at Seattle Pacific University where he serves on the doctoral faculty and in principal and superintendent certification programs. He served as a public school principal and central office administrator for over 25 years prior to moving to higher education in 2008. His scholarly publications have primarily been in the area of formative assessment.*

Chapter 43

A Bridge to Change

Regine Nuytten

"If you set out to create change, be prepared to be changed."

Is it possible to be engaged in a completely fulfilling profession and still become the victim of nagging discontent? After eight years of teacher leadership opportunities, I had a growing layer of professional experience that was plagued by a heavy underbelly of uneasy, seemingly disconnected, questions. Why are some students more successful than others? What facets of students' lived experiences follow them into the school? How does the education system affect the many children in foster care who bounce in and out of our classrooms and lives? How do we design policies in order to fit the people that they serve? How do educational leaders shape policies in their work context? How are families affected by the policies that schools forward? Why is it so hard to gather families and organizations around the table to support students?

Yet, being inclusively-minded, I believed I had students' best interests at heart and I felt I had the right goals in mind. But the voice of one 10-year old changed all that. With one quiet, but targeted, statement, my self-perception as a caring human being and an inclusive educational leader was destabilized. "I am CFS, FAS, ADHD. I come from a reserve, I hate French, and I don't read. The more letters I have the more money they get for me. Every teacher I ever had hates me, and you're gonna hate me too" (Personal Communication, 2011). This stark reflection revealed a self-centred social justice orientation on my part that allowed me to function inclusively in the classroom, but was now presented as a challenge for change to move beyond this narrow context. I moved outside of these borders and toward opening up to change. In an instant, this student became the basis for years of sleepless nights, and the core of what connects the professional questions that I harboured. I realized that my professional lens was no longer seeing enough of the picture.

Frustrated and looking for avenues to create change, I sought out a variety of other perspectives through official leadership positions in administration and graduate work at two universities. But answers did not immediately come my way. Instead, I was puzzled by systemic barriers, like the labels affixed by our educational support/funding silos, streamed academic programming processes, inclusive education legislation interpreted locally into exclusive practices, as well as restrictive catchment regulations. All of these examples seemed to draw lines of demarcation in the lives of under-served students in care in Manitoba; the 'haves' and the 'have nots', the 'seen' and the 'unseen', those that 'matter' and those that 'don't' in the conversation around equitable educational access.

As a vice principal I see the effects of systemic tensions, but find that I have little power to affect substantive change in a provincial system where 4-year political mandates make it difficult for sitting governments to move beyond the needs of the most vocal groups. As a beginning educational administrator, I am also becoming aware of the embedded analysis cycle, positives versus negatives, that underscores so many day-to-day decisions around budgets, funding, staffing, personnel decisions, and timetabling to name a few. Micro-economic imperatives encourage us to dwell on opportunity cost, as decreased funding limits the allocation of dwindling resources. Across the country, public school principals who voice their concerns about student needs and equitable educational outcomes find themselves pushed and pulled to choose the lesser of two evils, or the loudest voice at the table. But what is the price? I realized that I needed to find a bridge to change. Little did I know that the greatest change would be in me.

It was not until I had the opportunity to wrestle with the tensions that come from viewing these systemic trajectories, seemingly pre-scripted, play out for vulnerable students, that I also examined my own positionality, biases, and assumptions through a full-time doctoral pro-gram. This examination encouraged me to move outside the public edu-cation system, to draw on the leverage that the dominant white education system attributes to, and embeds in, academic research. With a plan to move this knowledge base, and my experience, back into the public edu-cation system, I hoped to create a space for discourse in education that connects the voices already located in research literature with the voices of participants in my study (i.e., principals and former youth in foster care), in order to develop a better understanding of their needs.

In effect, the contradictions in my situation forced me to engage with internal and external conflicts and tensions in different areas of my life; these opened up for me a brand new *third space*. It helped me develop a better understanding of the situation. This *third space* strategy encouraged me to critically analyze the role played by personal and sys-temic values, power, and identity. It also clearly underlined the need to create a *third space* context to determine the impact that the joined expe-riences of inclusive principals and former youth-in-care voices can have on the educational outcomes of Manitoba's more than 10 000 children in care.

No one can predict how a move into educational leadership or research will affect you, and in that respect the two fields are very similar. Although much of my doctoral journey resides within the academic world, two years of conversations and reflections with my cohort colleagues sug-gest that the impetus for our need to connect educational leadership and research studies originated within our personal professional context. My journey of learning started when a young Indigenous student transferred into my class as a result of a foster care placement. How could I, as an educational leader, effectively influence the growth of others, who may have more power and influence, to affect the educational outcomes of children in care? A central tenet of my doctoral program, *'effectively influ-encing the growth of others'*, took me directly to Rosa Beth Kanter's TEDx (2013) talk. Her keys for leading positive change continue to inspire my vision, as I see a tightly knit connection between the shared-relationship goals seen in highly prevalent distributed, democratic, and inclusive educational leadership models, and the fresh discursive spaces created by the potential that the intersection with research provides in this area.

Her admonition to "show up or nothing happens," exists on the leading edge of this *third space*, which marks for me the intersection of two novel dimensions. First, it situates my inclusive educational leadership perspective, which focuses on a need to change the educational outcomes of Manitoba's children in care. The study establishes potential resonance as a politically oriented catalyst that can effectively elicit valid and credible information, in order to influence educational leaders, policymakers and academic researchers.

It is only by forwarding the transparent goals and biases within my study, offering the detailed findings in my literature review, and clearly outlining the critical/analytical stance of my theoretical and conceptual frameworks, that I am able to begin to make the connection for my intended audience. With the infusion of nuanced social justice language and ethics, I hope to hold up my vision and goals for potential supporters. High levels of reciprocal engagement, collaboration, and co-creation of knowledge, with inclusive principal participants, former youth-in-care, and educational leaders, have the potential to initiate the leadership/followership cycle, for both participants and my external audience.

This journey continues to test my endurance and determination to find a way to dismantle and/or deconstruct barriers. It is a quality that I find critical as a reflexive researcher, and inclusive educational leader, to overcome challenges within the study design, as well as exterior barriers that threaten to affect the study's viability. Both the educational leader and the researcher in me struggled with internal and external tensions when I reconsidered, restructured, and rewrote my proposal's sampling and methods sections multiple times, based on external pressures, in order to stay true to the study's intentions and goals. Finding new strength to move forward appears to be a daily mantra.

In the face of accessible, equitable, education outcomes, it was Kanter's final key point, "to lift others up and share success," that transformed me and now drives the purpose for integrating my professional and academic lives. The voices of leaders from these two spheres forward critical reflections that address the power imbalance, which exists in both leadership and research processes. Their reflections advocate a move beyond using a critical analysis framework, as they call on educational leaders to lay the foundation for more action-oriented research with potential for transformative engagement and empowerment. In other words, if we want to better understand and affect the situations and experiences of underserved groups in education, it is necessary for those of us already legally positioned in this space to change, to step outside our comfort zones, and actively create a *third space*. This provides new opportunities for participation and discourse, which invite the voices of others, especially those most affected, in order to legitimize their voices and to share their experiences and expertise, rather than to appropriate their experiences based on our assumptions.

By realizing that the change has to start within myself, I hope to utilize my study to create a space or bridge that contributes to and integrates research and practical educational application to make children-in-care visible in the chaos of an educational system's leadership landscape that struggles to see and address the needs of its most underserved students.

Reference

TEDx Beacon Street (Producer). (2013). **Six keys to leading positive change: Rosabeth Moss**
Kanter. Available from https://www.youtube.com/watch?v=owU5aTNPJbs

About the Author: *Regine Nuytten has worked in Winnipeg, Manitoba as an inclusive educational leader since 2001, and continues her work there now as a middle school vice principal. As a 'Yes I Can - Manitoba Educator of the Year' recipient, and presenter at the 'Transforming Heart, Instruction, and Soul' conference, her passion is focused on improving educational outcomes for all students, but especially those underserved within the present educational framework. Regine is currently a doctoral student at Western University.*

Chapter 44

Building Collaborative Cultures in Unique Educational Settings

Charlotte Arbuckle

S tudent learning is at the center of all of our work in schools. As principals, it is critical to ask ourselves, "How can we create optimal conditions to support teaching that is progressive, educationally sound, and supportive of personalized learning for every student?" We know that teachers become stronger, more effective teachers through collaboration with their peers. We know there is a direct connection between performance and collaboration; when teachers collaborate, students perform better. As Robert John Meehan has written, "The most valuable resource that all teachers have is each other. Without collaboration our growth is limited to our own perspectives." Teacher collaboration is a key condition for ideal twenty-first century learning environments.

Over the span of eight years, I have served as the principal of two schools. Both of the appointments involved complex learning sites and programs, compared to standard community schools. My direction at both appointments was to build and foster a collaborative learning culture for all teachers under my supervision, regardless of program and teaching assignment.

My first principalship comprised five distinct therapeutic programs, primarily grades 7 to 12. All were partnerships with Health Services or a non-profit organization. Each program had school staff and therapeutic staff providing educational programming and behavioral, emotional, and clinical support for students. Teachers had to work closely in collaboration with their therapeutic counterparts to provide educational programming for their unique students. In order to build a stronger teacher practice, it was crucial to support collaboration and collegiality with teaching staff from the various sites, which geographically spanned 20 kilometers. At the same time, I knew that I had to develop an educationally sound professional culture.

Four years later, and less than four years ago, I moved to a different principalship. This new principalship also came with the direction to build a collaborative culture. In this context, there are four unique programs. The primary difference in the two assignments was the new principalship did not include therapeutic settings; rather, there are thousands more students, and a proportionately larger number of teachers and support staff. Another existing condition when I took up this role was extremely low morale amongst the teachers.

As outlined, this assignment consists of four programs. There is a homeschooling program, both blended and parent-directed, grades 1 to 9, housed at one school. The other three programs are located at a larger site five kilometers away, and include: a junior high (grades 7 to 9) online program; a senior high (grades 10 to 12) online program, which presently consists of 500 full-time students and more than 7000 concurrent students in a current school year, and; a Career Technology Centre with 600 concurrent students, on-site, engaged in various career technology courses such as culinary and pre-engineering. "Concurrent" indicates the students also attend a community school in addition to taking one or more courses within our online program. Online teachers are supported with flexible work schedules and work sites, which means some of the staff do not work on-site much of the time.

Both of my principal positions were similar, in that I led and am leading a multitude of unique programs which were or are disconnected professionally, geographically, and culturally. In both of these positions,

I have been able to build strong professional cultures in which teachers from various subject areas, programs, and grade levels collaborated with each other. My strategy was similar in both situations. To begin with, I explored the challenges of building a collaborative culture amongst my teachers. Some of the same challenges exist in accomplishing this task with the diverse sites that exist in our community school. Sometimes teachers do not feel that they have anything to offer each other when they are not teaching in the same building, or do not work with the same student population, grade level, and subject. Another challenge that is often prevalent, with high school teachers in particular due to the number of staff in their department, is a tendency to work only within departments, both physically and academically, and not with the whole school. The teachers collaborate exclusively, not inclusively. This sort of department siloing can be very detrimental to the overall culture of the learning environment as it limits teacher interactions, and therefore teacher growth.

The challenges faced in both of my principalships, however, were heightened by our diversity in program, delivery, and geography. These unique challenges sometimes affected our ability to be flexible in our school organization. For example, no planning time was built in to any of the teachers' schedules. Each and every teacher taught a full course load each and every day. Therefore, there was no common time when all of the teachers were available on one site, let alone amongst sites.

My entry plans for both principal assignments started with recognizing, supporting, and familiarizing myself with each teacher - in a short time frame and at all sites. This intentional, early, relationship building moved beyond the "fireside chats" approach to focus on teachers as individuals. Discussions were often informal, and involved getting to know each individual as a teacher and a person, with a focus on their strengths and passions as an educator. Many interactions occurred in the classrooms in a non-threatening way, with or without students present. Simultaneously, I explored the history of each program through the existing leadership model both at the school and at the jurisdiction level. How, when, and why had the program started, what the student population was, what the societal, economic, and political drivers were, and what the expectations of the parents and the community were.

I stated to each staff member that student learning is at the center of all of our work. I committed to each staff member that my leadership would center on supporting teacher collaboration, which would then directly support student learning in their classroom. I communicated to each staff member that I would set up a structure and opportunities to support collaboration amongst all teachers.

In order to ensure that collaboration became the modus operandi of the learning sites, I needed to provide these opportunities for all teachers to connect and collaborate. There were many ways, some more visible and some less, that we introduced collaboration into our working environment. At a glance, we started all non-instructional days together with a formal meeting. Also, all teachers were asked to meet together at one site once a month. I assured teachers that if I was asking them to travel across a city to attend professional development, the time together would be targeted, concise and meaningful. Nobody would feel that their time had been wasted.

The professional development opportunities and topics primarily centered on inquiry, task design and assessment, and working groups were often multi-disciplinary across subject areas and programs. The professional development was also designed to foster building respect for each other, their disciplines, and their student populations.

I believe that every teacher has something viable to offer to the learning community. In order to facilitate an environment where the teachers felt like they were contributing, we began by sharing evidence of student learning. As such, the sharing started in a simple and non-threatening manner. Confidence was built, all staff were commended on their contributions, and the excitement of being together grew exponentially. Collaboration occurred. Over the years, at each site, I felt my role shifting from being an active, front and center leader to an energetic bystander or facilitator as teachers took the lead in creating viable and valuable opportunities to collaborate together. How has this experience influenced my leadership? My understanding is clearer of the correlation between being both a leader and a manager as a principal. I needed to establish the structure for collaboration to occur, and then I could become a leader of learning.

Working with diverse populations fosters diverse thinkers. The teachers I work with (and have worked with in the past) have the motivation, curiosity, and creativity to become stronger, more effective designers of learning. The established structure gave them the opportunity to collaborate naturally and have fun together. Those structures continue, but the teachers also created their own times to collaborate, whether face-to-face or online.

The cultures in each of the settings are fun, engaging and dynamic. Teachers enjoy each other's company, and seek each other out. But the true benefactors are the students who, due to high levels of teacher collaborating, are leapfrogging forward in their learning.

About the Author: *Charlotte Arbuckle (B.Sc. Hons, B.Ed. M.Sc.) is the principal of CBE-learn online, Career and Technology Centre and CBEHomeschooling for the Calgary Board of Education (CBE) in Calgary, Alberta, Canada, as well as being a registered psychologist. As an avid educator, who believes passionately in the teaching and learning of all students, she actively pursues leadership experiences with diverse populations of students and educators. In her 35 years at the CBE she has held many diverse roles as a teacher, consultant in special education, and administrator in the schools.*

Chapter 45

Change: Make it Happen!

Damien Aherne

The Lay of the Land

I n the summer of 2013 I was excited about moving into a principalship at a small school in the south suburbs of Chicago. Ten years prior, I was a music teacher who loved my work and my students. However, I was ready for a new professional challenge.

I was the third principal in three years. In addition, the building was under construction. The installation of a new air conditioning system during my first summer restricted access and complicated the transition process. I did not have an office and I conducted interviews for new staff at the other school buildings in our district. In fact, I did not officially move into my office until three days before school started! The challenges were stacked before us, but I was excited to be part of the team and felt ready to tackle each one.

Having just completed my third year as principal, we experienced many changes during that time. What follows are lessons I learned through the change process.

First Things First

As a new principal, try not to make too many changes during your first year unless it is absolutely necessary. During your first year, watch, learn, and listen; these should be your primary goals. If change is necessary, have conversations with the people who the change will impact and get their input. If time allows it, and if your school has a leadership team, then also discuss the change with your team. It is important to include your staff in the decision-making process.

Decisions, Decisions, Decisions, and More Decisions!

So who gets to decide? At the end of the day, the principal will make the final decision. That said, how you reach your decision is as important as the decision itself. No doubt, some decisions will occur quickly, such as whether to evacuate in an emergency situation. When you do have the opportunity to allow the team to be involved in the decision making process, take the time to do it. Including others in the decision-making process and outcomes shows transparency and builds trust over time. It also shows that you do not know everything and you respect your team's perspective on what will influence and affect the school. Keep in mind what Todd Whitaker (2002) advises in his book, *What Great Principals Do Differently:* Base every decision on your best teachers!

What Will Change and Why?

Top down change does not last. For lasting change, let the ideas come from within the staff, then give the staff room to collaborate, time to believe, and the support to get it done. With online forums like *Pinterest, Instagram and Twitter,* great teachers have become masters at networking and adapting ideas that inspire changes. The challenge as a building leader is creating an environment of risk takers.

Take a Chance!

Risk takers are people willing to think 'outside the box,' have their ideas challenged, be uncomfortable, and not back away from what they believe because of fear. With that, many people will not take risks if they do not feel connected to or respected by the organization. So how do we create an environment of risk takers? As a building leader, you will need to assess your staff, their strengths, weaknesses, talents, and passions. You will need to develop strong relationships that build trust. You will have to be consistent, fair, honest, and competent. You will have to support and address those staff members who are persistently negative. People will need to feel safe before taking a risk - and negative people like chaos, not safety. Create an environment of trust through transparency, collaboration, and expertise. The principal may be the instructional leader, but the teachers are also the instructional experts. Encourage and support your staff in becoming leaders and they will take risks. They will change the world.

Resistance

You will rarely get everyone on board with every change, especially non-mandated changes that people can influence. In his book *The 80% Approach,* Dan Sullivan (2013) talks about getting the first 80% of any task done first, then continuing to work another 80% of the remaining 20%, until your goals are complete. The key is getting to your first 80%. Take the same approach to having your staff on board with a new idea or change. If 80% of the staff is on board, implement the change and work on the remaining 20% over time.

Passion

True passion drives change. If you are truly passionate about your goal, you will make it happen regardless of the challenges. In his book *Better Than Good*, Zig Zigler (2006) talks about feeding your passion through inspiration. Inspiration feeds passion, and passion feeds change. Seek out new ideas, have a growth mindset, be inspired, and make it happen.

Recommended books that will inspire growth and change:
   Schools Cannot Do It Alone by Jamie Vollmer
   Shifting the Monkey by Todd Whitaker
   What Great Teachers Do Differently by Todd Whitaker
   What Great Principals Do Differently by Todd Whitaker
   Leading School Change by Todd Whitaker
   Transforming School Culture by Anthony Muhammad

The Six Secrets of Change by Michael Fullan
Leading in a Culture of Change by Michael Fullan
Change Forces by Michael Fullan
The Principal: Three keys to Maximizing Impact by Michael Fullan
The Principal: Traversing the High Wire with No Net Below by Don Sternberg
Up the Organization by Robert Townsend
Building a Culture of Support by PJ Caposey
Leading Change in Your School by Douglas B. Reeves
Better Than Good by Zig Ziglar
The Energy Bus by Jon Gordon
Leading with Questions by Michael J. Marquardt
Fish by Stephen C. Lundin, Harry Paul, and John Christensen
Who Moved My Cheese by Spencer Johnson
Our Iceberg is Melting by John Kotter
Good to Great by Jim Collins
Flow by Mihaly Csikszentmihalyi
Creating Innovators by Tony Wagner
The 10x Rule by Grant Cardone

About the Author: *Damien Aherne is a 4th year principal of an intermediate school in the South Suburbs of Chicago, and is currently in his 16th year as an educator. He serves as the South Cook Regional Director Elect for the Illinois Principal's Association and is a doctoral candidate at the University of St. Francis in Joliet, Illinois. He is also in his 12th year as an adjunct professor at Moraine Valley Community College where he teaches music history. Damien lives in Frankfort, Illinois, with his wife and three children.*

Chapter 46

Leading Change

Tina Garza

The story began 20+ years ago when I was challenged with the notion of becoming an educator. Coming from parents with an education background, it was clear that it was a possibility. However, I had not a clue on how to proceed and follow in their footsteps, let alone lead a team or a campus.

Over time, interactions with students are what guided my path to best practices, and then into leadership positions on my campus. I am convinced that to strive toward, and achieve, greatness as a leader, you must have experienced the life of a teacher and paid close attention to the customers – the students. My experiences as both a department chair and a campus leader opened my eyes to the ins and outs of a school. By the way, there are no books that teach you these pieces. You learn how to use those pieces through trial and error and with the guide of a mentor; use those resources to your advantage as you plan experiences for the customers. Humility is an important characteristic of an administrator because you must learn to do self-system checks.

As an administrator, you must be self-aware, conscious and deliberate in everything you do when it comes to making decisions affecting students. Initially, the decisions I made were based on my instincts and involved three parts: me, myself, and my upbringing. Self-motivated decisions were not successful because I did not have the buy-in from the stakeholders. I learned that to have a responsible roll out, you must include the all the important partners in your conversations and decisions, and lead so there are diverse activities on campus.

Our campus, Harlingen School of Health Professions, is a diverse campus that includes professional learning communities at various levels within the organization. To ensure that communication is seamless and all stakeholders are involved, we meet weekly to discuss, brainstorm and execute activities that include best practices for our students. When I hosted conversations as a campus lead in my early years, meetings were a "check-box" agenda. I discussed the topic and checked off the box because it was covered. Now as a principal, the conversations are more meaningful and a few points could take 15-30 minutes to discuss. Everyone's perspective is an integral part in the puzzle and needs to be heard and taken into consideration. A sense of equality in roles and responsibility is imperative. Leadership comes in many forms and sometimes you must let go of the reins for great things to happen. Developing leaders on campus should become a norm for you, because inevitably you as the principal will not be able to manage it all.

Our students have achieved great success following our project-based learning practices, despite some of the neighboring district's experiences and failed attempts to successfully include these practices in the classroom. In our state, we received the highest number of distinctions that we were eligible for based on the size of our campus and our course offerings. But these achievements do not rest solely on the principal. It is crucial for the principal to listen to the others on campus and involve them in important decisions. New campus initiatives, concerns that arise school-wide, and academic challenges are just a few of the decisions that are made collaboratively so that all the stakeholders have buy-in. The goal is for the individuals in the building to be committed, not compliant. To accomplish this, meeting norms are created through a collaborative process. Individual opinions are shared and then merged to represent the group. Time management, a skill mastered by each member of the group, and collaboration with a positive problem-solving attitude are contagious; by the same token, they are just as difficult to manage. Individual accountability and commitment in pursuit of a goal are vital, as is the flexibility in determining the exact steps.

When it seems that the desired outcomes are not being produced, you must have the strength and the vulnerability to admit when a mistake happens, or when a given direction, strategy, policy or procedure is not working. As a leader, you come to a point when you realize that you are unable to cause change on your own. Stakeholders must be a part of the conversations. You need to meet regularly and be transparent. As an individual continues to evolve and develop, the reality is that to affect a large institution you should surround yourself with individuals who have the same goals. How you arrive at that point is the work that must happen. If you are included as a part of the onboarding process, selection of those individuals should be your focus.

Creating a culture is the next challenge. Once the goals and achievements have been found, the team will work towards those goals and as the leader, you must be able to trust others, trust your instincts and trust your intellect. Intentional leaders of change continually reflect on life, debrief, capture lessons learned, and act.

About the Author: *Tina Garza has been involved in education since 1994 in Harlingen Consolidated Independent District. She serves as principal at Harlingen School of Health Professions, which opened its doors in 2014. She participated in the design of the campus and, through opportunities afforded by the district, was able to design the cornerstones of the campus, paving the way in education and health care preparation. Her endeavors will not stop at this campus and she looks forward to continuing to grow in her educational experiences.*

Chapter 47

A Journey of Safe, Caring and Inclusive Schools

Susan Schmidt

This chapter took place in Pembina Trails School Division in Winnipeg, Manitoba, Canada. The division hosts over 13000 students, and is proud of the accomplishments of being an inclusive school division that develops programming and plans for all students in their classrooms and communities. The focus of this chapter is the journey of one school and one principal in Pembina Trails.

I was interested in formal leadership and was encouraged by others to exercise my leadership through chairing committees, running assemblies and being teacher-in-charge. A posting for a one-year term vice principal came up and I applied. In my mind, I believed that it was only one year and if I did not like the role, I could go back to my lovely Resource and Reading Recovery position. As it happened, I was never a vice principal. The school division decided that a principal role would be where I would begin. The experience was life changing for me. It created a passion that was unexpected and energy to do whatever it would take to make the school experience for children safe, caring, and inclusive. The school was in an economically disadvantaged area. I had been in the school many times for meetings and my children had played soccer on the school field. I did not pay attention to the surroundings.

I started my first day with my new red business suit and my principal shoes on; the school did not seem too bad. The second day a rough looking man came in to the office yelling that there were bullies in the school and I needed to do something about them immediately or he would. Little did I know that although I was scared and shocked that someone would behave like that in a school that moment provided the impetus for change.

I told the man that we would address his concerns and I would get back to him. He was very unsettled and I was nervous for the safety of the students within the school. My intuition told me that I needed to report his behaviour to the superintendent and the police department. I was right; he was known to the police. I asked for help and a partnership began with the police to support the school. The school division was also incredibly supportive and checked in often to support the success of the school. Several meetings occurred with the parent, the police, and me to set the standard of behaviour in the school. The staff noticed and began to pay attention to the serious nature of the situation. An early leadership lesson was to treat struggles like nuggets of gold.

The nuggets of gold came to a head early that fall when a large group of parents attended the parent council meeting to share a very serious concern about bullying at the school. When the staff heard that the parents were attending they all came and sat with me. Tempers were high and emotions ran thick that night. During that evening, parents stood up and shared stories of fighting, unsafe behaviors, and cruel, ongoing use of nasty language.

The staff wanted to respond with presentations on how the school had addressed bullying in the past. Imagine my surprise when the first volunteer who wanted to present to the group was the school secretary. She shared history and invited families to work with us. The second person was a classroom teacher who reviewed what the school had done in the past in classrooms. The third was me, and perhaps that is why my leadership change that night was my shift from teacher to principal. I was challenged to change myself and embrace the situation as an opportunity for growth. As Victor Frankl said, "When we are no longer able to change a situation - we are challenged to change ourselves." The emotion and tension of that night gave the school the urgency to change. Together, we needed to discover new strategies, evaluate the old, and recreate the vision of the future.

That meeting was in early October. After the meeting, many staff members came to me at once and said we need to work together to find solutions to this serious issue. We began to enroll division and community supports. I found myself telling anyone who would listen that we needed help and there was no time to wait.

Early on we decided that supervision was needed everywhere. I appealed to the staff to increase their time out on recess duty, and they did. The families identified bullying occurring in the change room, so we added supervision there. Students previously had entered the school at any door, were often running in the hallway and the beginning of the day was chaotic. Although the community resisted the change, we assigned entrance doors and I put forth the expectation that we all greet students at the door.

Our entrance door campaign was simple. Teachers taught - and expected - students to say hello. At one point, students collected data on how many hellos they heard, and what they saw as a reaction when there was hello. Students reported their data on the PA in the morning. The school became calmer. We worked with students on how to enter the school.

The second action after that meeting was that a class studied the nutritional habits of their classmates. They created a presentation to share with me and the school board. The results from their study found that many children did not have milk in their diet and even fewer ate breakfast. As a staff, we created a simple form to look at the behaviors we noticed and then we began a simple experiment of offering food. Immediately we saw change. Hungry children need to eat.

We decided that eating represented a universal approach to a daily routine, and was in line with our strong belief of inclusion. We believed the morning start to be a way to teach respectful behavior, and decided to build a culture in which all of us could be together and eat and enjoy a successful start to the day. We had $50.00 to start. A parent came and said she would go to her local church for help. It worked, and from there we built many community partners who became volunteers, we developed after school programs and best of all when students were out in the community they saw people who cared.

The staff, students, and the community identified the same vision of the future. "We know that students learn best in conditions where they feel safe, accepted, appreciated and included" (Dean and Whyte, 2005). In fact, schools need the base of these beliefs to be inclusive. Both staff and leadership worked tirelessly to achieve our vision.

The trend of character education has been alive in schools since the 1990s. At our school, it was clear that the parents expected a response and action. They were watching, and we did not have time to delay the plan. At this time our school was presented with an opportunity to take part in a three-year Justice Canada project, with the goal of crime prevention/reduction. Two other schools signed up and we entered the most incredible teaming and professional experience together. A wise leader once told me to always be on the hunt for treasures. Little did I know that during that chaotic time this opportunity would come along and would have not only enduring gifts at the beginning, but would continue until the present time, expand and travel through schools and the school division and the province.

The focus of the project was to collect data, create common language and focus in the schools, give professional learning opportunities, and build the capacity of the community. Numerous initiatives occurred throughout that project. The data collected showed tremendous growth in academics and a significant reduction in suspensions, bullying, and fighting.

The vision of the project was to Create Safe, Caring and Respectful Learning Communities. One of the key areas of focus was the work in the Respect programming which embodied the principles of character education, shared leadership, goal setting, service learning, curriculum integration, protective factors, and interactive instructional strategies. The school recognized that the outcome of respect could create an overall positive school climate that allowed for more time teaching and on task. Martin Luther King said, "Intelligence alone is not enough; intelligence plus character, that is the true goal of education."

The key in the success of the project was always celebrating the strengths of the students, the staff, and the school. The school had a rich culture of strength-based programming and very strong beliefs that all students needed to be included, appreciated, and celebrated.

The project was intense and we needed perseverance to keep focused on the many goals. As in all implementations there was enthusiasm at the beginning, but then there was a dip that we all needed to be conscious of to stay on track on the journey of where we wanted to be. As the school focused on reducing negative behaviors like bullying, the school also saw an increase in the behavior. It was a rocky road at times as we were concerned that the results were not quick enough. We needed to continually show to the community that the school was making progress. As the leader, I needed to be the holder of the dream and keep repeating to the staff what the goal was. As a principal I needed a team to work with. We created a divisional team with two other principals and a divisional leader. We met monthly and brought successes and areas for growth to each meeting. Over time we each understood each other's schools so well that we could find solutions and initiatives to support each other. Our plan developed further and we began finding creative ways to develop opportunities for our teachers to visit each other's classrooms and plan together. The depth of the teaming and collaboration was incredible. The school developed school-wide respect agreements, a respect definition, and a school song. The agreements were thoughtfully developed with students, staff and the community with the goal being for everyone to understand the expectations in the school.

The key success in the school was that the agreements had input from students, staff, and parents. Parents and staff signed the agreements and there was congruency between the school and the classroom and Pembina Trails School Division Standard of Behaviour. We posted the agreements in the school and had all students and staff sign them. We were on the same page, and the expectations were visible and taught on a very regular basis in the school. We reviewed them constantly with the community. They were how we did business and they were the standard for the culture of the school.

The story of change for me as a leader was my own growth and understanding of safe, caring, and inclusive schools. As a beginning principal, it was an honor to be involved in a project in which, even after the three years of the involvement with Justice Canada, there was a desire and determination for the team to continue and develop. The curiosity as a principal was to see if, when any of us in the project moved schools, we could take the initiative successfully to other schools. The work expanded and still continues to develop after 14 years. Each school approaches the work differently. Schools have added their own personality to reflect their strengths and areas for growth in their school and the community. What would I tell other leaders? If an incredible opportunity comes along, embrace it and learn from it.

Remember the parent who was aggressive? When I left the school, he apologized more than once that he behaved poorly. He said he did not understand what we were doing and provided me with great feedback. He said that there had been disrespectful behaviour by some students. He also said that the work we did changed the culture. His greatest change was that he learned as a person to be better and kinder to others. There is a nugget of gold! What else changed in the school? The data showed us bullying was reduced by 80% and fighting by 90%. Suspensions became almost nonexistent. Academics improved. Community involvement increased from one volunteer to over 100. Trustees commented that they did not get phone calls with complaints. The team got stronger and stronger.

We start our journey as school leaders with our own bias of who we think a school principal is and what they do. I dressed for the part, prepared myself with courses and thought I knew. Until you live the role, and lead your staff, it is almost impossible to understand what is needed. There is always more work to do, more research to help guide leaders and a new group of staff and students. We need to keep focused on the culture of the school. Students deserve schools where they are safe, cared for and included. I was so fortunate to work alongside the most talented group of students, staff, a school division that cares and a community that was willing to trust us with their children. My greatest thanks to all of them for supporting our journey together.

About the Author: *Susan Schmidt is an Assistant Superintendent of Student Services in Pembina Trails School Division in Winnipeg, Manitoba. Susan has been a classroom teacher, resource teacher, and Reading Recovery teacher. Susan was the principal in three schools. She is passionate about safe, caring, and inclusive schools. She believes strongly that all children can learn and that everyone has gifts to be shared and nurtured.*

Chapter 48

Supporting a Collaborative School Culture

Marie Lourdes Ssemanda, Ed.D.

I remember the phone call from my superintendent breaking the news to me that I had been appointed Principal of Maple Hurst Elementary School, like it just happened yesterday. It came a couple of weeks before the Christmas break. Although it has been nine years already, I remember the day with fondness. I believed it was the best Christmas gift I ever received; I felt great about it because the truth is, I had worked so hard to get where I was. So, I carried on that excitement throughout the two weeks of the Christmas holidays.

Little did I realize that the staff members of Maple Hurst were not so thrilled about my arrival! They had experienced a turn-over of four principals in recent years, so they figured that it would only be a short time before I took my exit too. Filled with enthusiasm, I arrived bright and early on the first day of school. I was looking forward to meeting the staff, students and parents. However, on the first day of school, I realized that this was not going to be a "walk in the park." I had my work cut out. I recalled what my former principal told me upon finding out that I was appointed principal of Maple Hurst. She said, "Be careful what you ask for! Maple Hurst has its own problems." Those warnings rang true when I walked into the main office. I was surprised to see the cold reception I received from the staff members. Although they were polite, I noticed that they did not want anything to do with me. The secretary did not even lift her head up to look at me when I entered the office. She completely ignored me as if I was not there. Not fazed by the cold treatment, I said good morning warmly but she just mumbled a reply out of duty without even looking at me. I carefully sat my briefcase down on the table in the main office and scrambled to find the key to open my office door. The secretary did not make any effort whatsoever to help me, although she kept the master key in her desk. She just continued to do her paper work as if there was no one there. This kind of treatment continued for weeks. Then it turned into months. Some staff members, including the secretary, would talk about me negatively among each other and with parents. Other staff members undermined any changes I tried to implement and refused to participate in anything I proposed, like divisional meetings. Some staff members talked to each other and laughed during staff meetings instead of listening; these behaviours disrupted the flow of the meeting.

I quickly realized that something needed to be done to improve the school climate. I noticed that some staff members seemed to control others. Most the staff members had been in the school from anywhere between 8 to 20 years. Those staff members seemed to dominate and intimidate the ones who had been at the school for less than 5 years. They had no voice at all. A few followed whatever the veterans asked them to do for fear of being ostracized. The division between the staff members was painfully visible.

I consulted with my principal mentor regarding how to deal with the "toxic" culture which seemed to have permeated the core of the entire school. I also alerted my Superintendent about my observations in regards to the staff interactions with each other and the parents. I strongly believed that if it was not for the support of my principal mentor, Superintendent, central staff and a few staff members, I would not have been able to make progress in improving the school culture. I knew that having a school culture which exudes positive energy was very beneficial to all staff members, students and parents. I questioned myself, "How am I going to change this culture?"

I realized that I needed to build a school culture that promoted collaboration among staff members. The first strategy I used was to build a strong relationship with the few staff members who were willing to work collaboratively with me. I brainstormed with them and we came up with some strategies to improve the school culture. It was imperative to include staff in co-creating the mission, vision and values. The divide became more prominent between the veteran staff members and those who were newer to the school. A few staff members felt caught in between the two groups because they wanted to join the newer group (as they presented a more positive outlook on the school climate). This divide was creating an atmosphere of "us" and "them." I vowed to work harder to create a collaborative school climate. I believed that all staff members, or at least the majority, needed to buy in and make it our shared vision.

It was agonizing for me to observe how a few miserable people can poison the school climate through their negativity. I reminded the staff members regularly why we are working in a school. We are in the business of educating students through our words and actions. If we could build a collaborative school climate our students would be the beneficiaries of our efforts. During the monthly one-hour staff meetings I began sharing the data from the students' report cards and standardized testing data to try to identify the students who are struggling. I insisted that they must meet as a division monthly to share their assessments and keep track of the progress the "marker" students were making. I introduced this because I noticed that some teachers were using the same outdated strategies but were expecting different student results. That was not going to happen.

I embarked on setting high expectations for the students and staff. This was intended to get the staff members out of their comfort-zone and help them grow their mind set. Since the school was in a low-income area, the staff members tended to set low expectations for the students. I reminded the staff during staff meetings and divisional meetings that living with challenges did not mean that the students were incapable of learning. It took me at least three years for the staff members to slowly begin to believe that everyone needs to work together in collaboration to help the students achieve to the best of their abilities.

I made some changes in staffing. I switched some teachers from one grade to the next to ensure that each teacher was placed in a grade that best supported student learning needs. Some staff members, however, did not want to change from the grade they had been teaching for many years, so they transferred out. The transfers created staff positions that were filled with new, open-minded, staff members. They were willing to work collaboratively towards creating a positive school culture in which everyone felt valued, respected, supported and included.

I tried to lead by example. At recesses, on many occasions, I would put on my supervision safety vest and go out on the school yard. This gave me an opportunity to model to the staff members that they are all expected to wear their safety vests so that they are visible to the students and each other. There was some resistance from a few staff members at the beginning; however, the resistance came to an end through my modeling and the fact that the few resistors were outnumbered. Most the staff members recognized the benefits of wearing the safety vests. The use of wearing safety vests decreased the number of discipline issues that happened during the year because the staff members were visible to all students. By my second year at the school, all staff members complied.

I visited the classrooms on a regular basis. This staff was not used to the principal visiting their classrooms. Initially they looked startled, stopped whatever they were doing to talk to me, and asked me if I needed something from them. I explained to the teachers that I was not there to judge them, but to support them by providing feedback and providing the resources that might help them to meet the students' learning needs. Some teachers, however, felt that they knew all they needed to know, were closed to any recommendations given and did not change their teaching practices at all. They continued to teach behind closed doors.

Conversely, other staff members wanted to learn and took every opportunity given to them to improve their practice. They shared best practices with each other and worked eagerly with the various resource teachers that I had invited to our school to provide professional development in-services. Others started to co-teach and model various literacy or mathematics strategies for each other. I learned along with them. This practice helped staff members understand that we are all in this together.

We learn together and support each other to improve our students' learning.

On the social level, I introduced monthly staff luncheons. Every month, three staff members signed up to bring in food to share with the whole staff, and those lunches helped bring them together. This gave us an opportunity to talk and get to learn more about each other. However, the first year I introduced this it was shot down by a few staff members. We had it just two times and when their turn came they stated that they felt pressured to participate.

The following year, when we welcomed new staff members I reintroduced the idea and this time it was very well received. The staff members took turns bringing in food on the dates they had signed up for. The only problem we run into is that some staff members had to do lunch supervision duty, which made it difficult to join in when everyone was eating. To smooth this problem over, I invited some parent volunteers to help supervise the students during lunch time. This gave the staff members on supervision duty an opportunity to be able to join everybody to eat together.

Although the school climate was moving in the right direction, a few staff members continued to find means to sabotage progress in the school by sharing disparaging comments about staff to other staff and the students' parents.

At the beginning of the new school year, with the support of my superintendent, I invited the consultants to Maple Hurst to lead our collaboration team sessions with all staff members. The first session took place over half a day, and focused on finding out what each staff member wanted to see in the school. We all wrote down these values and at the end of the session handed in the papers to the facilitators.

In the second session, which was a full day session, the facilitators began by giving us a task where we needed to complete a questionnaire, "What Colour is Your Personality?" After completing the questionnaire, we were divided into groups of the colors we identified with such as, yellow, green, blue and orange. Many staff members enjoyed the opportunity to learn about themselves, and also about other staff members' personalities.

The next exercise was to individually write four words that summed up what we valued. We then joined with a partner and had to collaborate together using our combined eight words, collapsing them into four words that we both agreed on. Then we joined with two more people and again had to collapse the words we collectively had into four words. We then joined another group, making us a group of eight, and did the same thing, coming up with four values we valued and finally in a group of sixteen collapsing the words again into just four values. We were divided into four groups, and each group was given a value; for example integrity. Each group had to write a value statement clearly stating what that value would look like, feel like and if anyone came on our "bus" what would they see and feel. Then we brought the statement each group had come up with and posted it up for everyone to see. Each statement went through several revisions, until we all agreed that we had captured the essence of what we all wanted. By agreeing, we were holding ourselves accountable that we would work toward making changes. No one would be pointing fingers at anybody else because we were all responsible for contributing to the "ingredients" we deemed necessary for the school culture we all wanted to work in.

The collaborative school culture is still a work in progress. However, I am now beginning to see that there is a light at the end of the tunnel.

I have come to realize that I may never get one hundred percent of everybody working collaboratively, but, if I have eighty percent, a collaborative school culture can be built. One thing to understand is that creating a collaborative school culture cannot be achieved overnight. It takes time and patience. Further, you must keep in mind that you build the collaborative school culture by building leaders among your staff, so that when you leave the school the remaining staff will be able to sustain it.

About the Author: *Dr. Marie Ssemanda has worked as an educator in a variety of elementary schools for more than eighteen years, as a teacher, vice-principal and principal. Ssemanda obtained her Master of Education degree from Brock University and Doctor of Education from the Ontario Institute of Studies in Education, Toronto University. She lives with her family in Hamilton, Ontario.*

PART VII

Reflections On Educational Leadership

Self-reflection becomes an important learning tool throughout the ebb and flow of a principal's career. Organizational concerns for leadership succession and sustainability permeate principals' reflections on organizational leadership. Reflections on educational leadership help to inform principal preparation programs and craft differentiated leadership development opportunities for experienced principals. Throughout the life-cycle of a principal, principals engage in learning as both mentor and mentee. It takes a school community to raise the collective efficacy, inclusive of all stakeholders. Principals learn from both the youngest students and the wisest Elders. Reflections on educational leadership synthesize the theoretical knowledge realized through individual and collaborative capacity, and practical knowledge that comes from job-embedded experiences. Principals seek to give their very best, every day, in the service of others.

Chapter 49

Leader to Leader: On Lessons Learned during Practice that Inform Principal Preparation

Israel Aguilar, Ph.D. & Dessynie Edwards, Ph.D.

Introduction

The principalship provides one the opportunity to facilitate school improvement by tapping into the interests, skills, and talents of others around you, the principal. After all, moving a school forward is not an easy task, right? It would be safe to say moving a school forward is complex given that problems of practice have more than one solution. For example, the needs of the people inside the organization are important, and have implications for the technical work one does during the day (i.e. check email, fill out evaluations, create budgets, etc.). The challenge then becomes how to meet the demands of the organization while staying in touch with the needs of the individuals who make up the organization. As former school leaders and current professors of school leadership programs, it has been our experience that adhering to the processes that inform practices (i.e. cultivating relationships, self-reflection, auto-ethnography, SuperVision, social justice) involved within school improvement yields expected benefits and products (increased student achievement, improved quality of instruction and actualized teacher and leader effectiveness). Today, we the authors, teach in a principal preparation program and help pre-service leaders understand that the journey towards school improvement starts when one sees the work of the principal along a continuum of processes that inform practice. It is our aim with this piece to help current principals reinforce the work they already do in schools, while also providing insight into our practice that continues to inform our teaching with aspiring principals. As such, we conceptualize this article as a conversation between leaders (us) to leader (you). Perhaps our lessons learned along the way will inspire others to also name their practice as we have done.

Israel's lesson learned: Assumptions will stump change, but leaders will foster relationships to develop others' pedagogy.

Between 2012-2014 I served as a school leader in a large urban district located in north Texas. The first year, I met a special education teacher who said that special education (SPED) trumps the services of the bilingual program for any student who was identified as exhibiting a learning or physical disability and spoke a language other than English. Apparently, students who were supposed to be provided with instruction through both programs were automatically denied the opportunity to instruction in their native language. While it may have been easy to assume ignorance or negligence was the case, I made the effort to understand why students who were both English language learners (ELLs) and who had a disability were mostly being served through only one program: special education. This type of decision required committee input, so I wanted to understand why the SPED teacher believed one program trumped the other program automatically. Without consideration of variances between students, any teacher could perpetuate exclusion and violate students' rights to a free and appropriate public education.

Still, I was patient and observed the behavior, the messages, and the written reports from the special education teacher. It appeared the educator exhibited deficit thinking and saw languages other than English as a curse rather than a blessing. I had two options: address the obvious bias in the name of achieving differentiation (product) but risk making things worse for the students, the teacher, and myself, or; build a trusting relationship with the educator (process) and anticipate the teacher will be more willing to change.

Slowly, I got to know Ms. Brown. She was young and energetic. She loved her job and the students loved her, but she confessed she felt alone as the only special education teacher on campus. Through more conversations with her, and through more observations of her teaching, I came to realize that, while she was well-intentioned, she did not know how to best meet the needs of diverse students who exhibited more than one difference. In her mind, one's ability was the only difference she could address. Acknowledging more than one difference made the teaching and learning process too messy for students who were supposed to be instructed in a native language while also receiving modification and accommodations.

To ensure that the teacher would not feel threatened or discouraged to change, I engaged another faculty member who could support the special education teacher with the design of instructional goals for students who spoke another language other than English. This entire process took much of the first year. At times, I questioned if this was worth my energy, but then I remembered why I was there in the first place. The job of a school leader is not something that can be characterized with quick fixes. Rather, the change of one's beliefs takes time. Leaders who are oblivious to that stump change and risk making matters worse between leader and teacher. Eventually, Ms. Brown saw that it was harder to work with students who exhibited multiple differences. It was my job to provide the opportunity. This took away time from the constantly growing number of tasks (i.e. return phone calls, return emails, and attend meetings) I still needed to get done. The lesson learned here is that all the phone calls, emails, and meetings do not matter when the people inside the building are suffering or in need of assistance. To develop one's pedagogy takes time, and building a relationship with someone who needs assistance understanding differentiation is part of the process that will render school improvement.

When I tell this story to my current students, many immediately want to criminalize Ms. Brown for her lack of understanding. Others say that she should have known better and could be terminated for the misplacement of many students. As such, the challenge is also to help the pre-service leaders understand that relationships are important; in this instance when given the opportunity to change, the teacher did meet the expectations. This process was exhausting, and I often felt it would be easier to find a replacement. Yet if I did this, I would feel like a failure; after all, I am leader who teaches. If I did not take advantage of the opportunity to teach another faculty member about social justice and why it is important to consider all angles or aspects of students then I, too, would have perpetuated the vicious cycle of deficit thinking that continue to plague schools. Ms. Brown did not have to respond to my requests for a chat. In fact, there was a lot against building a relationship with her. She was only part-time on campus. She had a classroom in a portable building that was about a 10-minute walk from the main building, and she never could stay after school because she had to pick-up her own children. Despite the technical tasks that still needed to get done, I was able to reach her when it mattered most. That required me as a leader to engage her with questions and potential solutions or resources. Because I knew Ms. Brown loved her job, I never assumed she wanted to hurt children. Instead, I saw that she was creative and energetic. I believed she could change her practice. This process did not stump change. Rather, it set the stage for it. While time consuming and emotionally draining, supporting teachers is not a choice. Rather, a privilege. I hope current and aspiring principals see it that way, too.

Dessynie's Lesson Learned: A Principal learning to lead, by changing, teaching and learning.

What were you expecting students to learn and be able to do? How do you know that all students met the learning objective? How did your instruction accommodate all learners and learning styles? How do you know that all students/scholars were engaged? What adjustments can you make to the lesson to ensure all scholars master the learning objective? These are appropriate inquiries that a principal, as an instructional leader, would ask a teacher during an observation debriefing or an instructional feedback session. However, in my case, as a principal and instructional leader of a large urban elementary school, these are the questions that a novice teacher asked me as we debriefed the 5th grade science lesson that we co-taught. Yes, as a principal, I planned instructional delivery with teachers and engaged in co-teaching with my instructional faculty.

I came to the consideration of and decision to use co-teaching as an instructional leadership strategy after an instructional catastrophe, for which I take full responsibility. During the previous school year, only twenty-one percent of the 5th grade class met the expectations on the science state assessments. The scores on the interim district assessments had also been indicative of instructional issues. I was a diligent and committed observer of instruction, and offered instructional feedback consistently during the year of the catastrophe. The teachers were receptive to the feedback and made as many adjustments as they could. The shocking truth is that I failed to supervise, guide, coach and support the teachers' instruction for student achievement. Collectively, we failed to effectively teach and prepare seventy-nine percent of the 5th grade students.

As I reflected on what I referred to as an instructional catastrophe, I considered my previous leadership roles and experience as a school leader. Approximately nine years before the instructional catastrophe, I had served as a middle school principal at a state approved public charter school. Prior to my middle school principalship, I was a high school special education teacher, high school academic coordinating teacher, department chair, high school administrator and district-level administrator. I also reflected on the benefits that were realized for students with special needs in the inclusion classes that I taught and facilitated in general education environments. The students, those who were eligible for special education and those who were not eligible, were the recipients of instruction from two instructional experts, a methodology expert (the special education teacher) and content expert (general education teacher). The teachers received reciprocal benefits, as they sharpened their content knowledge, accommodation and modification skills and overall pedagogy.

The year of the 5th grade science instructional catastrophe, I had returned to the principalship at the elementary campus, after serving more than seven years as a district level administrator in a large urban school district's Department of Special Education. In essence, I was a novice elementary principal leading a team of mostly novice, and a few experienced, educators. I was learning to lead in the elementary school context, while occupying the leader's seat.

My instructional catastrophe, coupled with my experience facilitating and implementing inclusive education programming and my acceptance of my status as a learning leader and novice elementary principal, taught me a major leadership lesson. I learned that collaborative planning and co-teaching offered reciprocal benefits for the students/scholars, classroom teacher and principal. The students/scholars were the beneficiaries of high quality, rigorous instruction planned and delivered by knowledgeable educators committed to their success. The novice 5th grade teacher, as she reported, gained confidence, courage, credibility, and individualized coaching from our co-instructional experiences.

The teacher's self- confidence was raised because through reflective processes she had opportunities to formulate and provide feedback and receive instructional feedback. The teacher became more confident with the content and pedagogy by having her principal as an instructional-thought-partner. Being courageous involves taking risks. The teacher was more open to taking instructional risks because of motivation and support from her principal/supervisor to self-reflect and strategize to mitigate risks. Credibility encompasses acknowledgement and recognition of efforts aligned with goals. The novice teacher also gained significant credibility because she shared accountability, responsibility and results for improved student achievement with the school's lead teacher, the principal. The novice teacher was the recipient of real-time, individualized coaching that included praise for her successes, probing for self-reflection and polish points to provide specific instructional revisions and ensure immediate changes in practice.

The reciprocal benefits for me, as the principal, included risk-taking with high yield results. As a group, district elementary principals had been cautioned and dissuaded against instructional delivery in their schools' classrooms. This caution and dissuasion was predicated on the practices - or maybe leadership malpractice - of a few principals who over-emphasized accountability. These principals assigned instructional coaches to classrooms to teach and some principals took over classes, delivered instruction and remanded teachers to the sidelines, as observers of instruction.

I had never taught 5th grade science, therefore, my learning curve was similar to that of the novice teacher. I proceeded with co-teaching, even though I had received a cautionary warning regarding teaching in my classrooms. I also acknowledged the risks of making my practice public and exposing my vulnerability to my faculty. However, transparency and making practice public were expectations that I had for teachers. I demonstrated courage by engaging in practices that were not supported by the district. Co-teaching with my 5th grade science teacher also bolstered my confidence with the content, pedagogy and instructional coaching mechanism. I gained credibility with the 5th grade teacher and my entire faculty because I demonstrated my ability and willingness to be challenged and change my instructional leadership practice. I was soon inundated by requests to co-teach with other teachers. The 5th grade scores increased by forty-eight percent following the year of our co-teaching. Co-teaching was not a panacea, but co-teaching proved to be an effective instructional leadership strategy for this context.

There is an assumption that an appropriately prepared, certified and effective principal possesses the knowledge and skills to supervise instruction and pedagogy for any content area, at any grade level, for all student demographics and in any school context. The question is, how does the principal learn to lead to meet the needs of everyone and actualize school improvement in varied school contexts? One answer to this question may be found in the instructional formats used in classes that vary by content, grade levels, teacher expertise and student demographics. One such instructional planning and delivery format used by teachers involves three components. The first component begins with the identification and modeling of the learning objectives. This component is referred to as 'I Do' because the teacher is modeling the expectations. The teacher then develops opportunities for students/scholars to practice the demonstration of learning with teacher guidance and facilitation and student collaboration. The second component is known as 'We Do.' The third component of this process is the independent work related to the learning objective, and the demonstration of the learning by each student, which is referred to as 'You Do.' I contend that this same instructional planning and delivery format can be re-conceptualized for use by a principal to provide instructional leadership and facilitate school improvement. I utilized this format when facilitating instruction in my graduate and doctoral courses with pre-service principals and instructional leaders. This format also aligns with the co-teaching model that I used when I learned to lead.

Conclusion

The principalship is an exciting position because of the opportunity one has to help develop the skills and knowledge of others. Furthermore, it is our contention that school improvement is possible when the leader understands that the processes involved take time, energy, vulnerability, self-reflection, and commitment. We hope our lessons outlined here will inspire aspiring and current principals to rethink practice so that their tenure as a school leader is one filled with moves towards school improvement, not stifled by assumptions, fear, or even mandates.

About the Authors:

Israel Aguilar, Ph.D. is an assistant professor of educational administration at Texas A&M University-Corpus Christi where he teaches about principal leadership for social justice. He has served in the capacity of administrator and teacher in large urban districts across Texas. He can be reached at: Israelaguilar01@hotmail.com

Dessynie Edwards, Ph.D. has 27 years of experience leading, teaching and learning in the PK-12 arena. Most recently, she served as the Assistant Superintendent of School Leadership in a large urban school district in Texas. She currently teaches in the principal preparation program at Texas A&M University-Corpus Christi. She can be reached at Dessynie.Edwards@tamucc.edu

Chapter 50

Misguided by a Light

Terry Kharyati

A t the age of thirty I interviewed to be a vice-principal at Western Quebec School Board's largest school. When asked why I should be hired, I remember saying, "If you want someone that will relate to students and get the best from them, hire me." For lack of a better candidate, they did. Seventeen years later, I am writing about how misguided my response was.

Six and half years ago my eldest daughter Emily was born. Quickly, I realized just how tough our students have it. I was an educated professional who had no idea why things were going so poorly for me as her caregiver. I could not read her cries as effectively as her mother or her grandmothers. I did not understand why she was so unhappy with me, and why I became so stressed when alone with her. The self-professed "relate to students" guru was not relating well with his own infant daughter. My wife, an educator, sat me aside and said, "Don't try too hard. She is behaving like she is supposed to, just be patient with yourself and read a little about this stage of her life." The problem was, I was focusing on her behaviour. I was worrying about my ability, or lack thereof, to change her cries to smiles. I suffered from a low self-efficacy as a parent.

When I returned to work I began to more deeply understand that my entire career as a professional educator had focused almost entirely on changing student behaviour. I had spent 11 years working on a better late policy, how best "to do" detentions, how to suspend students in a restorative way, have zero tolerance for drugs and violence, and how to work diligently on motivating or consequencing "those who could but weren't." We had set up a tiered system of student interventions and met with parents diligently to make sure all the adults were informed about the students' behaviour and attitudes towards their own schooling. I had spent a career as 'the disciplinarian' in what was once seen as a very tough school. I spent all my time on student behaviour, and all my nights and weekends on the business of being a school manager.

I was tired. The same students failing. The same students in the office. The same speeches and the same outcomes. I felt ineffective. I stopped believing I was right for the school. And another school year ended with relative successes.

Over the summer, I was revising the student agenda - almost 30 pages of policy-driven clarity. I was proud that every aspect of school life was explained, and every expectation came with an explanation and a consequence. It was a very well organized, central aspect of our pedagogical conversations with parents, students, and staff. Next, not long after revising the staff guidebook, I took a moment to have a beer with a respected central office colleague. He asked, "Why, after all this time, and after all your hard work, does your school still classically underachieve with regards to your student academic outcomes?" I had no answer and no excuses. I did not know. I fell asleep on our sofa that night ready for the writing of my resignation after breakfast.

The beginning of the school year started, as had 11 previously, with student induction assemblies, the reading of the student agenda (every page) during classes the first few days of school, and announcements reminding everyone about the expectations we, as adults, have for student attitude and behaviour. We were going to make sure the students knew our expectations of them. We were good at this part of schooling.

During the second week of school I became frustrated with issues that seemed to always arise around this time of year: staff missing lunch supervision duties; students leaving classes during class and wandering the hallways; students being marked absent when actually in class; staff not reading a memo about a student and missing crucial information needed to effectively work with said student, and; students sent from the same classrooms and same teachers to the office for intervention because of their 'misbehavior.' Different year, exact same issues, almost identical responses.

During October, teachers became increasingly upset with each other over the scheduling of extra-curricular events; events designed to increase student engagement but often scheduled such that they interrupted class time. The most upset teachers were clearly concerned about the impact of these events on the yearly pedagogical plan for courses our students were required to pass in order to graduate. These were two very intense perspectives about elements that positively influenced student achievement in different ways. In the end, the issue created hard feelings between staff. Again, I was feeling like I was ill-equipped to truly lead this school. Different year, exact same issues, and again, self-doubt.

That November, I met with a wildly successful fellow Head teacher who was visiting from the UK. We discussed the many issues that were surrounding my latest round of self-doubting tirades. He said, "What are your professional standards for your staff?" I responded, "I expect everyone to be a professional." End of conversation. He responded with "If you don't set the expectations for the adults, like you do with the students, the adults will set their own expectations. Are you sure they share expectations consistent with yours?" I mumbled, "No, I am not sure."

The administrative team started looking at the way we communicated expectations to our staff. Quickly we realized that we had not made the expectations for adult behaviour explicit; therefore, rarely ever gave feedback on adult behaviours that were rooted in a constructive, growth-oriented, data-driven approach. Together, with my administrative team, we set on the journey to defining and clarifying expectations for the adults in the system, including how we would react both when the staff knew what we expected and when they did not. Made sense to me.

We started with 'Rubric 1', created by our staff about the legal obligations of a teacher in Quebec. Our desire for clarity grew as a staff. The most professional staff members appreciated the standard that we were setting (as the standards being set were rooted in good pedagogical focus), and the struggling staff appreciated the structure that only comes from clear expectations, feedback, and growth-oriented support. We created a drive to clarify the processes that governed our everyday lives as staff members in a school community that truly wanted to be the best they could be. Buy-in was not an issue in that we did not strive to achieve it specifically, rather it came naturally as staff began to feel the comfort of knowing they were doing a great job according to a set standard that challenged everyone and was applied to everyone. We developed policies that helped ensure that class time would be kept uninterrupted while allowing for proper planning and full engagement in co-curricular activities. (We considered everything to be co-curricular.) Collaboratively we developed a whole-school pedagogical plan, and it was my job to focus on implementing that plan with a data-driven practice. Everything we did had to be aligned with our mission: to educate our students in a social and subject-specific curriculum which we defined and publicly communicated effectively.

The same tenets that led me to believe that I was going to get the best from students were the ones that I used to get the best from a talented, feisty, intelligent, motivated, eclectic staff. I realized that the one constant in the school system was our students, and the variables were the adult behaviours, which I came to realize, for the most part, can be consolidated and managed. Setting a standard for adult behaviour led to fewer office referrals because students were experiencing a more consistent classroom experience from period to period, activity to activity.

The staff knew it was expected that they were going to be held to a high standard. This meant I needed to follow-up and give growth-oriented feedback on staff performances. There was less staff to staff conflict and we stopped interrupting critical teaching time. We became a people-oriented, process-driven school that focused on adult behaviour as the antecedent of student outcomes. That was the buy-in that made the biggest difference.

For the past six years I have started our first staff meeting with an excerpt from a CBC interview with Phyllis Diller, the great comedienne. When asked after her retirement what the secret to her lasting success was - she said, interrupting the end of the question, "When they weren't laughing, I never blamed the audience." In the context of what became of our school culture, the professional standards established forced us to look inward to find an answer with a student, and forced us to look inward to find answers with staff and complex situations alike.

Light is a very real force in my life now, but I understand that it can be blinding at times; it can create safety and warmth, and it can, unintentionally, be a distraction. I willingly followed a light in those early years because it helped illuminate a worldview and value-system in which I had the skillset and the willset to work with students who were not achieving, and guide them into becoming motivated and engaged learners. I carried that light as a teacher and a principal and it shone brightly. As I become more aware of the limitations of my worldview, a new light led me to see that by providing students with a structured, balanced, positive and safe school environment, led by a talented, united, and committed staff, all kinds of lasting and replicable successes are achieved. The light that previously only existed when I was around my students now was being radiated by every adult in the building. The light that we can share with the adults can mean that everywhere, in all corners of the school, the same, consistent, bright light can keep kids warm, able to see the supports that exists in the school. Many forms of light continue to shine in that school long after my departure.

About the Author: *Terry Kharyati, having struggled through high school and CEGEP himself, began his university training with the goal of becoming a teacher; to give back to the leaders and teachers who had helped and mentored him along the way. His drive and passion for helping a range of students to learn and grow was evidenced early on, and he seized leadership opportunities whenever they presented themselves. Terry was a teacher, vice-principal, and principal for 23 years and is now serving the Western Quebec School Board in the central office role of Secretary General/Director of Programs and Evaluation. He is a proud husband and a father of three beautiful girls and lives in the community he proudly serves.*

Chapter 51

It Matters in the End

Debra Berner

Throughout my career, I have worked very hard to create a positive school climate, and meaningful relationships with my staff and students. I am continually seeking ways to do these things better. I read current literature. I seek out professional development. I review data until I know each of my students' faces, strengths and needs. I also use my personal and professional experiences to help me. I am the parent of two grown children and the sibling of a sister with special needs. I have been a special education classroom teacher, assistant principal, assistant to the director of special education, executive director to the Chief Operating Officer, director of student services, and now, I am in my tenth year as an elementary school principal. Even though I am what one would call "seasoned," I know I cannot be the best at everything and do not always have all the answers. One thing I do have is patience, and the motivation to try anything and everything to keep my students and school safe to ensure that learning can occur and success is evident.

I often get questions from staff members aspiring to be principals about how to best handle disciplinary issues while still teaching the kids and commanding their respect. "What does a positive school climate look like and how can I get there?" I am not an expert in growing a good climate but one thing I do know is that it must start from the top with the school leader. Let me share an experience that continues to be successful for me and fits in with my personal philosophy about discipline and school climate.

I want to preface this by saying that I have always had fabulous kids in the schools I worked, and have to remind others and myself that they are just KIDS and often will make inappropriate choices. It is our job, as 'surrogate parents,' to teach them along the way, just as we would our own children, and never forget to remind them that we still believe in them no matter what.

Every spring when we are getting ready to do our State assessments, I visit all of the classrooms getting ready to test that morning, give them a pep talk, and proceed to pass out peppermints to "clear the cobwebs" in their heads. I also make up small survival packs for the staff to get them through the week and put any leftover items (that year it was lollipops) in a basket on my conference room table to staff to take.

This one particular morning, I discovered that two of my 5th grade students, who were also my morning announcers of the month, had been stealing the lollipops from a basket on my conference room table where they do the announcements. I did not realize they were the culprits as the candy had been on the table all week for staff to grab and go. I just assumed that the bowl was gradually becoming empty because of the popularity of the type of candy. Well, I was definitely wrong!

As I circulated amongst my three 5th grade classes handing out the peppermints and giving my pretest pep talk, a fifth grade young man came up to me and offered me a lollipop...yes, one of MY lollipops, unbeknownst to him. After declining, I immediately looked over to my two announcers who also were in the same room. As one looked down and the other looked away, neither would catch my eye. I was definitely not going to cause any additional test anxiety by acknowledging the situation so I did not say anything and left.

As soon as the test was over, I went up to their room and requested that the two of them come out into the hall. I asked them if they knew why I was there. They both did and both also began to cry when I told them that we needed to call their parents and then discuss what we should do about this. They cried the whole way to the office - mind you, this was a 10-year-old girl and an 11-year-old boy, not one of my primary students.

Once in my office, they called their parents, who were glad I called (but not happy with why I called). I told the parents that I was not going to suspend them, but rather keep them in at recess to do a project. I do not believe in suspensions for things like this. I want to spend time with the kids to help them learn why what they did was wrong and often find alternatives to suspension. Therefore, I gave them a rubric with questions. The first question was to define *petty theft,* and to write me a synopsis of what it was and how what they did might fit under the category. Of course, I also included the usual questions of who was hurt, what you would do next time, etc. However, the main thing I wanted them to learn was how their actions affected me (and others) and what they could do to help solve the problem.

With agreement from the parents, I chose to keep them in at recess until the project was completed to my satisfaction. Although I did not ask her to, the young girl came back the next day with hers completed - as well as with a bag of lollipops that she purchased with her own money. The young boy spent the next few days in my office at recess because he took a little longer writing his and did not have the same type of home support as the young girl. That is not to say that his parents did not acknowledge the infraction; they handled it their own way and by their own rules at home.

Both children never did this at my school again, and when I followed them through middle and high school, this was not an issue there either. At our 5th grade Farewell Ceremony at the end of the year, each came up to me with their parents thanking me for taking the time to work with them rather than just suspending them for a day or two. Both students told me that the experience would never be forgotten, and both would always remember what *petty theft* meant!

Nevertheless, just because the intervention I came up with seemed successful - learning had occurred and the students understood its purpose - was it the right way to handle the situation? Some teachers thought the kids should be suspended; others thought they should have paid back by losing more recess time. Most thought it was a good way to teach respect of self and others. I still believe it was a good option, and rewarding in this circumstance. The rewarding part for me was that the students learned many *somethings*: something about respect, something about caring for others, something about the consequences of their actions and, most importantly, something about adults - I did not get angry and give up on them when they made this mistake.

Behavior management. Discipline policy. School rules. PBIS. Restorative Justice. All of these terms float in my head. All are things I have learned about and used throughout my 38 years of working as an educator. If I can give any advice, it is to remember that our job as an educator is to teach - to teach everything we want our kids to learn about academics, relationships, and life itself. Use what works for that particular situation, use what you know, use a strategy that gets your students to think, to reflect, and to pay back. Be the role model of what you want them to be and allow them to make mistakes. Take the time in each situation to teach them along the way, never stop believing in them, and always let them know that you care about them.

I am still learning, trying to find the best fit for a particular situation ... that is my job. As I said, I do not have all the answers, but I know what matters. Education matters, and is vital to a student's future success in life. It matters that a school should be intellectually challenging, motivating, safe, and supportive of students regardless of their needs. Relationships matter, and are the key to making a school climate filled with trust and respect. It is my job to teach my staff and then our students what matters.

I want my students to feel safe, valued and encouraged each time they walk into my school. Their success is measured by the positive academic, social, and emotional growth they make during their time in school. That is why I work so hard, always asking questions and never accepting that my work is done; it will always be a work in progress, looking at what matters in the end.

About the Author: *Debra Berner began her career in 1979 as a special educator and continued working with students with all types of disabilities until 1999 when she left the classroom to begin her administrative career. She has also worked at the central office level, most recently as the Director of Student Services. She is currently in her 10th year as an elementary school* *principal and is now the proud principal of Lakewood Elementary School, Montgomery County Public Schools, Rockville, Maryland. Ms. Berner also is an adjunct professor for Hood College, where she teaches aspiring principals everything they need to know about student services and special education.*

Chapter 52

Requiem for a Career: The Good, the Bad, and the Privilege

Scott Lowrey, Ed.D.

Somewhere I recently heard a stranger say, "I have had a life that is fair. Not great, fair." Fair enough. This comment continues to resonate with me. If principals thought about it long enough, I suspect that they would come up with an entertaining, lengthy list of solicited and unsolicited advice offered up from others once it became known that they were navigating this career trajectory. Upon reflection, this solicited and unsolicited advice can be a daily occurrence. Some advice is good, "Listen twice as much as you talk, and observe twice as much as you listen." Some advice is bad, "Document, document, document." Moreover, some advice is privilege, "Remember that every day, parents send you their best child. They do not keep the good ones at home." As you go about your workday, commit time to reflect upon the wisdom that you have learned from each person encountered. Your heart will soar, and your head will hurt!

I am at a juncture in my career where I find myself thinking about what words of wisdom, hopefully, I would share with someone entering the principal role. Narratives from experience. A road more or less traveled. I remain a teacher; my passion is to nurture talent. I mentor a wide-range of educators at different phases of the career trajectory. Public education is the cornerstone of the health of our democratic society. I believe that there are three foundations to excellent teaching: engaging programs, cultivating relationships, and nurturing talent. Outstanding principals remain outstanding teachers.

I frame the moral purpose to the principal role as follows: the leadership that influences public education is foundational to the health of a democratic society; school systems exist to serve school communities, not vice versa; the moral imperative of improving student learning occurs at the school level by dedicated principals working with talented teachers; and, the primary goal of principal leadership is to realize collective community efficacy. Now I find myself asking what I would communicate (as someone towards the end of his career) to someone who was about to embark on their career: the good, the bad, and the privilege.

The Good

Public education is foundational to the health of a democratic society, and teachers are the foundation of public education. Through my dissertation research, it became clear that the ability to build relationships and develop people remains the essential umbrella competency of the principal role. Relationships can be fostered, forged or forfeited with every interpersonal interaction. Earlier in my career, a superintendent who I respected stressed that good leaders seek to frame challenges as opportunities. Every day, parents trust us to work with their uniquely talented children. As we can all attest, uniquely talented children, and uniquely talented adults for that matter, present both opportunities and challenges. People are funny, and kids are funnier. "Don't fight with walls, right mommy? That would hurt." How many times has a child ruined a perfectly good bad day? How many times has a child made a solidly average day a great day? This is why we teach, and why we lead. When the school day begins, it is about the students. Always.

Educational leadership represents the deep commitment to the process of learning. It is an ongoing, daily, individual, reciprocal, and collaborative, reflective practice in the service of others. On a personal level, I struggle as someone who exists in the gap between scholar and practitioner, seeking first to understand and then be understood. People learn from you. They watch, listen, and ask. People learn about you by how you treat others. Your words, deeds, compassion, sensitivities, and integrity are symbolic of your professionalism; wear them with honor, and make many proud. People watch, but they do not always know. Lack of knowledge is not an impediment to lack of commentary. There will always be critics. Hold yourself to the highest possible personal, professional, and ethical standards, and admit when you mess up. Internal accountability, founded upon the moral commitment to serving others, trumps external accountability almost every time. Are your words always congruent with your actions?

There are many sources of great pride for the principal. The school community that you serve becomes your family; you celebrate and grieve together. The measure of success is the success that you create in others, not in yourself. Success in others comes in many ways: The child who learns to read or the staff member who learns the meaning of unconditional. The teacher finds and utilizes the hidden curriculum to foster greater inclusion in the learning environment. There is the colleague who learns that you are struggling, shows up at your door without an invitation and offers strength. There is that mirror image at the beginning and ending of every day that highlights that you have given the very best in the service of others. Great principals were and remain great teachers. I would like to say that great principals were also great students, but am uncomfortable to offer that view as a universal principle.

The Bad

There have been many difficult lessons along the way. Somewhere, sometime, someone will tell you to have faith in *the process* even when *the process* is flawed. Do not look for rational when confronted by irrational. Think about that for a minute, and always be true to yourself. One of my doctoral students at Western University recently helped me to better understand this statement by re-framing it as follows, "Have faith, not in the process, but rather in yourselves." There will be times when your faith in the process will be fundamentally shattered. For example, the promotion that you, or a highly respected colleague, worked hard and in good faith to achieve goes to another, and the feedback is incongruent with the interview performance, profile within the system, and professional accomplishments. One colleague stated, "Don't assume that you have enough information to be pessimistic." Fair enough.

Middle management means that you are accountable to those both above and below you in the hierarchy. This accountability can sometimes mean that you are responsible for the decisions made by others even when they are wrong. You will be required to wear decisions that you do not own. In theory, your decisions should be made on what is best for kids and community. Occasionally, disconnects between theory and practice occur.

Ethical behaviour is not a function of one's place in the organizational hierarchy. As principal, I have been cautioned for following policy, not following policy, and not following a policy that does not exist. I would like to say that the ethical behaviour is increasingly exemplary as one works their way up towards the highest levels of the hierarchy, but my observations and experiences have been different. Inculcating by example may prove to be catastrophic for organizational health and wellness. You are never wrong to follow district policy; however, not all direct supervisors follow their own advice.

The Privilege

I was building student profiles with a young teacher when she shared, "I need to get to know the students first as characters, and then get to know them as learners." Simple yet profound. This statement can be applied to your work with staff, community stakeholders, and community partners. Never lose faith in a child because they will never lose faith in you.

Conflict is the gateway to building relationships, and is rarely personal. Every interaction, formal and informal, provides you an opportunity to cultivate a relationship. Principals are much more than instructional leaders; their greatest moral purpose is to build relationships and develop people. Community engagement is at the heart of public schools. Learning cannot occur in the absence of engagement.

Children are both wise and intuitive; serve them well. I remember the saddest Sunday of my life, and arriving to work Monday morning. On most levels, this represented a bad decision. I learned a lot about wisdom and compassion that Monday from a student named Michelle. I have always known enough to seek wisdom from a child. Every day, this knowledge is reinforced; I have experienced this since my first day of my educational career. Michelle plunked herself beside me whenever possible every day for several weeks, and rarely said a word. Small. Quiet. Compassionate. Moreover, I learned from her. I learned that the world is a better place when we put the needs of others before our own. Children always come first in the eyes of parents and grandparents. Watch the interaction between a grandparent and a small child as they exchange glances for that one instant during any gathering of community. Remember, every gathering of school community is a celebration of children, family, and community.

Concluding Comments

As you finish reading this chapter, I suspect that I will be closer to making a decision regarding retirement and transitioning into the next phase of my career. The principal role is not for everyone. We all have many narratives to tell. There is so much to share for those now embarking upon the principal journey. Nevertheless, it is time to pass the proverbial torch. Weigh the good twice as much as the bad, and deeply consider the privilege twice as much as you weigh the good. The health of a democratic society is a function of the leadership that serves public education. Your leadership has made a difference, but has it left a legacy - bigger picture, longer term, and greater good.

About the Author: *Dr. Scott Lowrey is an Elementary School Principal in Hamilton, Ontario, Canada and Assistant Professor (Limited Duties) at Western University. He received Canada's Outstanding Principals (COP) recognition in 2005, the inaugural year of the program, for initiatives* *relating to early literacy and the creation of a multigenerational contin-uum of community partnerships encompassing society's youngest to society's most senior. Scott holds a doctorate in Educational Administration from the Ontario Institute for Studies in Education of the University of Toronto, and was nominated for the CASEA Thomas B. Greenfield Dissertation Award (Canadian Association for the Study of Educational Administration). Scott was inducted in the McMaster University's Alumni Gallery in 2014.*

Chapter 53

"So ... You're a New Principal"

Catherine Canzani

I'll never forget my first day with my shiny new title of principal. I pulled into the school to meet the outgoing principal, Anne, and as I stepped into her office I was mesmerized by her bright red dress, her efficiency as she packed her things, and her confidence in the idea that I would be just fine.

One week later, having walked through the mostly-empty hallways for a while, I sat at the cleared-out desk and wondered what in the world I was supposed to do - and how to go about doing it. I quickly saw that there was plenty to get started on; a quick check of my emails confirmed that I had 27 to reply to, three reports to fill in, a grant to apply for and five requests from my second school (yes, I was not only a new principal but had two schools to contend with) to call them immediately. There was an endless stream of teachers showing up at my office door with "just a quick question," most of which I did not know the answers to. There were parents with transportation questions and students who needed an intervention plan in place before they showed up for their first day. The welcome back barbeque needed organizing, and the first staff meeting needed planning. You get the idea. Somehow, I made it through and lived to tell the tale.

I remember meeting my mentor early in the year (a mentor is a *must*), and, as she pulled her briefcase on wheels into my office, she looked me up and down and said, "You obviously got the memo of how to dress as a principal." I smiled to myself. Could it be that I looked as crisp and in-control as Anne had in her lovely red dress and high heels? Was it possible that this very experienced former principal could look at me and see someone who was ready to fill the role of principal? That image was quickly crushed as we sat down; all of my doubts, fears, stress, and insecurities came flowing out. What are mentors for, right? My mentor, Julie, looked at me and said, "You look fine. You *look* like you know what you are doing. Just remember this – for the next few months, while you are learning the ropes, think of yourself as a little duck. On the surface, which is what people see, you are calm, serene and ready to lead. Nobody needs to see your little legs paddling madly under water."

My legs did paddle madly for the rest of the year, but I learned some skills that helped me to cope. One of the most important things I learned was to buy time when I was not sure of how to answer a tough question; unfortunately, sometimes there just was not enough time. For example, I was at my smaller school when I got a frantic call from my secretary, Linda, at my bigger school. "There's a dad sitting outside the office," whispered Linda. "He's got his camera and he says he's going out at recess to take pictures of the kids who are bullying his son." Without missing a beat, I asked Linda to put this dad on the phone.

I had no idea what I was going to do but I began asking this father a series of questions, trying to determine his level of sanity, his level of rage, and his ability to reason. After ten minutes of trying to feel him out, I told him he could go and watch his son *without* his camera. When I hung up the phone, I suddenly had a sinking feeling that I had made the wrong decision. I knew that I had exactly four minutes before the bell rang for recess; I called the school back, had Linda put the dad back on the phone and proceeded to tell him that he could not go out at recess, and that I would meet with him the next day. Luckily for me, he left with his camera slung over his shoulder. His parting shot to my secretary was, "That's one flaky principal you've got there." At least safety was maintained and I felt good about my decision.

This leads me to my second lesson any decision you make has to be a decision you feel good about. As a principal it does not matter how much you weigh the pros and cons, and listen to different opinions – when you make a final decision, someone will most definitely not be happy about it. Whether it is moving the photocopier to a new location, changing the way lunch hours work, planning professional development for your school, or even making changes to the lunch menu, you are sure to have upset someone. I quickly learned that if I could lie in bed at night and feel good about the decision I had made, because I had made it with my head and heart and all the necessary information, I was able to handle the inevitable fall-out. It was the times where I did not listen to myself that left me tossing and turning all night.

When you become a principal, people automatically assume that you now have some sort of power over students that magically makes them do what you ask them. I hate to be the bearer of bad news, but I quickly learned that this is not the case. I remember a call over the intercom system to attend a class upstairs to help remove a student from a class. There was a conflict between a replacement teacher and a student with ASD. The issue escalated because the student did not get the specific chair she wanted during math class. I walked into the classroom with eighteen sets of expectant eyes on me. In the middle of the room was the fifth grader, yelling, "I don't care what you say. I am not sitting in this chair. I want one of the blue ones!" I scanned the room and found two students in the blue chairs holding them possessively. I attempted to reason with the student, "Maybe you can have a blue chair later. Right now they're being used." Her voice got louder as she began to chant, "I want a blue chair. I don't want an orange chair. I want a blue a chair!" All 18 sets of eyes were still watching me – the replacement teacher's eyes biggest of all.

It was one of those "make it or break it" moments. I took a deep breath, stood up tall, using my alpha presence like I had learned in my Neufeld training, looked at the student and said, "I see you're really frustrated right now and that you really want a blue chair. Pause. Come on down to the office with me and we can discuss it." To my surprise, she got up and followed me out the door, still yelling, "I want the blue chair!" I got a little lucky, but, nevertheless, in the students' books I had won the battle. It worked out for me that time but you have to realize that the homeroom teacher has a lot more sway with students than you ever will.

What was my learning here? Work with your teachers when a student is in crisis. Find the adult that the child is closest to in order to talk them down. Offer to take the class so the teacher can deal with the student. Giving a direct command to a student in crisis might work, but then again...it might not. Do not put yourself in a position where the entire student body watches you lose to a student: it sends a message, and it's a very loud one.

If you are a brand new principal, wondering how to tackle this challenging job, just remember a few lessons. Take it one day at a time. Make decisions with your heart and head. Find a good mentor. Do not assume that you automatically have the power to make kids behave and keep floating calmly on the surface even if your legs are paddling madly underwater.

About the Author: *Catherine Canzani, McGill graduate, has been a teacher with the ETSB school board in Quebec for the past 23 years, teaching elementary, high school, and vocational education. In 2015, Catherine decided that she was ready for a new adventure, and embarked on becoming the principal of two schools with the ETSB - Waterloo and Mansonville. After only a year and a half of experience, she already has many interesting stories to tell, and is hoping to support newly appointed principals in their learning journeys.*

Chapter 54

Should I Stay or Should I Go?
The Career Decision!

Curtis M. Clough

As a 27-year educator with experience in many districts, states and arenas, I am sharing my thoughts on career pursuit as a 'building leader.' The toughest decisions you will ever make are those regarding your career. Do I want to be an administrator? How far do I want to go in my administrative career? Each decision has an impact on both you and your family that can be either positive or negative. On some days you will be really frustrated from your workday and your family will take some unintended grief from you, as you are only human. Certain reactions to bad days do occur despite our best efforts. Understanding that the "change" has occurred is key to transition into your first administrative position.

You may need to make tough decisions regarding when to remain in or leave a position. Your effectiveness as a leader is based highly on the fit you have with the organization you are serving. Schools are never a status quo business; they change in personnel and philosophy based upon who leads. This constant movement puts you in difficult positions: Do you fit the new perspective? Are you willing to put up with the frustration that may occur when you are not the "right person" for the new organizational paradigm?

This may make you uncomfortable; however, the reality is that not all people are treated fairly. Certain power structures in organizations appear to be slanted to your disadvantage. You can play the game to remain in that position, or stay true to who you are while exploring opportunities that better fit your skills to serve students. This is a difficult principle to understand, but I have learned that you will know when this happens. Trust your instincts. In my career, my feelings and actions have communicated whether I was happy or unhappy, fueling my need to seek change. If you are unsure, I have found that asking those that are close to you will help you better understand how you are feeling.

On the other hand, you may not experience this at all as you smoothly transition into a position with little conflict. In my career, I have come to a keen understanding of the importance of relationships to get you through tough times. Your partner may know you best, and help you understand the situation clearer than anybody. If not your partner, then find somebody that you have confidence in, that knows "you." I am not saying breaking confidentiality laws, but talk through complex scenarios where someone can help clarify your thinking and then bring it to greater precision. As the leader, you are constantly under a microscope by your peers, staff, community, parents, and students. How you manage adversity goes a long way towards defining your success as a leader. Every day brings unique challenges; mistakes will be made. Building relationships with people who you can trust to help you navigate stormy waters and persevere is essential to successful leadership. Great relationships are reciprocal; one day you are the mentor and one day you are the mentee. I have been both throughout my career with many different people. I have utilized critical friends to help give me perspective, and to avoid burnout and anxiety. Your feelings are real and having these important people in your circle can confirm whether a new career direction is necessary to maintain health and wellness.

Furthermore, you will experience times in your career that you desire to take on a new challenge, either because you do not see a clear direction in your current position or have accomplished what you desired and need a new challenge. Positions and organizations, by nature, become stagnant when the message remains status quo despite changes in the current educational environment. Sometimes you need a change to energize your growth as a leader. Comfort in a position can be good, but comfort can lead to a "routine" that does not fuel your passion to be an outstanding leader. I have faced this conundrum many times, as have other administrators who came before me. If you are not being challenged, why stay in a position that is not fulfilling your professional goals? If you have achieved everything, seek new challenges that expand your skill set and professional growth opportunities. I have contributed to the national numbers that suggest educational leadership role-specific life expectancy ranges from 2 to 4 years. I have learned that in order to achieve your professional goals, you must be true to yourself and worry less about what may be perceived by others.

It has been my experience that three board members can make the life of a principal miserable because they hold the power of your next contract, despite many having no formal experience in education beyond what they learn at workshops or from their own unique perspectives. I believe so much in myself, and that I could find another job that would want to have my skills and talents to make education better. If your ambitions are for bigger and better, do not settle to make board members or supervisors happy. The moral imperative of principals is to do what you feel is best for the kids. After all, we do these jobs to help kids succeed.

As you embark on your career journey, you will come to better understand your fit with the organization and become a more effective leader. If you are uncertain of aspects of the job and are feeling uneasy as you begin, that is fine. This is a learning experience. I have found the one constant that works for me as a leader: make sure that you stay true to yourself. That will help you to navigate your career trajectory. Each job has its own challenges/opportunities, and if you are feeling uneasy, there is a reason. Trust your instincts, and they will lead you. Do what makes you happy while feeling good about the job.

In my career reflections, not every relationship is a good one – and some may be toxic. Avoid toxicity so you can be an effective leader. In my experiences, people try to bring down others to look good in the eyes of peers. If this occurs, examine the organization's ideals and goals and reflect to see if they are a fit for your desires, goals and ideals to be an educational leader. Your fit with the position is critical to being success-ful, so do not be afraid to take on new challenges, even if this means you need to move on to another district, city or state.

I would not be the leader I am without the totality of my experi-ences in the positions I have held. Each position is like a piece of the jigsaw puzzle that is the big picture of your career and life in leadership. Take the good and bad from each experience, and be willing to take risks so you can achieve maximum career potential. Tough decisions are a part of the job but the toughest decision is to whether you should stay or go from a position. A true test of leadership is if you fully understand what makes you and others tick. Change is good. Managing change is a great way to learn and grow as a person and leader. This may not be everyone's path, but if you desire a new opportunity for your career do not be afraid to make the leap to see what happens on the other side. It will turn out okay. I have learned so much about myself with every leadership experi-ence, and I am a better person and educator for it.

About the Author: *Curtis M. Clough has 27 years of experience in public education with 16 years of administrative experience in K-12 and postsecondary education. He currently serves as the Principal of Cordova Junior-Senior High School in Cordova, AK after serving 20 months as the Educational Administrator for Career and Technical Education for the Alaska Department of Education and Early Development. He has been actively engaged in the training and development of future educational leaders by serving as a mentor to future principals and superintendents in his various positions. Currently, he is working on several leadership manu-scripts in his spare time and has started and educational consulting business to train teachers and educators in best practices for Career and Technical Education and program development and evaluation.*

Chapter 55

"Oh, Lord, Why Did I Say That?"

Helen Evans

I just finished a conversation with an irate father of a grade 8 student in our very busy middle school. It was late Friday afternoon and I, the newly appointed vice principal, was the only person in the office at the time. Frankly, I cannot remember what the issue was that caused this father to come storming into the building, fuming over some action that had happened with his lovely son. Nevertheless, angry he was, and I was the stationary target.

I did, however, utilize a newly learned skill: attentive, or active, listening. Therefore, feeling like a true fake, I began employing the techniques of *really paying attention* to what he had to say. The conditions were perfect ... no one else was in the building (sigh), I was about to leave, so my work matters had been temporarily laid to rest. I invited Mr. Angry to sit down, turned to face him and presented what the instructor in Attentive Listening called 'open body language;' welcoming and inviting ... at 4:30 p.m. Friday afternoon, a stance we all try to assume readily.

Leaning forward slightly, I asked him to tell me about his concerns. I rarely interrupted, only to summarize his comments or to seek clarification for understanding. I nodded and made intelligent comments, like "a-ha, I see." I recalled the instructions for active listening: do not let your mind begin the process of rebuttal; and, seek first to understand.

It was interesting watching this father's body language. He continued to vent his anger at me and pelted loud questions. However, (following the script) when I asked for clarification (resisting a defensive position worthy of Johnnie Cochran), he started to calm his voice and to speak more slowly. I made sure to verify his emotions of confusion and frustration. Voila! I actually saw his shoulders sink from their ear-high station and his neck appeared, in all its glory. He had lost his uber-offense position. That's when I asked the dreaded question, "What would you like me to do for you?" I realized that maybe I asked him the wrong question. Maybe I set myself up for failure. The horrors! What if he asked me to do something I could not do? What would happen if I denied his request? Could I? Would I? Oh, Lord! I am just a first year vice principal.

Here was a stark example of the benefits of attentive listening. He looked at me and said quietly, "Nothing, I just needed someone to listen." Best lesson learned ever. I maintain that the world consists of many people frustrated that their stories are not being heard. Schools owe them an obligation to be full partners in learning experiences. When we remember the profound affect intentional listening has on both the listener and the speaker, we begin to amass the power we need to make true changes in learning.

Hindsight: I understand now, after years of being a principal, that I could have responded to him by asking for time to seek more information, using the principle 'unless there is blood on the floor or police at the door, you have time to say, let me get back to you on that." Then, those are the *other* stories and lessons learned from behind the principal's door.

About the Author: *Helen Evans retired from the principal role after 35 years as a teacher/school leader in the Etobicoke and Toronto District School Boards. Her experience as Chair of the Toronto Principal Association (TSAA), featuring 1000 vice principals and principals, inspired her to create and to coordinate a unique, 10-day international exchange with other principals in New South Wales, Australia, and presently with Nordic leaders, offering shared knowledge with like-minded leaders and immersed learning involving an action research component.*

PART VIII

In the Principal's Office

I have often wondered why the threat of being sent to the principal's office was supposed to scare students towards improved behaviour. Moreover, I remember learning that the most effective behaviour management strategies involved providing engaging programs, collaboratively developing classroom expectations with students, and fostering positive, respectful relationships where educators know their students as both characters and as learners, and know what is important to their students. Our book represents narratives from a significant number of years of experience from those serving public education from the principal's office. What goes on in the principal's office? Transactional leadership? Yes, duties as assigned. Transformational leadership? Yes, absolutely. Transformative leadership? Yes, unconditionally. But equally important, is maintaining a work-life balance heavily predicated on humour.

Chapter 56

The Library

Shawn Wightman, Ed.D.

M any years ago when I first became principal, I had to over-come many obstacles and challenges that I was unprepared for (i.e., grievances, lack of funds, student discipline, parent concerns, state/federal mandates, etc.). Thankfully, I had a colleague, Dan, who was a veteran principal in the district that I could talk to.

Dan, whom is perhaps one of the greatest principals and storytellers I have ever known, was a BIG & Tall man—standing 6'2" and weighing nearly 400 lbs. One of the things that made him so great was his unbe-lievable sense of humor. Just hearing him laugh and seeing him grin was contagious enough to influence anyone in the room. Because of this quality, and many others, he was greatly adored by all his students, par-ents and staff.

On Fridays, when we got paid, Dan and I would meet at a local tavern to have a few drinks, tell stories, and discuss some of our troubles. We had a "code word" for the bar we would meet at; it was "Library." Whenever we would see each other at meetings or in passing, we would ask, "Are you going to the library with me this Friday after school?" Everyone would look at us like we were crazy—library, after school, on a Friday; those two must be out of their minds (probably thinking it was an inside joke or something). **Even so, I recall one particular library meeting, early on in my career as principal, when he told me this story...**

When I was first hired on as principal, I proudly moved my things into my new office (i.e., certificates, degrees, family photos, professional literature, etc.). While at my desk, I noticed in the top drawer that the former principal had left a large sealed manila packet. On the front of it, written in bold capital letters and underlined, read "DO NOT OPEN UNLESS YOU ABSOLUTELY NEED HELP!" I found this to be rather peculiar, but didn't pay it any further attention, placed it back into my top desk drawer, and continued to setup my office.

During my first day on the job, things got very, very hectic. Teachers were complaining to me that the copier machine wasn't working, a fight broke out on the playground before school, parents were in the office screaming profanities at one another about a car accident they had in the parking lot, and Child & Adult Protective Services, in conjunction with the local police, demanded to speak with a particular student about their home situation. At some point during the day, I turned to my secretary and asked, "Is this typical?" She brazenly looked at me, shrugged her shoulders and said with a nervous chuckle, "Welcome to Candy Land!" It was at that moment that I realized I had a lot of work to do.

After about a month of continuous problems, I encountered a situation that I will never forget. The state's achievement test scores were publicly released from the previous school year and my school's scores were the lowest in the entire state. Every assessment area and grade level was literally, "rock" bottom. It wasn't long before I was bombarded with emails and phone calls from news reporters wanting to talk with me. To be honest, I didn't know what to say or do until a reporter ambushed me in the school's parking lot.

"Hey you, aren't you the principal," asked a reporter as I closed my car door. The reporter aggressively pursued me with her cameraman as I anxiously walked to the building. Like a predator, she followed me and informed me that she called numerous times and sent me multiple emails to contact her about the school's poor performance. I apologized to her and tried to explain that I was just too engrossed in what needed to be done at the school (i.e., handling student concerns, planning for professional development, getting the copier machine fixed, etc.), but she wasn't having that. As we entered the building, I turned to her and politely told her that I would be more than willing to speak with her, but needed a moment to put my things away. She reluctantly agreed and peevishly stood in the office waiting for me to call her into my workspace for the interview.

After hanging up my coat and putting my briefcase down, I sat down at my desk in my office for a moment. At that time, I strangely remembered the manila packet I first saw in my desk with the designation "DO NOT OPEN UNLESS YOU ABSOLUTELY NEED HELP!" I briefly snickered to myself and said, 'What the heck,' and opened the large envelope.

Inside the envelope were three smaller envelopes left by the former principal for me. Solution #1, Solution #2, and Solution #3 were written separately on each of them. The envelope with "Solution #1" had a stickie note on it with the following instructions: "Open these envelopes in sequence. The solution to the problem will then be revealed to you." I thought to myself, 'This is some real bullshit,' and then opened the first envelope. Inside was a note and all it said was, "Blame the former principal." Seriously, I'm not kidding, "Blame the former principal."

I paused for a moment and decided to go with it. I invited the reporter and her cameraman into my office and explained to them that I had just started working as principal in the school a few months ago and inherited the test scores from the previous administrator. I also elucidated to her that the staff and I were planning some extensive professional development to improve teacher effectiveness in the classroom; this seemed to work and they eventually left.

Later that evening, I received a phone call from my superintendent. He was quite unhappy that I didn't communicate to him that the television station was at my school and I conducted an interview about our low test scores. I expressed my regret to him and explained that the former principal was incompetent, thus throwing my predecessor under the bus. He seemed to be ok with my comeback, but demanded that I call him whenever the media arrived to report a negative story about the school; I assured him that I would.

Things seemed to calm down at the school for the next several weeks. The copier machine was working, there were no fights, accidents in the parking lot, or visits from Child & Adult Protective Services or police officers. Heck, my teachers were even applying the skills they learned from our professional development sessions together. Nonetheless, it wasn't too long before a student was injured on the playground due to a hinge breaking on one of the swing sets. In this accident, the child broke both legs in the fall (compound fractures). I immediately had my secretary call 911 and frantically ran out to the playground to where the child was laying. It was complete pandemonium. Kids were screaming/crying, noon-hour-aides were trying to keep the large crowd back, and the injured student just laid there, alone, in complete shock. I just couldn't believe what I saw; two compound leg fractures, nobody willing to comfort the injured student, and everyone just losing their minds. I immediately took my suit coat off and blanketed the child, directed my noon-hour-aides to take the students back to their respective classrooms and waited for the paramedics to arrive. While waiting, I held the child's hand and told her that everything was going to be alright.

Within minutes, the paramedics arrived and I found myself riding in the ambulance to the hospital with my student. This was a very difficult moment for me; seeing an innocent child going through such pain and agony. 'How could this happen?' I asked myself over and over again; parents don't send their children to school to get hurt or injured. They send them to school to make friends, have fun, and learn; this obviously wasn't the case.

As we pulled up to the emergency entrance the child paradoxically thanked me for saving her life; she was then whisked away on a gurney to receive further treatment. Her mother arrived shortly thereafter and was absolutely hysterical; understandably so. She called me every degrading name imaginable; I took her verbal abuse and eventually walked away.

When I returned to work, the news media were waiting there for me; I asked them for a moment before meeting with them. I entered my office very emotional and upset about the calamity and couldn't think straight. Be that as it may, I had to meet with the media about what just transpired. Consequently, in desperation, I reached into the top drawer of my desk again and opened Solution #2. 'It worked before, maybe it will work again,' I thought to myself.

The solution read, "Blame the materials, equipment, or infrastructure." Bingo! I gathered my composure, stepped out of my office, and confronted the media. During my interview, I first informed the reporters that the child was going to be ok and that I spoke with the mother. I also faulted the swing set the child was playing on and that the district would be conducting a thorough inspection of the playground. This seemed to work and they all left.

Later that evening, I received another phone call from my superintendent. He was absolutely livid. Suddenly, I realized that I, once again, failed to communicate to him that the television stations were at my school. I immediately apologized to him again and that the victim was going to be alright. I also explained to him that the hinge on the swing set failed, which caused the accident and that I requested a safety inspection for the entire playground. He was satisfied with my actions, but warned me again, that I must contact him whenever the media arrives to my building to do a negative story; as before, I guaranteed him that I would.

Finally, it was the last day of school and I was feeling pretty good about how things moved along since the playground accident. The copier was still working, my students and parents were getting along, and there were no visits by Child & Adult Protective Services or the police. Moreover, the student who broke both her legs earlier in the year was out of her casts and walking again. Then suddenly, all at once, the fire alarms started ringing. There was a fire in the building and smoke was everywhere! Be that as it may, everyone followed the procedures to evacuate the building perfectly. The staff and I kept the kids away from the building as the firemen arrived to do their work; they put out the fire within minutes. After this, the fire chief approached all of us and told the group that we were not to return to the building until his department investigates the location and cause of the fire. Thankfully, the day was almost over and we only had to wait fifteen minutes before students were to be dismissed.

Many of our parents started to pick their children up early and were released by my staff one by one. I was ok with this, because my staff knew these families very well and it wasn't long before parents and the media started arriving. They wanted answers. Unfortunately, I couldn't call the superintendent, because this was at a time when there were no cell phones. I sluggishly walked over to the group of reporters, all the time thinking about what I was going to say to them. I have to admit, I was tempted to go back into the building to read what "Solution #3" said before meeting with them, but was unable to do so because everything was blocked off by the fire crew. I cautiously met with the media and first informed them that everyone was okay; nobody had been harmed and that every child and staff member was safe. I also expressed to the group that we don't know what exactly caused the fire. One reporter, the same who stalked me for the achievement test scores interview earlier in the year, crudely shouted out, "How soon will you know what caused the fire? Can you tell us anything else?" I quickly replied with, "As soon as the fire department and I complete our investigations, we will let you know." She smugly rolled her eyes and sauntered away with her cameraman; so did the rest of the other reporters.

As the last bus rolled out and all my staff and students left the school campus for the summer, I asked one of the firemen if I could enter my office to get my things. He approved. As I entered my office I saw my answering machine's message light blinking on and off. I hit the "Play Messages" button. There were a number of communications from parents on it, but the last one, of course, was my superintendent. He demanded that I call him immediately. To tell you the truth, this wasn't at all surprising, but before calling him back I meekly opened the drawer of my desk to open the last envelope. Inside was "Solution #3" and it said, "You stupid jackass! Write three more solutions. Place them in separate envelopes and seal them all in a large manila packet. You're FIRED!"

Dan and I both screamed laughing; what an incredible story. Dan recapitulated everything in a simple acronym: CHARACTER. In every decision and action, principals must have principles. He also went on to say that principles must be committed, honest, and accountable. They must be respectful, accepting, and care about what matters most – kids. Finally, principals have to be trustworthy, empathetic and responsible. All this is a mark of a true principal leader.

Committed

Honest

Accountable

Respectful

Accepting

Care

Trustworthy

Empathetic

Responsible

The aforesaid is so true, and I always hark back to it from time to time. CHARACTER is at the core of a true principal leader. It doesn't matter if you are a teacher, student, or parent; everyone knows the difference between principals that have it and the ones that don't.

On a side note, I couldn't help but ask whether or not he called the superintendent back. Dan replied, "Hell yes, I called him back! That son of a bitch fired me; as expected. However, this got the school community in an uproar. Teachers, parents, kids and the like filled the Board room at a meeting one night and they let the superintendent have it. The media, including that asshole reporter, felt sorry for me and wrote wonderful articles as if I were a modern day saint (instead of a screw-up). In the end, the superintendent was canned and I got my job back."

"Wow; seriously? That happened?" I probed.

Dan paused for a moment, looked me dead straight in the eyes and began to howl uncontrollably. What a sucker I had been. I was completely enthralled by his entire story, which was total bullshit. He had made the whole thing up.

"You got the bill?" Dan cagily asked.

"Yeah, I got it — short arms, long pockets," I responded and we both left the library, each fully entertained...

About the Author: *Shawn K. Wightman, Ed.D., is Superintendent of Marysville Public Schools in Marysville, MI. His interests involve the development and use of effective classroom instruction strategies that improve student achievement. His most recent publication focuses on the effects of story performance on fourth and fifth-grade students' comprehension and oral reading fluency of narrative and expository texts.*

About the Editors

Darrin Griffiths, Ed.D. has held leadership positions in schools in Toronto and Hamilton-Wentworth District School Boards since 1997. Currently he is the principal of Mountain View Elementary School in Stoney Creek, Ontario, Canada. Darrin is also a Senior Lecturer (PT) with Niagara University, where he teaches masters level courses on educational leadership and curriculum. He is the author of *Principals of Inclusion: Practical Strategies to Grow Inclusion in Urban Schools* (2013), and co-editor with John P. Portelli [OISE/University of Toronto], *Key Questions for Educational Leaders* (2015). More recently, Darrin edited *Save Our Teachers' Souls: Professional and Social Well-Being in a Managerial Environment* (2016), a book by Danielle Cassell and Victoria Door [Keele University, UK]. He is co-editing an upcoming book with James Ryan [OISE/University of Toronto] titled *Case Studies for Inclusive Educators and Leaders* (May-June 2017).

Scott Lowrey, Ed.D. is an Elementary School Principal in Hamilton, Ontario, Canada and Assistant Professor (Limited Duties) at Western University. He received Canada's Outstanding Principals (COP) recognition in 2005, the inaugural year of the program, for initiatives relating to early literacy and the creation of a multi-generational continuum of community partnerships encompassing society's youngest to society's most senior. Scott is also an annual participant with the COP Academy (COPA) Executive Leadership Development Program (Rotman School of Management of the University of Toronto). Scott holds a doctorate in Educational Administration from the Ontario Institute for Studies in Education of the University of Toronto, and was nominated for the CASEA Thomas B. Greenfield Dissertation Award (Canadian Association for the Study of Educational Administration). The title of his dissertation was *Canada's Outstanding Principals: A Mixed-Methods Investigation of Leadership Development, Transformational Leadership, and Principal Efficacy.* To relax, Scott enjoys the Stratford Shakespeare Festival and Canadian music (i.e., Trent Severn, Blue Rodeo, Lee Harvey Osmond, Whitehorse, Gordon Lightfoot, and Kathleen Edwards). Scott was inducted in the McMaster University's Alumni Gallery in 2014.

Made in the USA
Lexington, KY
27 July 2017